The Maker of
DUNE

Insights of a Master of
Science Fiction

Frank Herbert

Edited and with introductions by

Tim O'Reilly

BERKLEY BOOKS, NEW YORK

THE MAKER OF DUNE

A Berkley Book/published by arrangement with
the authors

PRINTING HISTORY
Berkley trade paperback edition/May 1987

ISBN: 0-425-09785-4

A BERKLEY BOOK ® TM 757,375
Berkley Books are published by The Berkley Publishing Group,
200 Madison Avenue, New York, New York 10016.
The name "BERKLEY" and the stylized "B" with design are
trademarks belonging to Berkley Publishing Corporation.
PRINTED IN THE UNITED STATES OF AMERICA

FRANK HERBERT

"An astonishing science fiction phenomenon!"

—*Washington Post*

"Herbert's novels are infused with that rare quality of being indisputably magical."

—*Los Angeles Herald Examiner*

"Herbert is one of the most thought-provoking writers of our time; by focusing on an 'alien' culture, he makes us examine what the true definition of 'human' is."

—*Pacific Sun*

"Herbert does more than carry events forward: he deals with the consequences of events, the implications of decisions."

—*St. Louis Post-Dispatch*

The Maker of Dune

Contents

An Understanding of Consequences

Do Not Fold, Spindle, or Mutilate

Introduction

Frank Herbert has something important to say to you.

He wrote more than twenty novels (including the world-famous *Dune* series) and several volumes of short stories. His stories and novels are prized as much for their powerful and often unconventional insights into human nature and social organization as they are for his vivid storytelling. However, no one will charge him with writing simple-minded allegories or one-dimensional stories designed only to flesh out a concept. Rather, his stories are packed with enough highly charged, closely woven ideas that most readers find themselves turning their thoughts again and again to one part or another of what they have read. Both the stories and the ideas "stick" in the mind.

This is Frank's first collection of nonfiction. It includes essays and introductions written for various collections of science fiction, as well as feature articles written during his long career as a newspaper reporter and editor. It also includes a number of interviews conducted especially for this book and never before published elsewhere.

I first became interested in putting together this collection while writing a critical introduction to Frank Herbert's work.* The clarity with which Frank explained some of his basic concepts in these essays made them invaluable for a critic. It seemed to me that they would be no less so for the general reader.

This is not to say that an understanding of the concepts

* *Frank Herbert*, Frederick Ungar, New York, 1981.

1

presented in these essays will make everything in Frank Herbert's novels fall into place. It is more that they provide clues with whose aid the enterprising reader can hope to trace (without unraveling) some of the myriad threads that make up the cloth on which Frank's stories are so lavishly embroidered. The richer novels, such as the *Dune* chronicles, become even more stimulating as they become more intelligible, while those which a reader might have thought trifles by comparison with the greater works take on new fascination. You'll get a fascinating glimpse behind the scenes of some of the best science fiction ever written.

This is also not to say that these essays and interviews are of interest only to those who have read Frank Herbert's novels. They have a cogency and a fascination of their own: the observations of a man who, in his own words, spent his life "stretching time in a different way than most people." He said:

> During the period of writing a story, I'm living in that time, which is in many respects dramatically different from what we find around us right now. After finishing the story, I pull out and come back to these primitive times.

> The word primitive has a peculiar meaning to a lot of science fiction writers. If you have stretched your mind out, for the story's purpose, twenty thousand, a hundred thousand years into man's future, and then come back to these times, you look at these times in many respects the way you might look if you were suddenly pushed back into Shakespeare's time.

When asked about the source of his ideas, Frank said:

> I'm a muckraker, a yellow journalist. I ask myself: "What are we ignoring?"

He's tackled such subjects as ecology, artificial intelligence, gene-splicing, and the nature of leadership in our society, each time asking: "What are we ignoring?"

In reading these essays, you will see that Frank Herbert has something to say to you right now, not just twenty thousand years in the future.

But be warned: There is a danger in knowing too much about an author's intent. The very best stories speak to us on levels non-fiction can never reach. When we identify with a character in a novel, the ideas, experiences, changes in that character change us, too. We are touched, we are *moved*, sometimes quite literally.

What we understand, on the other hand, we often feel we have control over, and can safely ignore. Understanding can be a barrier to change.

In some of the pieces included here, Frank has made a special effort, as he did in his novels, not to leave you with easy answers, to make you draw your own conclusions from what you have read, and perhaps even to act on them. He has tried to undermine the understanding that takes the world for granted, and to strengthen the understanding that comes when you find yourself struggling with an idea, intellectually or emotionally moved but unable to pin down just what it is that has touched you.

If you come away from this book wondering as well as satisfied, as perplexed by the new puzzles that have opened up as you are fulfilled by those that have fallen into place, these essays will have done their job.

—*Tim O'Reilly*
Newton, Massachusetts
September 1985

P.S. Frank Herbert died on February 11, 1986. He was a fine man, and all of us who knew him will miss him. This collection of essays is now doubly precious, since Frank himself is no longer available to spin dreams for us, but lives on only in the gift of words he has already given.

Crisis, Anyone?

I found the following two pieces the most helpful in understanding Frank Herbert's basic outlook on life and man's place in the universe.

It is a universe of uncertainty, infinite and ever changing. It is stable only in the minds of human beings who close themselves off from its diversity.

Such a universe is frightening to a person in love with security. To a person who trusts in his or her own flexibility, his or her own potential for growth and change, the unknown is the headiest wine.

Readers of science fiction have long known this. They dream of a future that will bring radical change to the humdrum lives they live. Even disaster and dystopia may seem attractive, because they bring with them the heroic dreams of individual efforts to meet and overcome enormous difficulties.

What too many of us forget, wrapped up in dreams of imaginary worlds, is that we live in the most exciting of imaginary worlds. The uncertainties of the real world far exceed those which fiction models. And so do its possibilities.

Frank noted: "It is a mistake to talk about the future. I like to think of futurism as an art form. There are as many possible futures as we can create."

I like to think of Frank's work as a series of training manuals on how to live in the real world. Here are the first two lessons.

Listening to
the Left Hand

When I was young and my world was dominated by indestructible adults, I learned an ancient way of thinking that is as dangerous as a rotten board in a stepladder. It told me that the only valuable things were those I could hold unchanged: the love of a wise grandfather, the enticing mystery of the trail through our woodlot into the forest, the feeling of lake water on a hot summer day, the colors (ahh, those colors) when I opened my new pencil box on the first day of school . . .

But the grandfather died, a developer bulldozed the woodlot, loggers clear-cut the forest, the lake is polluted and posted against swimming, smog has deadened my ability to detect subtle odors, and pencil boxes aren't what they used to be.

Neither am I.

There may be a quiet spot in my mind where nothing moves and the places of my childhood remain unchanged, but everything else moves and changes. There's dangerous temptation in the nostalgic dream, in the expertise of yesteryear. The nameless animal that is all of us cannot live in places that no longer exist. I want to address myself to the survival of that nameless animal, looking back without regrets at even the best of what was and will never be again. We should salvage what we can, but even salvaging changes things.

The way of this change is called "process" and it requires that we be prepared to encounter a multiform reality. Line up three bowls on a table in front of you. Put ice water in the one on the left, hot water in the one on the right, and lukewarm water in the middle one. Soak your left hand in the ice water and right hand in the hot water for about a minute, then plunge both hands into the bowl of lukewarm water. Your left hand will tell you the water of the middle bowl is warm, your right hand will report cold. A small experiment in relativity.

We live in a universe dominated by relativity and change, but our intellects keep demanding fixed absolutes. We make our most strident demands for absolutes that contain comforting reassurance. We will misread and/or misunderstand almost anything that challenges our favorite illusions.

It has been noted repeatedly that science students (presumably selected for open-mindedness) encounter a basic difficulty when learning to read X-ray plates. Almost universally, they demonstrate an inability to distinguish between what is shown on the plate and what they believe will be shown. They see things that are not there. The reaction can be linked directly to the preset with which they approach the viewing of a plate. When confronted by proof of the extent to which preconceptions influenced their judgment, they tend to react with surprise, anger, and rejection.

We are disposed to perceive things as they appear, filtering the appearance through our preconceptions and fitting it into the past forms (including all the outright mistakes, illusions, and myths of the past forms). If we allow only the right hand's message to get through, then "cold" is the absolute reality to which we cling. When our local reality has attached to it that other message: "This is the way out," then we're dealing with a form of "holy truth." *Cold* becomes a way of life.

FALSE LIMITS

We must begin to see ourselves without the old illusions, whatever their character may be. The apparently sound step can drop us from the ladder when we least expect it. Herman

Kahn's opus on the year 2000 never mentioned environmental concerns. A Presidential committee appointed in 1933 by Franklin D. Roosevelt to "plot our course" through 1952 had not a word about atomic energy, antibiotics, jet propulsion, or transistors. Such levels of perception are worse than inadequate; they impose deadly false limits. They beguile us with a promise that "we know what we're doing."

The man with broken bones stretched out beneath his ladder doesn't need to look at the rotten step to know what he did wrong. He believed a system that had always worked before would work once more. He had never learned to question the mechanisms and limits imposed by his perceptions.

In questioning those mechanisms and limits on a larger scale we move into an arena dominated by the powerful impositions of genetic heritage and individual experience, the unique influenced by the unique. Here is the conglomerate of behavior-biology, the two so entangled they cannot be separated if we hope to understand their interlocked system. Here is "process."

You and I, while we strive for a one-system view of this process, are at the same time influenced by it and influence it. We peer myopically at it through the screens of "consensus reality," which is a summation of the most popular beliefs of our time. Out of habit/illusion/conservatism, we grapple for something that changes as we touch it.

Must we stop the river's motion to understand *riverness?* Can you understand *riverness* if you are a particle in its currents? Try this:

Think of our human world as a single organism. This organism has characteristics of a person: internal reaction systems, personality (admittedly fragmented), fixed conceptualizations, regular communications lines (analogue nerves), guidance systems, and other apparatus unique to an individual. You and I are no more than cells of that organism, solitary cells that often act in disturbing concert for reasons not readily apparent.

Against such a background, much of the total species-organism's behavior may be better understood if we postulate collective aberrations of human consciousness. If the human species can be represented as one organism, maybe we would understand ourselves better if we recognized that the species-organism (all of us) can be neurotic or even psychotic.

It's not that all of us are mad (one plus one plus one, etc.) but that all-of-us-together can be mad. We may even operate out of something like a species ego. We tend to react together with a remarkable degree of similarity across boundaries that are real only to individual cells, but remain transparent to the species. We tend to go psychotic together.

Touch one part and all respond.

The totality can learn.

This implies a nonverbal chemistry of species-wide communication whose workings remain largely unknown. It implies that much of our collective behavior may be preplanned for us in the form of mechanisms that override consciousness. Remember that we're looking for patterns. The wild sexuality of combat troops has been remarked by observers throughout recorded history and has usually been passed off as a kind of boys-will-be-boys variation on the male mystique. Not until this century have we begun to question that item of consensus reality (read *The Sexual Cycle of Human Warfare* by N.I.M. Walter). One of the themes of my own science fiction novel, *Dune*, is war as a collective orgasm. The idea is coming under discussion in erudite journals such as *The General Systems Yearbook*.

Assume this concept then. In it, the giant species-organism is perpetually involved with a moving surface of many influences where every generative encounter is felt as change throughout the system. Some of the cells (we individuals) feel the changes with the brutal impact of a napalm explosion. To others, the transition from one condition to another comes at such a snail crawl that it's barely noticed. But always the species, involved with its longer and larger career, responds to the changes at whatever pace conditions permit.

THE SPECIES-ORGANISM

Understanding that pace and its conditions requires a different approach to the total human system, that nameless animal of a species-organism. In this approach you no longer can listen only to the right hand that tells you "this is the cold way it has always been." You listen as well to the left hand saying "warm-warm-warm." Somewhere in between left and right you begin to get a glimmering view of things in process now. That glimmering offers the following observations:

- Something like pheromones (external hormones) interacting between members of the human species to weld groups into collective-action organs. (How does a mob unite and hold itself together?)

- Isolation cues that separate groups into identifiable substructures, a system possibly influenced by diet. (Aside from accent and mannerisms, how do members of the British upper class recognize each other?)

- Conflict igniters, possibly sophisticated abstractions of primitive postures and vocal signals. (How do you know that the man coming toward you is angry?)

- Glandular responses to changes in territorial circumstances, responses of remarkable similarity throughout large populations, but with a more complex substitution system than implied by most observers. (Why did most of the occupants of Chicago's high-rise Lake Shore ghetto abandon it within three years, and what did that experience do to their life expectancy and subsequent behavior?)

In all of the above, you can expect a suppression of group and individual consciousness and an amplification of group conformity. But even if you answered each of these deductions to our present general satisfaction, you would only have begun the process of understanding. Expect that, too, to change.

In our culture, when you make this approach to process thinking, you immediately raise a conflict over whether we individuals (and the groups we form) are reacting on the basis of information. Classical theories of individualism and free will that underlie consensus reality in our society assume a lawless character for the species as a whole. ("Human nature will never change.") Classical theory assumes that we are profoundly different from blind cells, that human individuals are informed, and that their reactions can be ascribed to a rational basis except in cases of accident and madness. To assume for the species as a whole a response pattern partly habituated (and thus unconscious by definition) threatens belief in *reason*, whose raw stuff (information) is assumed to be openly (consciously) available to all.

But television directors, politicians, the psychiatric profession, advertising/public relations firms, and sales directors are seeking out predetermined preferences to exploit mass biases. In a very real sense, we already are conducting conversations (communicating) with the species as an organism. For the most part, this communication is *not* directed at *reason*.

Process and the species-organism represent a complex mixture whose entire matrix can be twisted into new shapes by genius (Einstein) or madness (Hitler). The course of this process can be misread by an entire species despite wide evidence of disaster. To understand this matrix, consider the problems of rat control. We've learned that a quick-acting poison doesn't work well in eliminating rat colonies. Grain treated with a fast poison tends to kill only one or two rats from a colony. Rats translate the message "grain-kill" without any need for verbalizing. We can, however, kill off entire colonies with a slow poison such as Warfarin. When one rat must go back to the grain seven or eight times before dying, other members of his colony tend not to make the lifesaving connection.

This gives you an idea of what limits may apply to a species' time sense. The presence of a threat may be known, but its context can remain frustratingly diffuse. What is this strange new lethal disease attacking my fellows? It calls up an ancient scenario out of primitive times when our beliefs were geared to living in the presence of an outer darkness that pressed upon us with terrifying force, mysteriously and inescapably painful. How do you placate the angry spirits of the poisoned waters?

THE LINEAR HABIT

Many things complicate our ability to recognize threats to the species. Not the least of these many may be contained in the observation of Sören Kierkegaard: "Life can only be understood backward, but it must be lived forward."

This Janus-faced view of life comes right out of the old linear swamp. It carries an attractive sense of reality, but it assumes that our affairs flow with an absolute linearity from way back there to somewhere wa-a-a-ay up front. This allows for no optical illusions in time, no compressions or expansions, and it ignores much of our latest computer hardware (ten billion years in a nanosecond) as well as other odd Einsteinian curves and spirals that intrude upon our consensus reality. It's well to recognize the low probability that one lonely cause underlies any event that inflicts itself upon an entire species. Neither Hitler nor Einstein sprang from a spontaneous and singular generating event. Worldwide pollution has no singular origin.

Yet, the linear orientation of our perceptions (1, 2, 3 . . .; A, B, C . . .; Monday, Tuesday, Wednesday . . .; January, February, March . . .) makes it extremely difficult to break away from the belief that we occupy a universe where there are straightforward linked cause-and-effect events plus a few other odd events we call accidents. We are habituated to a noncircular, noninclusive way of interpreting a universe whose circularity and all-inclusiveness keep cropping up in the phenomena we investigate. Events of tomorrow *do* change our view of yesterday; an ancient Greek's accident is our better-understood phenomenon. The linear habit remains, however. It dictates that we consign accidents to the unconscious. We keep loading the unconscious with events we do not understand. This burden inflicts itself upon our sense of reality.

Devotion to that linear consensus leads us inexorably into a confrontation with the mathematician who tells us: "We inevitably are led to prove any proposition in terms of unproven propositions." He's telling me that all of my pet beliefs inevitably go back to a moment where I am forced to say: "I believe this because I believe it." Faith!

Mathematics and physics may yet drive the old realities over the brink. For instance, we now can project complex models of human societies through analogue computers and within a few seconds get impressive readouts on the consequences of paper decisions projected for hundreds of years. This is, of course, subject to the omnipresent warning pasted over computers operated by cautious men of science. That warning reads: "Garbage in—garbage out."

In engineering terms, we are looking for *resultants*—sums of social forces through which to examine our world. This often produces a more realistic approach than taking up the components one by one. Any auto mechanic knows there are engine problems for which it's better to make ten adjustments at once. Still, singularity as a belief confounds our attempts to "repair the system."

Technological playthings distort and amplify our performances to the point where we may believe we are *discovering* futures that we invent in the present. This may be the most elemental reality we have ever encountered, but the distortions born of mating our unexamined desires to our technology have tangled future and present almost inextricably. Future/past/present—, they remain so interwoven deep in the species' psyche that our day-to-day activities are often concealed from us. We put out our own Warfarin, unaware of lethal consequences and forgetful of where we have hidden it.

Few who examine our planetwide problems doubt that we live in a Warfarin world. The thrust of my argument is that we are not raising our awareness to the level demanded by the times, we are not making the connections between poisons and processes—to the despair of our species.

SUCCESS AS FAILURE

Planners often appear unwilling to believe that a history of success can produce the conditions of disaster. Rather, they believe that success measured in current terms is sufficient justification for any decisions about tomorrow. (To those who doubt that success can bring ruin to a community, look at the Boeing Corporation, a study of unusual poignancy in its demonstration of disaster brewed from success.)

You glimpse here a hidden dimension of powerful influence upon our survival. Here are the locked-up decisions predicated on capital investments and operating costs. Governments, large corporations, and service industries know they must build today according to long-range projections. Those projections tend to come from planners who know (unconsciously or otherwise) what the directors want to hear. Conversely, directors tend not to listen to disquieting projections. (Boeing's directors were being told as far back as the early 1950s that they had to diversify and that they should begin exploring the potential of rapid transit.)

Planning tends to fall into the absolutist traps I've indicated. Warm is better than cold, we'll listen only to the left hand. The limits under which powerful private assessments of "the future" are made predict mistakes of gigantic lethal magnitude.

If we define futurism as exploration beyond accepted limits, then the nature of limiting systems becomes our first object of exploration. That nature lies within ourselves. Some who say they are talking about "a future" are only talking about their own limits. The dominant pattern in current planning betrays a system of thinking that does *not* want to abandon old assumptions and that keeps seeking a surprise-free future. But if we lock down the future in the present, we deny that such a future has become the present—and the present has always been inadequate for the future.

My explanation of this pattern goes partly—where we commonly believe *meaning* is found—in printed words (such as these), in the noise of a speaker, in the reader's or listener's awareness, or in some imaginary thought-land between these. We tend to forget that we human animals evolved in an eco-system that has demanded constant improvisation from us. In a mirror sense, we reflect this history of mutual influences in all our systems and processes, including the human brain, our consciousness, and our thinking patterns. The virtuosity of our customary speaking response tends to conceal from us how this behavior is dominated by improvisation. This non-awareness carries over into that "talking" with our universe by which we shape it and are shaped by it.

It dismays some people to think that we are in some kind of a jam session with our universe and that our survival de-mands an ever-increasing virtuosity, an ever-improving mas-tery of our instruments. Whatever we may retain of logic and reason, however, points in that direction. It indicates that the creation of *human* societies probably should become more of an art form than a plaything of science.

To plan for the future, to attempt to guide ourselves into "the better life" projected by our utopian dreams, we are in-volving ourselves with profound creative changes and influ-ences. Many of these already are at their work unrecognized around us. Inevitably, we change our frames of reference, our consensus reality. It becomes increasingly apparent that today's changes occur in a relativistic universe. It is demon-strably impossible in such a universe to test the reliability of one expert by requiring him to agree with another expert. This is a clear message from those physicists who demon-strate the most workable understanding of our universe-in-operation. After Einstein, they tell us: *all inertial frames of reference are equivalent*.

This is saying that there is no absolute frame of refer-ence (local reality) within the systems we recognize, no way to be certain you have measured any absolutes. The very act of introducing the concept *absolute* into a question precludes an answer with sensible meaning. (Which hand will you be-lieve, the "cold" hand or the "warm" one?) It serves no pur-pose to ask whether absolutes exist. Such questions are constructed so as to have no answer *in principle*.

Accordingly, both Pakistan and India could be equally *right* and equally *wrong*. This applies also to Democrats and Republicans, to Left and Right, to Israel and the United Arab Republic, to Irish Protestants and Irish Catholics. Remember: "We inevitably are led to prove any proposition in terms of unproven propositions." We do not like unproven propositions.

If we face up to this consciously, that might cut us away from everything we *want* to believe, from everything that comforts us in a universe of unknowns. We would be forced to the realization that the best logic we can construct for a finite system (which describes our condition at any selected moment) might not operate in an infinite system. No matter how tightly we construct our beautiful globes of local reality, no matter how many little Dutch boys we assemble to apply fingers to any holes that may appear, we still have built nothing more than a dike, impermanent and essentially fragile.

BREAKING PATTERNS

It would seem that a futurist concerned with our survival and our utopian dreams needs to listen, to observe, and to develop expertise that fits the problems as they occur. But that is not the pattern that dominates human behavior today. Instead, we shape our interpretations of our problems to fit existing expertise. This existing expertise defends its local reality on the basis of past successes, not on the demands of our most recent observations.

The consequences of such an approach can be deadly far beyond the circle in which the planning decisions originate. And in the hierarchical arrangements of human societies it often is just one person who finally makes the profound choice for us all. The reasons behind such decisions can be perfectly justified by the contexts within which they are made. (Have I ever failed you before?)

In the universe thus described, we are destined forever to find ourselves shocked to awareness on paths that we do not recognize, in places where we do not want to be, in a universe that displays no concern over our distress and that may have no *center* capable of noticing us. God-as-an-absolute stays beyond the reach of our definitions, beyond our questions, beyond any demands we can articulate. The old patterns of thinking, patched together out of primitive communications attempts, continue to hamstring us.

Play a game with me, then, and maybe you'll understand what I am attempting to describe. Here's a list of numbers arranged according to a logical order. The solution to that order (see page 279) embodies what I mean when I suggest we leap out of our conventional limits. The numbers: 8, 5, 4, 9, 1, 7, 6, 10, 3, 2.

As you consider how the way we approach a question limits our ability to answer, I'd like you to reflect upon a short paraphrase of Spinoza, changed only to read "species" where the original read "body."

No man has yet determined what are the powers of the species; none has yet learned from experience what the species may perform by mere laws of nature (chemical, genetic or other) or what the species may do without rational determination. For nobody has known as yet the frame of the species so thoroughly as to explain all of its operations.

Science Fiction and a World in Crisis

Washington's Mount Olympus is a pile of dirt and rock with snow on its crown. I can see it out of my study window. It helps sometimes to look out at it and remind myself of Laotze's words:

> The soul may be a mere pretense.
> The mind makes very little sense.
> So let us value the appeal
> Of what we can taste and feel.

If you write science fiction in a crisis-ridden world, the value of the pragmatic reasserts itself regularly. You have to say to yourself: "As I see it..." We need to touch base on occasion the way Antaeus had to touch the earth. If we don't, we lose an important contact and we may write sentences such as this one from NASA's Apollo 14 documentary:

> Astronauts Alan B. Shepard, Jr., and Edgar D. Mitchell were climbing a steepening slope (on the moon); their maps indicated they were approaching their destination, the rim of Cone Crater where rocks may have remained unchanged *since time began. (Italics mine)*

Since time began?
You see it all around in crisis after crisis—how deeply we remain immersed in the Cartesian division between material and mental. It is virtually impossible for anyone conditioned in a Western culture to think with any empirical directness about Infinity—about a universe without begin-

20

nings and without end, a universe of continual temporary conditions, one merging into another forever.

Time does not begin in such a universe. A beginning may be only the moment you notice something move against that background which ancient India called "the void."

I found it necessary to begin this way because of something that happened to me at a recent cocktail party. The setting was so common to our culture that it has become a cliché—and so was the tall, heavyset fellow with the bushy black beard who came up to me with a question often asked of science fiction writers.

"You science fiction guys have imagined every problem the world could face. What the hell do we do about this planet that's ready to come apart?"

It is to laugh, but bitterly.

With alcohol-induced clarity, the fellow had just realized that the end of the Vietnam war had changed very little in respect to a world balanced precariously on the edge of an explosive finale. The threat of ultimate war is still with us and just as potent as ever.

But I've thought about every problem, so . . .

My God! Every problem? Not by a long shot on a rainy Monday. Otherwise I'd be out of work. In common with the rest of my fellows, I do not have the book of answers. Sorry. I do, however, know something about crises. They're the stuff of good stories. If you write fiction, you become fairly adept at solving unsolvable problems which (and this is crucial) you have first created that you may solve them entertainingly.

Straw men.

But every now and then, we hit pay dirt. Realpolitik catches up with fiction. Industry just happens to manufacture the device we imagined—Telstar, Waldos, the Bracone collapsible oil barge. . . .

Technology turns a corner around which we have peeked.

You can wake up, as did Cleve Cartmill in 1944, to find yourself answering the questions of suspicious minions from the FBI. "Yes, Mr. Cartmill, but you speak in this story of an atomic bomb. Where did you get that idea? And why did you set your story at Manhattan Beach?"

Cartmill had pretty well laid out the developmental process for an atom bomb, which was then the private domain of the top-secret Manhattan Project. It was a good story and John Campbell published it.

But who could believe such coincidence?

And who can convince a security-conscious minion of the government that there is no way to keep these things secret when knowledge about the steps leading up to such developments permeates an entire layer of world society. There is no way. Despite Descartes, mental and material do not separate.

But nobody seems to believe that a mere science fiction writer can think up such things out of his own head. The question has a definite accent to it: "Where'd you get that idea (pause), out of your head?"

The head of a science fiction author is not supposed to produce the stuff of real crises. We're supposed to entertain, to amuse, to provide interesting food for thought and, occasionally, to bring people up short with a gasp or two.

Vide *1984*.

Vide *Brave New World*.

When you think about it, you realize these two works have influenced our world. Neither *Brave New World* nor *1984* will prevent our becoming a planet under Big Brother's thumb, but they make it a bit less likely. We've been sensitized to the possibility, to the way such a dystopia could evolve.

If we're to understand the relationship between such fiction and a world of real crises, it pays us occasionally to look out at Mount Olympus and append some footnotes.

With the exception of the fancy eugenics, *BNW* presents us with a society that might've been planned by a committee of behavioral psychologists. In many ways, it resembles nothing more than a worldwide *Walden Two*. The universal infant conditioning, the College of Emotional Engineering, and the system of World Controllers ruling by scientific behavioral modification would appear to meet with approval of

W-Two author, B. F. Skinner, who, you may recall, has been described as the world's foremost social engineer.

Both Orwell and Huxley were concerned with the ability of our democratic institutions to survive the onslaughts of overpopulation and rising industrialism—mass business, mass government, mass automation, etc. They were concerned with their own understanding of that concept which we call "freedom."

Pause now and consider certain practices by the United States federal government, by state and local authorities here and elsewhere in our world. Consider wiretapping, mandatory lie-detector tests, the keeping of extensive files on citizens alleged to be dissenters, refined electronic surveillance, manipulation of the media, the deliberate distortion of meanings in language. All of this foreshadows *1984*.

Make special note of the ways that have been developed to create demands for goods: the manufacture of goods so shoddy they break down at a predictable rate; a constant stream of "new" models which are not really new; advertising propaganda to maintain demand for goods that have little relationship to human survival (the appeal to sexual and status longings, etc.), and recall Huxley's words:

"As political and economic freedom diminishes, sexual freedom tends compensatingly to increase."

Does that sound familiar?

When people such as Theodore Roszak in *The Making of a Counter Culture* take up these themes, then science fiction leaves the realm of fiction and enters a shadowland between myth and reality. Roszak comments on the repressive desublimation factor in *"Playboy* sexuality" which has taken over American society: ". . . casual, frolicsome and vastly promiscuous. It is the anonymous sex of the harem. It creates no binding loyalties, no personal attachments, no distractions from one's primary responsibilities—which are to the company, to one's career and social position, and to the system generally."

Whether you begin from science fiction or from educational commentators such as Roszak, you can smell a crisis coming.

The promiscuity which Puritans thought would undermine the foundations of society has been co-opted by technocracy and channeled in a way that makes it serve the establishment—maintaining a state of non-freedom, of economic servitude, as well as stability for a social system that allows the technocracy to go its own way.

Our society tolerates drugs such as tobacco, alcohol, barbiturates, and tranquilizers because they serve a useful social purpose. They enable people to endure an otherwise intolerable existence, to remain on the production/consumption treadmill.

Perhaps *1984* isn't all that far away and we may already be living in a *Brave New World*.

In a society of Spocked babies and spooked adults, it gets easier to understand why marijuana, acid, and other drugs are tolerated to help keep the populace under control, especially when you add the mind-numbing properties of TV (audio-visual soma). Whoever said that the realities of twentieth-century industrial mass society cannot be endured without outside help may not be far from wrong and the phenomenon of the black-bearded fellow asking a science fiction author for "the answer" becomes more acceptable.

According to Huxley, the greatest triumphs of propaganda have been accomplished not by doing something, but by refraining from doing something. *Silence is greater than truth*. "We'll appoint a committee to study this problem." The assumption by most of today's social engineering types is that independence is not the natural state of man.

Vide *BNW*.

Misfits are removed to their island—"all the people who, for one reason or another, have got too self-consciously individual to fit into community life. All the people who aren't satisfied with orthodoxy, who've got independent ideas of their own."

When they begin feeling out of sorts, the people of *BNW* get a jolt from hypnopaedic memory telling them to take a gram of soma, to enter the "warm, richly colored, infinitely friendly world of soma holiday."

It's clear that both in science fiction and the crisis-beset "real" world, drugs (like magic) need to be taken seriously and considered significant socially as well as individually. Can't you visualize the sincere announcer on TV telling you:

"Drugs can be of significant value when used in a conscientiously applied program of personal hygiene and regular professional care."

In the foreword to *BNW*, Aldous Huxley begins his prescription for the revolution to bring about the world of his book by telling you that, first, the government requires a greatly improved technique of suggestion to make everyone susceptible to the propaganda of the new society. He includes infant conditioning and the use of certain drugs and a greatly transformed "norm" of sexual behavior from that which our fathers openly accepted. Where *BNW* pointed the way, Masters and Johnson or Katchadourian and Lunde follow to fill in the gaps.

You've read all of this in science fiction, of course, and made many of the comparisons yourself, and it's nice to think you're sitting there with the *avant-garde*, first to know what tomorrow's world will be. Let me recommend, therefore, that you study the records of history a bit more carefully. The sexual morality of *BNW* was the norm in the nineteenth-century Oneida colony of upstate New York. The Arab culture pioneered in the use of drugs to control the populace a thousand years ago.

If history teaches us that we learn nothing from history, then there may be little point in rehashing these observations on human behavior. Perhaps it'd be better to save this material for fiction, that world of perfection, which is where things operate the way I want. In the "real" world it has all happened before. There's no such thing as a new crisis, just instant replays on the old ones.

It's fun to play the game, though, and to hope that your newest window dressing on the old patterns will tell us something really new. After all, science fiction in its dealings with crises for the sake of story, does indicate other avenues open to us.

We can, for example, assume that behind any accepted

morality, fictional or otherwise, is the function of maintaining social stability. When emotions brought out by repression become socially disruptive, dangerous to social harmony, then the repression may be eliminated by the society itself. Our "new morality" so shocking to Middle America could be an evolutionary force to eliminate potentially disastrous social conditions. It could be the social organism's way of dealing with the need for sexual expression without the dangers inherent in producing too many new humans.

As you can see by the foregoing, the science fiction mind is always ready with alternative possibilities—which is part of the game of human change.

Much of our lives we're breaking camp from one set of known surroundings and heading off into an unknown *Other Place* which we hope will become just as familiar as today's surroundings. That's the stuff of science fiction and it is, as well, the stuff of world crises. The hierarchical levels of a future society may very well be sharply defined by categorical birth into different intelligence classes, a birth prearranged from conception. Science of the pragmatic world may give us the aristocracy of the IQ which previous aristocracies attempted to create by mating only with their "own kind." We may look back on *1984* and *BNW* as relatively mild and amusing examples of fictional exploration in social engineering.

Much depends upon the way we integrate the myth world of our wishes into the physical experiences that define who we are as an animal society. This is the crux of all attempts to diagnose current conditions and form some articulated whole that expresses the nature of world crises. If we say, on the one hand, that our world suffers from a certain kind of disease that brings on these recurrent crises, then under present conditions of dependence upon words, the disease we "have" becomes more important than who we are as a people. This could be why we, as a society, suspect the large social diagnoses of the engineers and psychiatrists. We know with a sure and ancient instinct that to be treated and "cured" of such a disease could take from us both the why and the who of our identity.

Certain pitfalls exist in our tendency toward overdependence upon the professional expert, the specialist. When we turn toward such counsel, we begin by admitting that we are helpless and require their *superior* guidance. At the very moment we seek such help, we have created a particular kind of non-symmetrical relationship: the professional, all-powerful and knowledgeable on one hand, and the dependent, abject one on the other hand. One side assumes all of the healthy viewpoint and the other side takes on all of the sickness. With a kind of suicidal totality, we turn matters over to the professional, saying: "Heal me."

This is the situation upon which the politician capitalizes and which psychiatry/psychology have been unable to resolve. Instead, the so-called mental sciences have been seeking political power for many years. This was to be expected as a natural outcome of their power posture. They assumed the position of *all-health* dealing with *all-sickness*. Such non-symmetrical relationships inevitably produce shattering crises.

Remember the old Chinese curse: "May you live in interesting times."

The Chinese of those days valued a serene existence. Their utopian ideal was based on a sophisticated appreciation of the world, on the guiding of the senses into heightened awareness. It's not surprising that Zen found wide acceptance in such a culture. The inner world obviously was where one dealt with consciousness. Thus, external crises were to be avoided. Ignorance, poverty, starvation, and disease were the evils. War was a class monopoly and was to be kept in its own place. Famous generals could not hope for the status of famous teachers. Fear was a tool of statecraft and was to be used to keep down the size of government. Apotheosis (transubstantiation to an immortal state with one's ancestors) was a necessary part of culture.

In such a setting, interesting times were times that changed dramatically, rolled on the wheel of crisis. Those old Chinese could have made common cause with Middle America. Both look to the ideal society as one of social unity, of togetherness as the ultimate social achievement. The distinguishing of one individual from another has to be held within tight limits. To be different is to be dangerous.

God bless the child who has his own. That's the catch phrase, but don't sing it too loudly except on Saturday nights.

This is both a pure and abstract notion. It is the seeking for solace against the physical isolation of the individual identity. It is a barrier against mortality akin to ancestor worship. It is also the stuff of paradox because it brings with it dreams of gods, of nations, and professional experts as the all-powerful arbiters of our lives. This necessarily creates the conditions of crisis because it fails to deal with change. It does not square with a changing universe.

Thus, we get the stuff of crises and of science fiction.

On this relatively small planet well out into the edge of a minor spiral galaxy, we have been simultaneously breeding ourselves an abundance of humans while creating an abundance of material things for a small proportion of that burgeoning life. Against a backdrop of false absolutes, we reduce the variables that we permit in our societies, in our individuals, and in our possessions. By our acts, we demonstrate that we want mass production of a standard human who employs standardized consumer goods. We execute this mass production of sameness in a largely unexamined, unconscious manner.

But *nature* constantly evolves, trying out its new arrangements, its new kinds of life, its differences, its interesting times, its crises. Against such movement, we attempt our balancing acts, our small sallies at equilibrium. In the dynamic interrelationships of the universe around us, we look for models upon which to pattern our lives. But that universe greets us with complexities everywhere we turn. To talk about just one element, carbon, for example, we are forced to deal with combinations whose complexities we have not yet exhausted.

You've read about such things in science fiction; you see the conditions around you which touch your own life. Still, you seek *the* answer.

Our land of plenty was supposed to lead the way to a world of plenty for humankind. Instead, we followed a more ancient pattern, becoming like the worst in those we opposed. We lead the world today in the potential for mass violence. The material doldrums of the 1950s trended gradually into this era, and instead of plenty we find ourselves in a world where, if we shared the world's food supply equally with every living human being, all of us would starve.

Malthus pointed the way. Science fiction has been filling in the possibilities of a Malthusian world ever since. If we experience massive human die-back in such areas as the island of Java, Malthus and science fiction will have been proven correct.

But at what a cost!

We approach this next level of crises as though we lived constantly in the presence of devils. If no devils appear, we manufacture them. *Give us this day our daily devil.* To counter the unconscious (and conscious) tensions aroused by such a process, we seek seclusion, individual privacy—all the while breeding ourselves out of that vanishing commodity.

Creativity of any kind has become the modern devil.

And the oddball is dangerous.

We want to end all conflicts. They not only kill us, they never seem to produce the glorious and victorious end conditions which we verbally attach to them. But now that the Vietnam war has been brought near a close, we awaken to the realization that we still live in a world threatened by imminent, totally destructive, mass conflict. We cure the disease and find we still suffer from it.

Paradox, paradox: the stuff of crises and of science fiction.

We walk across the ground of our fears and our movement stores up static electricity which shocks us every time we touch the *real* world. Somehow, we are not grounded to the universe. But we go doggedly about those tasks we consider necessary, emulating the muddle-through quality of the ideal nineteenth-century British public servant. And all the time, we fight to repress the sinking feeling that everything we do is useless, that the next crisis will leave us destitute.

Why can't the world be more like me?

Middle America *über alles!*

On the wall of a small hotel in Kabul, Afghanistan, there is a notice, which reads as follows:

MENU

Acid...$1
Opium..30 Afghanis
Heroin..70 Afghanis
Ask Abdul

The hotel, populated in season by large numbers of expatriate American youths, represents a full retreat from crises—retreat from crises into crisis.

You may find it strange that I read this and other signs as heralding hard times ahead for science fiction as we have known it. This is how I read it:

The current utopian ideal being touted by people as politically diverse (on the surface, but not underneath) as President Richard M. Nixon and Senator Edward M. Kennedy goes as follows—no deeds of passion allowed, no geniuses, no criminals, no imaginative creators of the new. Satisfaction may be gained only in carefully limited social interactions, in living off the great works of the past. There must be limits to any excitement. Drug yourself into a placid "norm." Moderation is the key word. And how the old Chinese would have loved that!

In a word, you can be a Bozo, but little else.

Rolling Stone in the fall of 1972 described this world of bozoness:

"Bozos are the huge, fat middle waist in the land. They clone. Everybody tends to drift toward bozoness. It has Oz in it. They mean well. They like their comforts. The Bozos have learned to enjoy their free time, which is all the time."

Among the secondhand, limited excitements permitted in the Bozo world would be reading science fiction, but its creators are in for harsh treatment unless they hew strictly to the well-worn concepts already treated by the field, unless they eschew anything truly new or pertinent.

No more *1984*s. No untimely accuracy. You must stick to such things as *Walden Two*, which is really Edward Bellamy brought up to date. You must look backward, only backward.

Creativity, however, requires wide open alternatives. It fits with the random chaos of the unknown universe and with those limited (and limiting) laws which we learn to apply for our temporary benefit. Science fiction has functioned well against such a backdrop. The more diverse our work, the more profoundly creative, the more luxurious the literature.

The luxury of unbridled investigation carries its own ongoing sense of excitement, one of the attractions of the best science fiction. What will I find around the next corner? This is one of the marvelous lures of pure science, as well. And pure science already is finding itself in the public doghouse. The levelers ask: "Why'd you bastards discover atomic weapons and lasers and bacteriological weapons and all that crazy stuff?"

One of the answers goes this way: "I was driving down this road, see, and there it was."

"But how'd you find the right road?"

"Well, I took that turn back there a ways and, you see, there it was."

The best science fiction and pure science assume an infinite universe where we can look up at the blue sky. That's our playing field. Eton is too confining. That sense of infinity (anything can happen) gives us the proper elbow room. But an infinite universe is a place where crimes of passion can occur, where any dream can be dreamed *and* realized. The reward of investigating such a universe in fiction or in fact is not so much reducing the unknown but increasing it, opening the way to new dangers, new crises. This implies disorder when what we suppose we're seeking is order. The story plot and the scientific law represent order, but chaos lurks at their edges.

Order equals law, a key word for humans.

Law indicates the form by which we attempt to understand order. It enables us to predict and otherwise deal with order. And we don't like the mathematician suggesting to us that we occupy a universe of multiple orders, plural, and thus of multiple laws.

Humans want beginnings and nice anthropomorphic motives and happy endings. But motives (intent) are not required against an infinite field of laws. The assumption of infinity opens quite a contrary view. Infinity does not require beginnings or endings. Intent does require them. The essence of infinity is no-beginning, no-ending. Without ends, there can be no ultimate (absolute) goals, no judgments, and the whole concept of sin and guilt (products of intent) falls apart. Such concepts as sin-guilt-judgment require beginnings which are cut out of an infinitive system, boxed-in, articulated and defined for human motives. They occur as segments of a *linear* system whose infinite surroundings must be represented as nonlinear. Such concepts are ways of dealing with finite, human-created and human-interpreted laws, and are only incidentally (in the fullest meaning of that word) related to infinity.

To project a god, a government, or a professional expert against such a backdrop, we set limits.

Law and order represent a system of dealing with interesting times such that we set our preordained limits upon crises. Law and order is a breeder of crises because it cannot predict everything that will happen.

To accept a universe where anything can happen, however, is to accept a hellish insecurity which is, in itself, an ongoing crisis. We don't know how to understand such a universe. The essence of something we don't understand is that it appears chaotic; it lacks recognizable order. There's a devil in anything we don't understand. It is menacing. It is an outer darkness in which we not only lose a recognizable ground upon which to stand, but we also lose all sense of identity. It is a vision of hell. We must defeat such a devil at all cost.

And we forget that we created this devil.

We say, instead: "This is who I am. This is my absolute god. These are my absolute laws. Get thee behind me, Sathanus!"

Thus, we strive for the illusion of all-knowing in an infinite universe where anything can happen. We seek the basic law to explain a never-ending All which stands as a seething backdrop, as the Vedantic void, that ultimate chaos from which any form of law or order must derive.

In *The God Makers*, I have a religious leader say it this way:

"We have a very ancient saying: the more god, the more devil; the more flesh, the more worms; the more property, the more anxiety; the more control, the more that needs control."

The lost existence of our Eden-Paradise gets further and further from a dichotomized, man-limited world, less attainable every instant. We must turn to science fiction for the temporary illusion, for the *prediction* that once again we will enter into the blissful universe of godlike order. You would be astonished at how often science fiction editors get the Adam and Eve story as the first effort of the aspiring writer. It has become the cliché of clichés in our field. We attempt to deny Eden's ultimate, unchanging conservatism, its essential boredom for the questing intelligence. The very language in which these concepts are couched provides a retreat to match the menu on the Kabul hotel's wall.

Santaroga Barrier puts it thus:

"We sift reality through screens composed of ideas. (And such ideas have their roots in older ideas.) Such idea systems are necessarily limited by language, by the ways we can describe them. That is to say: language cuts the grooves in which our thoughts move. If we seek new validity forms (other laws and other orders) we must step outside language."

We must stand silently and point at the new thing.

This represents an essential Zen concept.

Santaroga portrays an extreme reaction against many of the problems challenging human survival in the 1970s. Technology worship, endless economic growth, human alienation, the limitless powers implied by scientific investigation—all products of today's American-style society—are rejected by Santaroga's counterculture. Santaroga attempts to control change and thus to scale down both the physical and social pace of human life. Isolated, but with a purpose to their hibernation, Santarogans try to make better people for a static world which is necessarily depicted as a valley, a place of high walls, both natural and manmade.

It is the mind, not the artifacts of human ingenuity, on which Santarogans concentrate. However admirable their intentions, the result of their behavioral control is not totally positive. Santaroga is dangerously stable, poised always on the edge of destructive crisis. Its people seem happy but without individual vitality. They are not enslaved by technological innovation, but neither are they much concerned about creativity and personal development. Life for the Santarogan revolves around an archaic super-loyalty to the community which is deliberately akin to nation-state patriotism.

Santarogans indulge in their own form of the step-by-step behavioral engineering you see in *Walden Two*. They also remain self-suspended in time. They have chosen a rather static "good life" to escape the dilemma that Alvin Toffler's *Future Shock* details. The closed society creates its own Berlin Wall to keep out visitors, tourism, the threats inherent in things and people which are different.

Santaroga turns out to be Middle America and Old China brought up to date. As in *Walden Two*, Santarogans extol the merits of their society and permit selective immigration. Essentially, both Santaroga and *Walden Two* ask whether human happiness can be achieved through positive reinforcement techniques and tampering with chemical and psychological characteristics of the species. It is not a question to pass over lightly because every extant culture does those very things, although in a relatively haphazard manner. The difference is that *Walden Two* and *Santaroga Barrier* describe a conscious, "scientific" approach to social conditioning.

Why is it, then, that most people detect something sinister in such a process to produce humans who would behave in a predictable, although "socially beneficial" way? Behavioral control and happiness appear to be inextricably linked in the contemporary social engineering field. Most humans feel, however, that such tampering would not produce happiness, but would force us into new crises.

We have always distrusted Machiavelli.

Is it the coldness? The manipulation of humans by humans? Is it the inevitable separation into the *users* and the *used*, the abject seekers after help and the all-knowing helpers?

The character, Gilbert Dasein, sees the common identity of Santaroga thusly:

"In there behind the facade, Santaroga did something to its people. They lost personal identity and became masks for something that was the same in all of them . . . a one-pointedness . . . such that every Santarogan became an extension of every other Santarogan."

Arthur Clarke, in *Childhood's End*, states it baldly; his entire story represents a comment on differences. He is saying to you that, while men have been able to adapt to wide differences in climate, geography, and threats to survival, they have not always been able to adapt to differences in one another. In the end, the children of Clarke's Earth become what can only be interpreted as a single identity and that identity reflects the myth structure of Western man. Witness the way anthropological studies of acculturation focus on the difficulties a non-Western "underdeveloped" people confront while undergoing cultural assimilation by the West. Almost no studies have been done on the difficult adaptation problem faced by Western men when thrust into a non-Western society.

In fact, Western men tend to refuse such adaptation; we must force others to imitate us. One does not go native!

Why can't the universe be more like me?

Through what is probably a profound unconscious process, the flow of Western scientific/technological development takes on much the same characteristics. Most of science fiction has followed the same channel.

Nature, as a system of systems which we attempt to reduce to some kind of order, has been conceived by much of Western science as flowing from a unified field. Eastern researchers have taken a quite contrary viewpoint, saying that a unified field is inconceivable because even such a mental construct would tend to flow and change. To the Eastern viewpoint, seeking after a fixed, unchanging unified field is the ultimate in conservative thinking. It requires a god (or government, or society of professional experts) who must be worshiped by a mass consciousness that agrees slavishly with everything coming from the god, the government, or the experts.

It is a question of the relationship between human consciousness and the rest of the universe, whether by oneself or through intermediaries. Western culture, selling itself as the last outpost of individualism, has been as quick to stifle this characteristic as the East has been. The West has merely been less aware, and thus less candid, about the consequences of its major decisions. It is also a characteristic of the West that we must believe in absolutes. We demand them. Our language assumes them. We ask: "What *is* it?" And we say: "It either *is* or it *isn't*."

The verb "to be" betrays us.

Some of the East escaped this pitfall, but shared our tendencies toward the designed state, toward all-inclusive planning. We in the West seduced the East not through guns and massive power, but through engineering and planning. We captured most of the Eastern consciousness through engineered "contingency factors."

An engineer of my acquaintance, servant of a powerful industry, when asked how his industry dealt with unknown contingencies in its long-range plans, said:

"We put a very large item in the budget and label it *contingency.* When the unexpected problem arises, if it's something money won't solve, we borrow facilities from other areas. We patch together a temporary solution until we can fill in the gaps."

He went on to explain that the cost of such solutions was added later to the price which the public pays.

The question of absolutes—absolute solutions, absolute control—remains at the core of our science, our science fiction, and our approach to the solution of crises. It is, without a doubt, a battle of ingrained conservatism against outer chaos. Our utopian dreams of Eden are essentially conservative. We dream of a designed state wherein all the needs of the designers are secure. The main function of paradise is to entertain the needs of its human creators. Everyone must be a Bozo, happily comfortable, and thus limited in severely designed ways. There goes freedom of choice and in come *Santaroga* and *Walden Two*.

And God had better answer our prayers or we'll stop worshiping him. We'll vote for somebody else.

Few seem to have remarked the failure of demanding, ego-centered prayer as an argument for the current revival of satanism, witchcraft, and the like. The morality argument has fallen on hard times recently. Is it significant that both Barry Goldwater and George McGovern, candidates who offered themselves on morality platforms, lost by about the same proportion? There does appear to be an element of moralizing which says: "Why can't you be more like me?"

When the chips were down, the American electorate may have said: "I'll render my own moral judgments, thank you, and you can stuff that preacher pose."

"Judge not lest ye be judged."

In a sense, the struggles of our world, the crises arising from these struggles, and the stuff of our literary creations which reflect on the sensory universe represent a battle over human consciousness and its judgments. It's not so much the minds and hearts of men that are at stake, but their awareness, the ideas they are permitted. The struggle is over what is judged valuable in our universe. Some of the antagonists follow a valuable system based on what can be measured, counted, or tabulated. They call this attitude "realpolitik." Others base their standards on undefinable terms (undefinable because they change when we touch them) such as freedom, the rights of man, morality, the law of God. . . .

These latter concepts defy programming. They must be continually reinterpreted. Witness the provisions for change in the United States Constitution. Islam provided for *Qazi*, judges who rule on secular matters as they derive from the Koran. *Qazi* must be "adult, free, Muslim and unconvicted of slander."

Even as they are defined, these concepts fall outside current conventions of language which, as a set of symbols, remains finite and forever incomplete as a communications tool. Language opens up the reflection of thought, but by its very nature it also creates boundaries which appear insurmountable when posed against infinity. Language programs us, decides what we see and how we see it—what value judgment we place on anything we see. It is a root of prejudice and a limiter of perceptions as the embodiment of previous experiences which have been judged and catalogued. A new occurrence, pervaded by past perceptions, can be misconstrued. Power—secular and religious—is grounded in language. To assault the barriers of language is to do something dangerous to those who hold power because you open the way to new validity forms, new relationships, new *laws*, new ways of ordering society. Language represents an intervening force when we articulate our dream utopias. It prevents the realization of dreams. It is a sea of paradox, the substance of interesting times, curses and blessings and interesting stories.

Without language there would be no science fiction. What a crisis that would be!

Remember that Thomas More, the author who gave us the word *Utopia* and the dream of uniformity which the Old Chinese and the modern West find so enchanting, conceived his paradise in the form of the army—as does Skinner in *Walden Two*, as the pure-gospel Communists do, as the ancient Essenes did, as they did in the Oneida Colony. . . . The rule appears so very simple:

"From every person according to his ability and to every person according to his needs."

This requires, however, that someone pass judgment on the needs and abilities, setting limits for them. More's *Utopia* provided public kitchens, public clothing repair shops, public laundries, etc., and guidelines for public behavior. I invite you to run your own survey. Ask people who have served in a branch of the military if they judged that a utopian existence. Personally, I recall an unspoken military commandment: "No individual crises allowed!"

Walden One, as seen through Thoreau's prejudices, was a place where the physical universe and the human spirit were to be interwoven harmoniously. Thoreau permitted no machines. Only the simplest things that the earth provided made up his tools. He professed himself perfectly contented in this condition.

Thoreau was not the first on that path. Rousseau drew similar surroundings for his "noble savage." St. Francis of Assisi employed his religious genius in rebellion against life-styles of the thirteenth century. To know God, it was necessary to discard all material possessions and marry nature. He said, in Christ's words, "The foxes have holes, the birds of the air have nests, but the son of man hath not where to lay his head."

And then there were the earlier Pan god prototypes.

Pan is still with us.

Religion says: "Love is the answer."

Science says: "There's infinite energy out there just waiting for the right blend of imagination and creativity to bring it into the service of man."

Rebellious youth says: "I'm going back to the farm."

The Black says: "I want it all; share it!"

The American Indian says: "Give it back before you wreck everything."

The social engineer says: "The key to our many problems remains in proper ordering and efficiency."

Listen to the social engineer because he has the inside track. Constant planning is a *Walden Two* obsession. That's familiar, isn't it? There we go again trying to impose our human order on an infinite universe.

However, when we narrow our frame of reference to the earth itself, as Thoreau did, it appears nature is a circle of delicately balanced systems which function efficiently only when man doesn't tamper with them. According to this view, man introduces chaos into what was originally a well-ordered plan, a system of symmetry and balances, and our attempts to establish our own kind of order open us to new complexities and crises.

But the desire for that abstract condition which we call *security* is implicit in our attempts to plan and order our lives. Disorder and chaos, the uncertainties of an infinite universe, threaten our peace of mind if not our physical comfort.

Against such a background, behavioral (social) engineers such as Skinner can be heard pleading with us: "Please! Let us plan the world in a way that will set our minds at ease."

Translation: "Why can't everyone be more like me?"

Because the mind at ease is a dead mind.

For civilization to exist as we know it, socializing processes must be strong and pervasively thorough. We are programmed in a multitude of ways, many of them operating unconsciously. By the time we awaken even faintly to the awareness that we have been socially conditioned, we find ourselves so indoctrinated that it's difficult, if not impossible, to break the old patterns. The reinforcements of the system are powerful, many of them rooted in our animal past, and such systems have been taken over entirely by the unconscious socializing programs. Our history also shows us that there has always been a majority in human society which never becomes aware of any need for change.

Survival pressures demanding that we evolve, grow, and change, however, continue to proliferate. We don't want to change, but the floodgates open abruptly and we are overwhelmed.

Crisis!

Western tradition faces such demands with the concept of absolute control. You control the force which seeks to change your world. You build a dam. You organize an army, a navy, an air force, a space service, more efficient police. You control the mob—even that mob in yourself. You control crime or the Mafia or the heroin traffic. Never mind that the control concept is in direct conflict with the American myth of individuality: the thing you fear must be controlled.

How the control concept works with the heroin traffic exemplifies what happens when we apply such pressures to a system without sufficient understanding of the system's internal behavior. Understand first that we have never discovered an upper limit to what the heroin addict will pay for his fix. The *demand impulse* of the system has a wide open upper limit, assumed as infinite. Result: New Yorkers no longer live in Fun City. It's Fear City, made that way by this lack of understanding about the drug traffic. New York at night is effectively in a state of siege reminding one of the Mekong Delta at the height of the Vietnam War. Remember? "The night belongs to Charley." New Yorkers know their addicts will pay any price asked of them—your life, your household goods, anything.

But our dominant approach continues to operate out of that judgmental edict: *Heroin is nasty! Suppress it! Control it!*

Even with our wildest control binge, however, the heroin traffic cannot be completely shut off. Some of it will get through. Remember the industrial engineer's comment on unknown contingencies? You put in a big contingency fund which is passed along to the consumer. Thus, some heroin will enter the United States because the head of a friendly government (or his uncle, or his sister) profits from the traffic; or because a federal agent has been paid off; or because a high United States military officer has become an addict and is forced to use his facilities in the traffic; or, finally, because there are just too many holes through which the stuff can enter the nation.

It may cost a bundle to corrupt a federal official, a general, or a member of the State Department, but what the hell! The consumer will pay.

Ultimately, even if you are not an addict, that consumer-who-pays is you.

Our control efforts do little more than raise the price of the heroin that does get through. There's no upper limit on that price; thus it's a wide open system.

If we really wanted to make a social adjustment to the heroin traffic, our actions would have to be somewhat different. We would have to accept first that our new approach would bring its own problems, that it would not be *the* final and absolute answer. But let's begin by assuming that it's not a good thing to allow a flow of money which can corrupt high officials and whole police departments. Let's assume that we want to stop that flow of corrupting cash. Very well; we take the profit out of the heroin traffic. We make the addict's fix available at a reasonable price—say for about fifty cents and under medical supervision. Then we prepare ourselves to deal with the other socio-medical aspects of the drug problem which would be certain to surface under these new conditions. We could do this by understanding that we would be *dealing with* our mutual problem, not controlling it.

The one-pointed view of the "control it" approach invariably seduces us into making faulty assumptions. A fundamental cause of depressed urban areas has been found to be an excess of low-cost housing, rather than the housing shortages which we assumed to be the problem. City tax bases and legal structures gave incentives for not tearing down old buildings. But aging industrial buildings bring a decline in employment. Residential structures, as they age, attract lower income groups who are forced to use them at a higher population density. Jobs decline while population rises. Then, we come in with our development schemes and add *more* low-cost housing. This attracts more people from the low-income group into the area where jobs are decreasing. Our well-intentioned efforts help to create what Jay W. Forrester of MIT calls "a social trap."

But that wasn't what we wanted at all, was it? My God! We have to control this sort of thing!

Pakistan wanted to control its mosquitoes because the insects are a vector in a runaway malaria problem. However, Pakistan already suffered from the *control disease* which it caught from our Western culture. Having only enough funds and other resources for about a seventy-five percent mosquito control program, Pakistan demonstrated how well it had learned from the West by going ahead with an incomplete program. Result: the surviving mosquitoes are now resistant to former control techniques and malaria is again on a runaway increase.

Attempting to control something "evil," we precipitate a larger crisis. This may be a general human tendency. We feel helpless and alone when faced with large problems. Loneliness influences us to grab for the reassurance of anything offered to us as *the* solution. We want someone to assure us he has the answer and if we'll only follow him. . . . It produces very odd behavior. The more complex a problem appears, the more apathetic we become; the more we turn away, the more strongly we grasp at a proffered solution which is presented with the promise of immediate relief. After all, Pakistan's seventy-five percent mosquito control program *did* ease the malaria problem, temporarily.

We know that a single-pointed attempt to solve a problem is more likely to increase that problem's complexity, make the problem harder to solve and, eventually, confront us with a crisis. The arguments for planetwide planning of human existence are relatively easy to accept, but the danger of massive, single-entry "solutions" remains as long as humans demand "immediate relief."

It is astonishing how many college-level young people writing scenarios for a utopian rebuilding of world society begin their scenarios with a worldwide disaster which kills off ninety percent or more of the human population. The scenarios then have the survivors (including the scenario author, of course) climb back to a planned civilization based on "nonrepressive freedom." The quote is from an actual scenario by a twenty-year-old college junior.

Many of these young writers turn to Herbert Marcuse and Paolo Soleri (strange bedfellows, indeed) for supportive arguments, and they draw heavily from the works of such writers as Robert Heinlein, Ray Bradbury, Arthur Clarke, Ted Sturgeon, Isaac Asimov, Alfred Bester, Jack Williamson, Tony Boucher (W.A.P. White), John Campbell, Lester del Rey, Hugo Gernsback, Henry Kuttner, C. M. Kornbluth, Frederik Pohl, Fritz Leiber, Murray Leinster, Judith Merril, Margaret St. Clair (Idris Seabright), Clifford Simak, Robert Silverberg, William Tenn (Philip Klass), Jack Vance, Poul Anderson, A. E. van Vogt. . . .

This is just a partial list of authors named as sources by students in university classes writing utopian scenarios. The science fiction authors are understandable in this list, but Soleri and Marcuse may need some explanation. Soleri provides them with the concept of arcologies (the single social superstructure, world village) and Marcuse outlines the psychomythology of rebellion. It is Marcuse who provides the justification for killing the world's population down to a "manageable" size. Soleri leads the scenario writers to think of mining "the old cities" for materials to construct new super-urban communities linked by high-speed transit. We in science fiction provide social and technological innovations— the frosting on the supercake.

Inevitably, the scenario writers come down to hard judgments, decisions about the limits within which people will be forced to live. Even with London a half hour from New York City and most of the world's surviving population living underground to free the surface for agriculture and other human requirements, the consequent accelerated demand for efficiency produces its own paradox which the scenario writers fail to resolve. They turn to more and more planning, a pervasive planning-octopus which reaches deeper and deeper into the individual life. Current concepts of freedom are abandoned "for the general welfare" and heavy social conditioning is accepted as "inevitable." The demand for more god produces more satan. In come the Skinnerians and another crisis lurks at the end of this road.

Well, the Club of Rome and MIT in their study of the limits to human growth warned us what was happening. They said humans cannot go on increasing their numbers anarchically or exponentially beyond specific limits on this finite planet. They told us that growth must be selective, oriented, governed—that is, *planned*. Equilibrium must be maintained between the human population and its habitat. But this equilibrium cannot be reached if world society remains in a state of imbalance. Social justice and peace have definite ecological impact. But people *en masse* are loath to face up to issues which seem beyond human comprehension and *control*.

World population, which took hundreds of generations to reach present numbers, will double its size in the next thirty years. That means more than seven billion people—all demanding homes, schools, industry, entire cities, highways, harbors, and all the rest of it. No relevant body of opinion has so far faced up to this challenge. There is no *they* out there working on the big answer. Some sort of global planning may be undertaken in this decade, but political pitfalls line the way. The problem may become too big and complicated to be dealt with at all before even the first hesitant steps are taken.

Now *there* is a crisis for you.

Science fiction has explored such fancies and continues to explore them, but the basis for today's world planning concepts remains firmly seated in a commitment to absolute goals—political and physical. The holders of power in this world have not awakened to the realization that there is no single model of a society, a species, or an individual. There are a variety of models to meet a variety of needs. They meet different expectations and have different goals. The aim of that force which impels us to live may be to produce as many different models as possible.

As things now stand, you can be doing something that doesn't need to be done, which in fact is threatening to the survival of the human species, and yet you may be surrounded by a system which says you're doing your job well. The question "Should you be doing this at all?" is seldom asked in a species-wide context. We remain caught in the old "realities" with all of their myth-based self-justifications.

Remember that a way to align your behavior with my desires is to get you to accept my definition of reality. Power rests in getting masses of people to accept your interpretation of events, and this is firmly seated in the structure of language. The words you use, how they are defined as descriptions of events, these carry the weight. Certain definitions are established (Freedom is freedom, dammit!) and these are imposed on our social experiences. The delusional content of the definitions is masked by social pressures. "Historical knowledge" (any past definition) is marshaled to support the way we interpret new experiences. This all occurs within hierarchical structures where the occupants of niches may change but the structures, their myths, and their delusions remain. *"There must be an absolute authority which will make everything right . . . eventually."*

What one learns best in this world is how to please those farther up the ladder of authority. Education and social pressures cultivate individuals highly sensitive to the demands coming down to them from above. Most people believe what they are told to believe. The hedge against the unexpected, our social contingency factor, is to continue believing in the possibility of miracles. Of course, if you read the story of Jesus carefully, you'll note that the employment of miracles brought profoundly disruptive crises.

I must take another look at Olympus and recall that it's the source of the most disastrous earthquakes which have struck the northwest corner of the United States. Even a pile of dirt can turn against you.

Perhaps tomorrow I'll call my friend, the industrial engineer, and warn him: "There can be no absolute contingency allowance in an infinite universe."

As long as that's a condition of our existence, the explorations of science and science fiction will continue to turn up exciting discoveries.

But look out for the crises!

About
Frank Herbert

In person, Frank Herbert was every bit as interesting as he is on paper.

I first met Frank in 1979, while writing a book about his work. He was on a publicity tour sponsored by his publisher, and I met him at their offices in New York. I was early for my interview, and had a chance to sit in on an earlier meeting. The interviewer was a short, stuffy, cigar-smoking man from New Jersey who knew nothing about science fiction, and less about Frank Herbert. (His company had decided to cash in on the science fiction boom by putting together a glossy fan magazine of some kind.)

The interview was brilliant. Frank both posed the questions and answered them, but the man was left thinking he had done a good job. As Lao-tzu said, "When the best leader leads, the people say 'We did it ourselves.'"

On tour, Frank was like that: intense, brilliant, eloquent—these are the words that came to mind. Each question returned an essay, a flood of thought. Frank looked at you with penetrating eyes, and used all the skills of a veteran reporter to discover your interests and evoke your questions.

After I had met him a few more times, the brilliant facade began to dim for me. I wanted to meet the real Frank Herbert, not the man on show. The very qualities which had first impressed me began to seem a barrier.

Much later, when I met him at home on his own turf, Frank was more at ease, less the performer, simply a man who writes for a living, whose ideas have ignited greater fires than he had planned.

The following two pieces give you a feel for Frank as he was at home in the Pacific Northwest. His love for the country and the life there shines through.

Country Boy

The following reminiscences about Frank's childhood are excerpted from my first interview with him, in 1979.

I grew up on the Olympic and Kitsak peninsulas in the state of Washington. And even when we lived in Tacoma we lived on the outskirts. It was sufficiently lightly populated that you could keep your own chickens and a cow.

So I was mostly a country boy. To the point where I really have trouble in a city . . . remembering streets. I know how to get there—because you turn right at the drugstore. It's a landmark consciousness. My pattern ability is deeply seated in a landmark consciousness rather than a label consciousness.

Another thing I've noticed about the difference between country and city is that you find many more self-starters, who aren't stopped by certain kinds of problems, coming from the country than the city. In the city, if your car breaks down, you go to the garage, and they're closed. You throw up your hands and say you'll come back Monday. In the country, if your hay-baler breaks down, you've gotta get the hay in, and you say, "Well, get me the tool kit."

I would also say that I was very heavily marked by a journalistic attitude of looking at the world. There's a particular kind of attitude that this sets up, and that is, if you want to find out, you go ask questions. I've never hesitated to ask anybody anything I wanted to know. Sometimes you have to get into a *quid pro quo* situation. Especially if you're asking an expert to teach you his expertise, or a sufficient amount of it that you can write knowledgeably about it. What you have to do, and what I did, is to knock on doors, and say, "Look, I can do something which may be useful to you. I can write. Do you have any papers you want written, or anything of this nature?"

And don't worry about your questions making you appear stupid. If they're stupid, you say, "Well, straighten me out." And I would say that attitude was crucial. In a very real way, that's a scientific attitude.

I've got a very catholic curiosity. Things interest me and I just go see if I can find out about them. I blew the minds of the *California Living* people. They wanted me to become their wine writer. And I wouldn't write about wine before I spent a couple of years learning how to make wine. And so finally I knew what I was doing, educated my palate to a degree, and went on from there. Then I'd write about it.

I had early Catholic training. My mother was from an Irish Catholic family. My father was not, and my father really won. I was a rebel against Jesuit positivism. I know how to win an argument in the Jesuit fashion, but I think it's flying under false colors. If you control the givens, you can win any argument.

I looked on schools, especially when I got up to the higher levels, as a kind of a cafeteria line. I wasn't interested in a degree. I was always interested in writing. I announced that to my folks when I was eight years old. I came down to my birthday breakfast, which was laid on to my precise demands, and announced that I was going to be "a author." And I never really deviated from that very much.

I thought that I was good at telling stories, that I could entertain—and did, from a very early age. I was telling stories at

Boy Scout campfires when I was twelve, thirteen, fourteen. I was known for it. You get great ego massages, you know, when you get called on to do it. But it's also good practice. It's good training ground. In a very real sense I was trained as a jongleur was trained, to entertain orally.

And as far as I'm concerned, the oral tradition is far more deeply seated in our psyches than the written tradition. And what you're really doing when you put words on a page is talking to the ears, through the eyes. And so you'd better be conscious of how the individual hears it, even though it's silent on the page. I mean it's a lot of things, not just rhythm. It's the associations of the sounds, some things beyond onomatopoeic considerations.

I call it a dance, too. It really is. I also call it a jazz performance. It really is a jazz performance. There is no other conversation in the universe that has ever been precisely like the one we're having now. And there never will be another one precisely like it.

You Can
Go Home Again

Last night, I looked out my living room windows at the 600-foot tower of Seattle's Space Needle and called myself a damn fool.

It was a beautiful, clear and sparkling night. The lights of the Bremerton ferry drew a mirrored pattern on the water as it headed for its glistening new pier on our Elliot Bay waterfront.

Off to the right, maybe five miles from me as the crow flies, the Alki Point light winked and turned, as green and shining as a glass of creme de menthe.

"Damn fool," I said.

I could see Mount Rainier's hump of ice cream behind the space needle. And out to the west there lay the whole line of the Olympic mountains frosted with moonlit snow.

It was so beautiful it made you want to shut up and just get drunk, from nothing more than looking.

Now, I'm supposed to help spoil that? "Tell California tourists about the attractions of the Northwest," they said.

And I, like a fool, agreed.

Do you really think I want you coming up here, filling this relatively clean air with your exhaust fumes, leaving your beer cans and garbage on our beaches, doing all the things we do en masse to destroy the earth which supports us?

What I do wish is that you could have shared, really shared, that moment of admiration for this lovely corner of the universe—that moment when I looked out our windows.

And there are other things I wish you could share.

A few weeks ago, my wife and I went up to Vancouver Island. We drove west along the island's southern tip to River Jordan, Port Renfrew, then north along the Gordon River to Cowichan Lake, to Duncan and back to Victoria down the west side of Saanich Inlet.

The gravel road along the island's southern tip alternately dips down to the beaches of the Strait of Juan de Fuca, then climbs to give you magnificent vistas out into the Pacific.

This is the important part—on that first leg of the circle we drove twenty-four miles, an hour and a half, without seeing another car or another person. On the Gordon River leg, we passed two cars containing fishermen. Between Duncan and the West Side Highway, we passed thirty cars—locals, sightseers, tourists. There was one California license.

On the main north-south highway, there was as much traffic as you'd normally encounter along 101 between Mill Valley and Santa Rosa on a Sunday afternoon.

Very few of these cars on the main highway (and none on the back roads) were dashing along, intent on getting from here to there. The dominant traffic mood was that it was a beautiful day in a beautiful countryside.

It took us considerably longer to make that round-the-tip trip than just driving over the connecting roads because we stopped frequently to get out and walk to something that attracted us—a view spot, a creek, a patch of driftwood on the beach.

Through it all, we never once got the feeling we were being crowded—either by people or their artifacts or their rich garbage.

How long has it been since you drove twenty-four miles without seeing another car or another person? How long has it been since you were lured into stopping your road locomotive and getting out for a walk in real wilderness?

It may give you an insight into what it means to live here if I tell you that what we regularly carry in the trunk of our car and what we have at hand, ready to toss into the back of the car.

Standard equipment in the trunk: fishing tackle for two,

a nested pan-dish set, a clam shovel and bucket, a small hatchet and cooking grill, hiking boots and a complete change of rough, outdoor clothing.

At home in one package, all set to toss into the car, are sleeping bags and a light shelter.

What I'm saying is that you live *with* the countryside here. If you're a native, as I am, you know where and when to find the best edible mushrooms, you know the best oyster, geoduck and clam beaches, you know sources of good spring water and campsites.

Just a few weeks ago, I dug butter clams on a beach where my father took me clamming when I was seven years old.

When we first returned to Seattle from the Bay Area, we chartered a small boat, what we used to call "a cabin cruiser," and took off for two lazy weeks on Puget Sound. The charter cost was $250, and we absorbed a million dollars in human renewal.

We picked up the boat at Shilshole Bay Marina, Seattle, and headed north in water which I have navigated in small boats since I was a child.

We spent our first night on the boat at Roche Harbor in the U.S. San Juans and our second night at Pender Harbor in the Canadian San Juans.

By the third day, we were at Nelson Island on the British Columbia "Sunshine Coast." A deep, fjord channel heads east there toward Princess Louisa Inlet. The channel appears to run directly into mountains so steep and tall they have to be seen to be believed.

That evening, a half hour after the high tide had begun running out, I stood on a beach at Nelson Island in one spot, without moving my feet, and filled a small box with fresh oysters, selecting only the smaller, tastiest ones.

While doing this, our youngest son Bruce remained on the boat having the time of his life catching red snappers— and watching the float-line to our crab pot.

Right there and then, I knew I had come home, and I knew why.

· · ·

Last week, we came home late one night from hearing Leontyne Price in concert at the Seattle Opera House and made the few preparations required for a hiking trip the next day in the snow country near North Bend. We have a special affection for the North Bend area in the Cascades because we spent our honeymoon there isolated in a Forest Service fire-watch lookout.

It was foggy the next morning and we had to creep out of the city in fairly heavy traffic, most headed for ski areas. When we reached our parkside destination (adjoining a national forest) the weather had turned to mixed rain and snow.

We were dressed for it and made the short trail loop we had planned. It was cold, snow fell from branches in great wet blobs, but the countryside held that lovely sense of enduring beauty and strength.

Of course, we didn't cook our dinner over an open fire. We stopped at a roadside inn where we knew they had a big fireplace and served magnificent fresh trout poached in wine.

There's a marvelous inner relaxation that can be achieved by first getting fairly tired in wild surroundings, then stepping into the warmly cushioned environment of an inn so good it has been at the same place under the same management for twenty-five years. This one's at Cedar Falls. There's another (Mary's) at Port Angeles, waiting for you to come down from Hurricane Ridge in the Olympics.

Another (Pearl's) sits at the Purdy end of a long sandspit near Gig Harbor below Seattle, all ready to welcome you with local clam chowder and homemade wild blackberry pie on your return from a day along Hood Canal.

This Northwest corner of our nation has its own special flavor, a thing built out of the relentless force of water— Puget Sound, the Pacific Ocean, countless rivers and lakes —and a lush piling of life upon life, that beautifully interlocking, inter-dependent circle which we call ecology.

We stand in the full view of mountains so young they still can fill you with awe. I was driving back to my office one day last week and was stopped by a view. I pulled over to the side of a city street here in Seattle, got out and looked.

It had been raining—yes, it rains quite a bit here—and the air had that clear quality. It was early afternoon and by just turning around in that one hilltop spot in the north end of Seattle I could see the Cascades, the Olympics, Mt. Rainier and, poking its tip above the houses to the north, Mt. Baker.

No more than two hours driving could have put me at any of these places. But my driving, multiplied by the thousands like me all around, soils this beauty.

I suddenly felt myself as the intruder.

We're still eating the salmon (a forty pounder) I caught last fall off La Push. We had it canned at a sports cannery at Clallam Bay. We're going to dig geoduc on a minus tide next week. Good friends who live nearby will spend next week skiing in the Cascades. Another couple we've known for years will be going on a weekend house party at Port Townsend, a quaint mill town with a Victorian atmosphere, up on the Olympic Peninsula.

A group of friends—students and staff, from the University of Washington—will spend next weekend at a wilderness cabin on the Duckabush River in the Olympics. We were invited to spend the weekend at Irish Cabin, a "retreat-type" near the Snoqualmie Forest.

I think we will go to Irish Cabin. The occasion is a weekend of "brain-jamming" with about forty other "concerned citizens" over the problem of maintaining this fragile and beautiful country in which we live.

What I'm saying is this—if you decide to visit this region soon—do it with love.

On Writing

Frank Herbert was not only one of the best science fiction writers around, he was also one of the most articulate on the subject of what is special about science fiction as an artform, and on how he goes about writing it.

The following essays give you a sampling of Frank's thoughts on writing.

The first piece, written as an introduction to the fifteenth annual collection of winners of the Science Fiction Writers of America's Nebula Award, reveals Frank's suspicion of science fiction criticism and the academic legitimization of science fiction.

When I first proposed to write my own book of criticism on his work, Frank asked: "As my granddaughter might say, 'Please don't dullify it.'" And as he himself described his own writing:

> I design what I do, as best I'm able, to entertain. Because if you don't entertain, nobody's going to read it. You might as well write it for the smallest possible circle of friends—yourself and your mother, as I usually say.

Too often, the small world of literary criticism is just that—the smallest possible circle of friends. Frank was justifiably proud of the fact that he managed to pack a lot of thought into novels that are profoundly entertaining.

The second piece, "Men on Other Planets," was written for Reginald Bretnor's excellent collection of criticism by science fiction writers, The Craft of

Science Fiction. *It reveals Frank's fundamental concern with finding the familiar in the strange, and revealing the unknown in what seems familiar.*

The third piece is a feature article on poetry that Frank wrote in 1969 for the San Francisco Examiner's California Living *magazine. While Frank was not a poet, poetry was very important to him as a tool in his writing, and the boundaries between prose and poetry often blurred when he was composing the intense passages that occur in his novels—passages that often stick in the mind like poetry. He claimed to use poetry as:*

> . . . part of the process of writing, of loading the prose. In a sense, I use poetry the way a batter coming up to the plate swings three bats. If I want a passage to be evocative, I will write it as poetry. Then I conceal the poetry in the prose, in the paragraphing. I work on the beat, to fit the total rhythm of what I'm doing.

Introduction to
Nebula Winners Fifteen

You probably don't know the first damned thing about my prejudices. Do you care? Yet without that knowledge, anything I write in this introduction to the Science Fiction Writers of America Nebula anthology is virtually useless. Do you know how this book came to be?

Most of the hard work was done by Peter Pautz, SFWA's executive secretary. Like the anchor man on the six o'clock news, I was called in when the material was all assembled. I have read it and now I'm supposed to give you the "definitive critique." That may improve sales but it can be lousy communications.

You want to know what kind of mental safari you are about to take in this book?

A well-known literary critic once asked me if I believed "science fiction *really* could aspire to the status of Art?"

The capital *A* was audible.

I asked him why he thought any writer should bother his head with such an asinine question. This is especially poignant because I have yet to meet a literary critic who knows contemporary art or Art from a four-letter word which includes the same letters. And yes, I pass the same terrible judgment on myself-as-critic. I think the only reliable critic is time, and I don't mean the magazine.

Does it endure?

Contemporary critics are useful mainly as they reflect your prejudices. They help you avoid things you would consider to be dreck. The Critic as screening system. It's not a perfect system and requires periodic reassessment, but where do you find perfection?

You begin to see my critical approach: Will future teachers inflict it on our descendants? Will our descendants enjoy it and keep it alive?

Even then . . . well, I ask you: Is "The Masque of the Red Death" *really* Art? It's entertaining. It's instructive as a comment on its times. It's required reading in schools. But is it Art?

What's Art? As far as I'm concerned, it's my dentist, Art Krout. You see, if critics don't know, how can you expect a writer to know?

This is not to say that writers and readers should be uncritical. Readers have to protect their eyesight and their valuable time. As a writer, if you're not self-critical, you're not trying hard enough. Your work could become sufficiently sloppy that it would bore even the most ardent fan.

Boredom! There's one of the enemies! Shoot the bugger down!

Look back on the Artists and Critics whose work has endured. They did not bore their contemporaries and they do not bore enough of us today that they are secure for at least another generation. Continue looking back but this time only at the works of enduring Artists. What did they have in common?

They tested limits, their own *and* yours.

They produced something new.

They entertained you. (Remember, stuff that endures does not bore.)

They often addressed very large questions, sometimes in miniature.

They touched a chord which we still call *truth*. (It rings true when you hit it.)

They took you beyond yourself to something you recognized as better. They reminded you of the best in your own humanity.

Ah, there's something: Art is humanizing.

What's that mean, that word there—*human?* You know a human when you see one and so do I. Two-word definition of human? "like me." At bottom, that's the litmus paper we all use.

If it debases you, if it makes you feel diminished, damaged and irrevocably pained, *and that's all it does*, it's not Art. It's something else.

No cheap shots. (My God! That eliminates most movies!)

You ask: "Will the stories in this volume enter those rarefied and enduring currents?"

Patience.

There appears to be some evidence, including this anthology, that sci-fi (we say "skiffy," not "sy-fy") is coming out of a formative phase into something which may endure. Check back with me in a few hundred years and we'll review this question on the basis of better evidence.

Then how did Peter and the rest of us come by these particular anthology selections?

We voted.

Was it an honest vote?

More honest than most.

There was a time when some writers and their friends lobbied hard for inclusion in this prized selection. It got so bad that a number of us considered dropping out of SFWA.

"Stop trying to buy my vote," I said. "It is a poor thing but mine own."

Reasons for the lobbying are obvious. You must know that inclusion in SFWA's anthology rings the cash register. And then there's all that "fame." Good sense appears to be winning, however. Attempts at vote trading and other lobbying efforts have died off because they produced unwanted negative results.

Each of us voted, then, on the basis of our personal assumptions, that set of prejudgments which we identify as private internal reactions. The results are exposed here in this book for you to judge. Now, like birds that have been kicked out of the nest, these stories face an uncertain future.

Keep in mind that these stories and articles are among the best available today in the judgment of professional writers. The best and the most dangerous honors come from contemporaries in your own field. It's nice to have the admiration of fans, yes. That means you've been entertaining and the effort was profitable. This is important because money means the writer has more time to write. When it comes to your fellow writers, though, they are doing what you do; and if they like your work, that's a rarefied form of praise. It can be very heady stuff.

Why dangerous, then? The danger comes in the movement toward the Academy and the reactions of Academe. It can be poisonous when Academics convince a sensitive writer that Academe knows best.

"We know what's Art," they say.

"Yeah! Tell me more!" the writer says.

Listen, they may know what *was* Art, but there's something like hubris in the claim to absolute contemporary good judgment. I'll let you in on a secret. They're guessing. Some of them may make lucky guesses, but don't count on it. The poison comes when praise for the wrong reasons fogs over the self-critical awareness of someone who might have become a great (read *long-enduring*) Artist. What wrong reasons? Only the Artist and time know.

It appears clear to me that these Nebula Awards anthologies may be one of the first steps toward an Academy. Now, that's not necessarily all bad. In the first place, an Academy is something like a double-edged sword with no handle. You can only pick it up by grabbing a sharp place. If you grab it too hard you'll be the first one taken out of the action. How many choices of past Academies have survived into our times? Not many.*

There's another safety valve in the recent reminder by a friend that we don't have an academy tradition in this country. We have schools, lots of them. Grant them good intentions, but we know what kind of a road is paved with good intentions. Some of those schools could be paving roads for lemmings. As for the waves and the movements and the other

*If you would like to keep score on current survival rates from "Best of . . ." choices, get a copy of Franson and DeVore's *A History of the Hugo, Nebula and International Fantasy Awards*. It's available at science fiction conventions and by mail from 4705 Weddel Street, Dearborn, Michigan 48125.

schools . . . well, all of the votes aren't in yet.

Whatever you do, don't underestimate the strength of science fiction. It flowered in this country for good reasons. We Yanks have a well-earned reputation for winging it, and that's exactly what science fiction does best. We rejected a lot of that European stuff a long time ago—unwarranted searches, monarchs, confiscation of arms, self-satisfied academics, funny food . . . I mean, they eat *snails!*

When it comes to European-style Academe, a lot of us crowd into Missouri. We are suspicious. Just what are they trying to sell us? We *know* that European Academe is Fat. This knowledge comes out of the same mythos which prompted a superb writer to tell me once that the best writing is done by people who are either lonely or hungry. Hunger has a long-standing association with Art—garrets, tuberculosis and all of that. Incipient tragedy drives us to greater heights.

Academe in this country has developed a different tradition, more homespun and strongly influenced by the Great Depression, when a thing we had suspected for a long time was demonstrated right before our very eyes: teaching was a safe and secure job even in hard times. They get tenure, you know.

This attraction of security accounts partly for a fact revealed by the results of World War II draft-deferment tests of United States college and university students—most of the then education majors were in the lowest 10 percent of the IQ scale. Maybe our existing intelligence tests are not all that accurate in screening for the best teachers, but they are a screen. And they obviously screen for people who seek some kind of sinecure. We don't know what effects might have come from having at least two generations of students taught mostly by people screened that way. And what of their influence on school administration?

The paradox of security, that grail which supposedly lured so many immigrants to these shores. Hell, the Indians didn't have security and we didn't import it.

To a free-associating science-fiction writer, security is a dirty word. Security has a well-known history of attracting the unimaginative, the noncreative, the people who prefer any yesterday to any tomorrow. We live in a society dominated by a bureaucracy top-heavy with people selected that way—security seekers. Those are the people who gave us Social Security—the biggest chain letter, the most monstrous Pyramid Club, the most outrageous con game in the history of government. You want one measurement of the con? Our bureaucracy has its own private retirement system, as does the Congress. They remain completely independent of the dissolving pyramid which they administer. They don't want any part of this thing when their own *security* is at stake.

Yes, this is pertinent to Academe, Academies, to this anthology and to science fiction in general. I remind you that science fiction is mostly about tomorrow. Is that a secure tomorrow? Hell, no! Do our fictional governments perpetrate outrageous con games and other injustices on their fictional societies? Indeed they do. Do we offer security with one technological fist while yanking it away with another hand? Oh my, yes. Is there any reflection of current realities in all of this? You be the judge. Don't leave that to an Academy or to Academe.

Which brings me back to the current love affair between Academe and science fiction. We are witnessing a complex phenomenon here. You can identify several dominant movements and mixtures of same in the muddy waters.

There are the Academics who praise science fiction as a lever with which to improve reading skills among the young.

There are those who see it as *what's happening*. It appeals to an urge for contemporary understanding, to a drive to be part of history.

Then there are the academics who came in through fandom. These bring a real interest in the exploration of outré ideas.

All of them analyze, and when they read this, I hope they appreciate taking their turn under the lens of the microscope. I say to them sadly that analysis does not always lead to understanding. It is possible to analyze the life out of a subject. You can make it boring. This has led many a fan to cry out in anguish: "Keep science fiction in the gutter where it belongs!"

To these fans I say: We don't gain a thing by fleeing in terror from the current academic enthusiasm. I agree that it is dangerous, but it also is unavoidable and may be beneficial in the long term. The thing to resist is those forces which push us toward a hidebound European-style Academy—forces found not only in Academe but even in fandom and, God forbid, among writers themselves.

In Europe, Academies not only were used to honor selected practitioners of the Art, they also were designed to control what *could* happen in a chosen artistic field. They were a source of funding and still are. As you might expect, they experience(d) a certain amount of lobbying and other kinds of politicking. Sound familiar?

Enter politics, exit Art.

Politics easily becomes the ultimate boredom. Witness how few people actually vote in the United States, a condition politicians say they would like to correct but which they are very careful not to correct. People recognize that when there is an elitist force at the helm, the single vote doesn't carry much weight. And that's the way it is in a politicized Academy.

Let's suppose that we have something Artistic happening in science fiction—new ways of looking at our universe, poking fun at dearly beloved assumptions while gathering greater and greater economic clout, more and more attention from a swelling population of fans.

That can be dangerous.

Art has always been viewed as at least potentially dangerous in this country, anyway, an attitude attached to our homespun traditions but rooted in far deeper things. Involved with the NEW as it is, Art produces its fair share of surprises. If you break through the limits everyone else believes contain that which is safe and secure, you *may* encounter something which flips existing power structures into new alignments.

Can't allow that! It's bad for business.

The truth is, it's good for business and always has been. However, it has been known to put some people out of business. Thus, political/economic power structures always want to keep firm control of Art. Thus Academies and all the rest of it. Do I have to be the one to tell these people that Art and Firm Control are mutually exclusive, that Firm Control is actually bad for business?

Now you have an idea of where I come from, and I can comment on the selections in this anthology with less fear of being misunderstood. I obviously believe there are some standards by which to judge contemporary work. This anthology contains good work—some of it may even be great. I enjoyed every bit of it, but I don't want that to dominate your judgment. Let me point out something, though, which could be overlooked. Publications of this type can be of extraordinary value to new writers. This is what's being accepted. This is foundation stuff judged by contemporary writers themselves. Don't think of us as an Academy but just as writers. If you write or want to write, go out and do something better. I truly want that.

Think of this volume as an example of where we are today. We writers liked this enough that a majority of us voted to include these works in our most prestigious publication. We do now, however, intend to stand on these laurels. What we write tomorrow may be much better. We will let time be the judge.

Men on
Other Planets

They're human.

You surmise this from the descriptions. They're bipedal. They have two arms with conventional hands. The head is in the right place with chin, mouth, nose, eyes, hair on top, visible ears. But they may be both male and female in one body, shifting from one sex to the other at the behest of strange chemistry (Ursula Le Guin's *The Left Hand of Darkness*) or they merely assume human shape for disguise (Jack Vance's *Star King*).

From *Star Trek*'s Spock through the Wellsian cannibals at the end of time, these humanoids stalk the worlds of imagination. They walk on other planets, in space craft or on an earth so changed that you would not recognize it without a program. Then again, it may be your earth, but changed only in ways which accent trends visible all around you— *Brave New World, 1984, 20,000 Leagues Under the Sea, Childhood's End . . .*

What price a glimpse of tomorrow?

Where does fiction end and fact begin? When is it another world?

In a real sense, Joshua Slocum is a man on another planet. He lives out a recurrent human fantasy in chosen isolation. That isolation aboard his tiny sloop, *Spray*, is so different from the ordinary lives of most humans it might as well be on the back side of a planet circling a star in the Draco Cluster.

When we put our fictional men on fictional planets, we are dealing with a phenomenon that has surpassed in popularity the onetime front runner, detective stories. Why, in this particular age, have we singled out science as the guilty party (or the hero) instead of the butler?

Whodunit?

We all did. But why?

When you begin to glimpse an answer to that question, you begin to understand the craft behind this genre. Cyrano De Bergerac understood this when he turned from a real life of sword and sorcery to send a fictional hero to the moon. Certainly most who practice the craft of science fiction today understand the problem.

At one level, to put humans on another planet requires that you make alien places and people understandable to contemporary readers. (Let posterity take care of itself in this regard; there'll probably be academics around who can translate us for *their* contemporaries.) You begin by creating an understandable human/humanoid/sentient in an alien culture and right there, even though you may not intend it, you will reflect in some way the current human condition on Planet Earth.

Your Time Machine will have the appearance of a horse-drawn sleigh. Your hero will go to the moon on a lighter-than-air balloon or be fired there from a gigantic cannon. It's interesting to speculate how the writers a hundred years from now will make this same comparison looking back at our obsession with rockets. No matter how hard we try, we cannot entirely escape our times. Some small point will drift into print and leave its mark. *Player Piano*, although a landmark in its day, already is rather quaintly out of date. We may be past *1984* already.

Yet the science fiction phenomenon remains and the *why* begs an answer. It is not in stick-figure characters playing at Cosmic Mechanic or Rover Boys on Pluto; it is not in our time-bound curiosities. You won't find the answer there. But you will find it in those penetrating accuracies which glitter on Captain Nemo's control panel, in Cleve Cartmill's devastating prediction about the manufacture of atomic weapons, in Arthur C. Clarke's almost casual revelation of Telstar twenty years before the launching, and even in my own 1952 warning *(Under Pressure)* about the coming crisis in fossil fuels. It's in all of these: in Samuel R. Delany's *Babel-17*. It's the solid sense of character reality in such creations as Harold Shea (L. Sprague de Camp's *The Incomplete Enchanter)* or Isaac Edward Leibowitz (Walter M. Miller, Jr., *A Canticle for Leibowitz).*

Star Trek's control-room drama may have opened doors for people with misconceptions about science fiction, or for those who had never been immersed in it previously, but this is not where the current popularity rests, nor does it explain the fascination of putting humans into other futures, other planets, other cultures.

No, we have other things going for us.

First, we are talking about futures. In an age when many people question whether man has any future at all, we bring the imagination to grips with a variety of survival patterns. We preach ecology and we damn it. We utter warnings about unforeseen consequences. We explore strange paradises.

Second (and probably most important) the creation of understandable humans in understandable alien cultures on understandable other planets has to reflect in some ways the present human condition on Planet Earth.

The key word here is *alien.*

Does your conceit lead you to believe that you possess an absolute understanding of Mao Tse-tung's utterances?

Absolute?

The conditioning of most cultures on this planet tends to set up absolute categories, each with attached judgments about good-bad, beautiful-ugly, saintly-evil, painful-pleasurable, sacred-profane. Western culture is particularly obsessed with this absolutism through its narrow vision of a linear pragmatism hitched to technology. We have been taught to believe that for every problem there is a scientific answer. Every problem. Any denial of such absolutes raises opaque barriers which block new understandings.

But in science fiction we're not talking about a real earth, are we? It's all imaginary, a game, entertainment. It's other planets, other people. The opacity is reduced. You can make out shadow shapes which may have a certain reality. An entertaining view of realities.

There can be more than one reality.

You see, Dr. Einstein, we heard you.

This is probably science fiction's major attraction, linked as it is to all of the old myth strings we humans carry around. We humans still deal in archetypes with our politics and our entertainment, in our sex lives and our hobbies. Whether they see it clearly or not, science fiction writers play in this same arena.

You don't believe it?

All right—here are some classic myth ingredients:

The hero on a search/journey (for which read in science fiction Captain Kirk, Isaac Leibowitz, Jerome Corbett, Paul Atreides, Susan Calvin and so on and on . . .).

The Holy Grail which the searcher seeks (for which read in science fiction "almost any utopian story").

The ability to talk to animals (the stories of extrasensory perception where humans enlist the help of animals and/or vice versa).

The shaman who understands great mysteries and can bring them into the service of humans (for which read "any fictional scientist"—or real one for that matter).

Furthermore, science fiction is full of father gods, falls from paradise, wise old men, tricksters, people who change persona with a change of name, virgin witches and great mothers.

We also have our share of sorcerers (and sorcerer's apprentices), all of whom are variations on the shaman/scientist.

And one of our creative problems has been to show how directly these myth creatures apply to the world around us. If you want a recent example, look at how many of the myth characters are personified in the Kennedy Clan. Who first came up with that Camelot label?

If you're going to put men on other planets, it's well to understand these things. In academic terms, what we do is to create our own intercultural ethic and aesthetic out of the structural parts already available all around us. This is partly a problem in anthropology. Therefore, the newcomer to this genre should be warned. Because such problems often deal with Western society's unconscious taboos, a few outrageous clichés recur with maddening regularity. Ask any editor in this field. The most common first story from a would-be writer of science fiction replays the Adam and Eve theme (as survivors of an ultimate war, as castaways from a derelict spaceship, as a life form introduced from elsewhere or else-when and so on and on and on *ad nauseam*).

Our taboos ring in other changes that deserve careful watching, both as sins of commission and omission. You recognize these taboos and changes by their assumptions. Here are a few to consider as a sensitizing exercise:

1. Man is the king of all animals. Thus his planets (plus any alien occupants) are beneath man; they exist only to be exploited.

2. Only man has language. (Remember Carl Gustav Jung's warning that we must discover another sentience in the universe before we can understand what it is to be human. This proposition grows more fascinating as we teach more and more chimpanzees to talk Ameslan.)

3. The only thing wrong with our universe is that humans have not yet invented the right machine. (Many of us have assaulted this assumption. Isaac Asimov did it with beautiful directness in *I, Robot*. Tongue firmly in cheek, I took it on in *Destination Void*. Kurt Vonnegut's *Slaughterhouse Five* plays this theme legato.)

4. All human behavior can be traced to a) genetics, b) conditioning, c) cosmic intervention.

5. Current labels are adequate to describe any changed condition. (It'll still be Communists vs. Capitalists in 3031 A.D.)

With rare exceptions, authors and/or editors well understand the area of the current most dangerous taboos. When you see a story described as "daring," depend on it, that story has at least touched on one of those taboos. Of all the literary genres on the current scene, science fiction ventures into these arenas the most often.

You don't believe these taboos exist?

Have you read any good stories lately (outside of science fiction) where an orgasm is the highest religious experience? Maybe the world never was ready for Tantrism. Okay.

But if you're going to create science fiction, these are some of the questions you must ask, some of the limits you must recognize. Having recognized them, you can appropriate them for your own. Your hero can have clay feet. Your holy virgin can be barren. The innocent child can lead his people to destruction. A nymphomaniac can be the most honorable person in your alien society. The sensitive and concerned liberals can be the ones who make the grossest and most deadly mistakes. World Government can be demonstrated as a complete disaster. A football game can be the supreme intellectual delight. The utter ecological destruction of the planet is man's sole key to survival.

Are you getting the picture?

What is it that you believe without questioning? What is it that serves as the main prop of your identity?

What kind of a story would come out of your discovery that your most dearly held beliefs are completely false? Your beliefs, not those of someone else that you wish to attack. This is no debating society where advocates meet to listen only to their own arguments. We might assume that the advocacy system is humankind's greatest flaw and attorneys (plus their legal structure) are essentially parasites destroying their host.

Invite paranoia and explore its contexts. Science fiction has done this often. There *was* something following the little old lady. And it ate the psychiatrist for dessert. Now it's cliché, but once it was new.

There you are: make it new. Listen to Ezra Pound. He was right. "Make it new."

Science fiction, because it ventures into no man's lands, tends to meet some of the requirements posed by Jung in his explorations of archetypes, myth structures and self-under-standing. It may be that the primary attraction of science fiction is that it helps us understand what it means to be human.

Any reader of science fiction turning to page one of a new story has an implicit understanding that the function of what he is about to read will extend far beyond physical descriptions. Except perhaps as analogue, the value of putting men on other planets is greatest when it ceases to be a contest with that life which can be seen when you look up from the printed page. You know that the story will take you through experiences that cannot be achieved through any other means than the story. In fact, it may inflict upon you an experience that could never take place at all, except perhaps in your wildest fantasies. Your implicit understanding reaches even farther, though. You know that this story can be measured against a scale of achievement where the supreme experience comes when (no matter any logical objections) you are made to believe that these events might take place just the way they are laid out in the story.

And right here is where science fiction is most attractive as an art form, but also where it lays out the most traps for an unwary writer. The temptation is to wallow in excesses, to inflate your sense of "how strange!" to such an extreme that it dulls the sensibilities or even repels. Something like this happened in the development of what are obviously science fiction's current clichés, the clichés which science fiction creates—the monster and the maiden, the variations on Adam and Eve, the aliens who come to earth as missionaries, Ezekiel's wheels as helicopter rotors, the planet as egg of an interstellar monster, and so on.

Make it new.

Even while using old themes, make it new.

It's by restraints and subtleties, by aftershocks, that you can create your greatest effects.

Were you really surprised when Charlton Heston discovered the remains of the Statue of Liberty on the Planet of the Apes? It had a certain time-stretching effect, but surprise? How much more interesting if he'd discovered a toilet bowl (more likely to survive the eons) or a perfectly preserved Landon button.

Readers and editors tend to say: "Oh, no! Not another cosmic egg story!"

Now, let's invert this argument for a moment and remind you that there's a supreme achievement in storytelling when you can take on one of these clichés and make it so vivid, so new in its construction that no one minds the cliché.

The argument here is obvious: don't cater to the lowest common denominator in those reactions available to you. Don't cater to the weakest reaction patterns. Don't go for the throat; go for the guts, but do it in such a way that the reader realizes that's what you've done *after the fact*. Make damned sure you know your story objective (and it had better be at least nine-tenths entertainment).

This brings us naturally to the pot of message often found in science fiction. Quite a few science fiction writers will tell you they are attacking our current culture head on. They really believe this. But if you look at the consequences of the most extreme efforts in this class, you find that they have merely reinforced the cultural characteristics which drew their most strident verbal scorn. This is quite often the ultimate effect of the most fanatical world-changers. Thus, while some writers avow that they are out to change (or even wreck) the culture which they despise (even while that culture is offering them a good return on their efforts), the polarizing effect of such writing tends to do quite the opposite. It exposes the values which have maintained the cultural characteristics dominating our society. The writer's ambivalence shines through all his preachings: he needs the society and the culture which he attacks. He's in a transactional relationship with it. This is the relationship that can be observed, for example, when you see large groups of medical practitioners behaving in a way that maintains a certain level of illness, that level which justifies the continuing function of the group *as they see that function*. The process here is an unconscious one but nonetheless real for all that. Such unconscious processes are fair game for science fiction because they are embedded in the society. Once exposed, they have a "the-king-is-naked" flavor and they are less social attack than social exposure. There are no guilty and no innocent. Every living human behaves to some degree according to unconscious processes. The trick is to recognize this and cast yourself (as writer) in the role of commentator rather than advocate.

This is a rather delicate line of reasoning to follow because it so easily raises opaque barriers. A physician reading the above paragraph, for example, could be thrown into an immediate defensive posture even though he knows (rationally) quite well that the word *iatrogenic* has real meaning in his practice. (Iatrogenic is defined as "of a neurosis or physical disorder caused by the diagnosis, manner or treatment of a physician or surgeon.")

It's one thing to know something rationally and quite another thing to behave as though that knowledge had real physical application in your own life (because how you view your life can be so securely tied to the way you *feel* your own identity).

Follow this reasoning with me, though, because it has a great deal to do with the whole process of putting fictional men on fictional planets. No human being on our "real" planet is completely free of his unexamined assumptions. And it is precisely this that science fiction does better than any other art form with the possible exception of cartoons.

We examine assumptions.

Certain phenomena have been locked up in the unexamined assumptions of our society. It's in unlocking these phenomena with their attendant assumptions, exposing the structure to view, that science fiction does its greatest, most enduring work. What other human activity ventures this deeply into the crystallized (and crystallizing) structures of our society and exposes these structures to a broader view?

It might clarify this to re-examine briefly one of the all-time classics in science fiction, the Foundation Trilogy (which isn't a trilogy but nine beautifully constructed stories, each a jewel in its own right). Let's just take up a few of the assumptions within Asimov's work.

1. The nine stories are firmly rooted in behaviorist psychology to an extent that would gratify B. F. Skinner. Foundation history, which is to say the human function, is manipulated for larger ends and for the greater good as determined by a scientific aristocracy. It is assumed, then, that the scientist-shamans know best which course humankind should take. This is a dominant attitude in today's science establishment all around the world. ("The Sorcerer's Apprentice," a symphonic poem by Paul Dukas, isn't a very popular work with this establishment. The plot from the Goethe poem deals with an apprentice sorcerer who tries one of his master's spells and can't countermand it.)

2. While surprises may appear in these stories (e.g., the Mule mutant), it is assumed that no surprise will be too great or too unexpected to overcome the firm grasp of science upon human destiny. This is essentially the assumption that science can produce a surprise-free future for humankind. There's another Skinnerian tenet. It says that you produce this kind of future by management. And *that*, with all of its paradoxes and inconsistencies, is another recurrent theme in science fiction.

3. It is assumed that politics in this managed future can be reduced to the terms, the conflicts and the structures as they are understood on earth today. This is an odd assumption by a scientist because it says that nothing new will be discovered about politics in all of those intervening centuries. We can close the Patent Office, so to speak; we already know it all.

This is not to detract from Asimov's achievement. You should understand that there are very strong literary and communications reasons why his was a good course to take at the time. All of us, and especially those of us who write science fiction, owe Asimov many debts. (From where I sit, I can see nine Asimov nonfiction titles on my working library shelves.) What I am saying is that Asimov, in common with all of the rest of us, operates within a surround of assumptions, any one (or combination) of which could serve as the jumping-off point for an entirely new series of stories. The assumptions are there and can be lifted out with this kind of analysis. In passing, it should be noted that these three assumptions can be found together or separately in many science fiction stories.

Now, see what happens if you assume an opposite viewpoint. To give you an example of how this leverage works in lifting out our unexamined assumptions, let's take a science fiction look at a current problem in the United States—hard drugs. Here are some of the transactional structures involved: guilt-innocence, control-controlled and life-death. Those are pretty heavy relationships and they operate within the assumption that we (in the form of our government) can manage absolutely all of the variables within known limits.

Now, we turn the systems over. We assume that we do not have a system of absolute and known limits, that we cannot control all of the variables and that our approach doesn't have to be involved with guilt-innocence or our own attitudes about personal life and death. Our aim would not be to solve *the* problem but to reduce its influence, throw it into a smaller arena.

This gives us the following: the hard-drug market operates within an open-ended pricing system where no top limit has ever been found. This means that if we cannot stop all of the hard drugs from entering the country, those we do confiscate merely increase the price of what does reach the market. That price is inflated to take care of bribes which can buy senators, congressmen, generals, diplomats, police, customs officers. (Remember that we're talking about billion-dollar slush funds.)

What happens if you lower the barriers and offer a fix at the corner pharmacy to any registered addict for fifty cents? Have you solved the drug problem? No. But you've cut organized crime out of the market. And you've removed the major source of new addictions. More than three-fourths of the present addicts were maneuvered into addiction by other addicts who became pushers to support their own expensive habits.

You've also relieved an important bureau (customs) of one of its primary tasks, one of its reasons for being. You've removed a major way that people feel innocent (by redefining an extremely large body of the guilty). And you've admitted that there may be some things that cannot be controlled absolutely.

In my hypothetical science fiction story, the three items listed in the paragraph above (plus pressure from professional criminal profiteers) would combine to resist any change in the present system. Here's an important story ingredient, conflict, combined with a currently recognized problem, all of which lend themselves ideally to fictional exposition. And if you put the entire thing on another planet you make it much more palatable to contemporary readers.

You're not talking about real places, real people.

Are you?

What we have in the science fiction techniques being explored here is the fine use of conjecture as a literary tool. Science fiction gives you the added elbow room of entirely new places for things to happen to people. It allows you to generate your own values for your alien places. It permits you to go beyond those cultural norms that are prohibited by your society and enforced by unconscious (and conscious) literary censorship in the prestigious arenas of publication.

And here is a real danger in the current trend toward academic acceptance of science fiction. If it becomes too prestigious, science fiction will encounter new restraints. In the Soviet Union, where all writing carries a high prestige mark, you don't find science fiction stories dealing with political systems at wide variance with the Soviet state. This may not be the best example to make the point; different modes of enforcement are accepted in the Soviet Union, but it does indicate what could happen to a free-swinging literary form when social norms change.

We still have, however, our virtually unlimited resource of unexamined assumptions and our arsenal of imaginative conjecture.

What if . . .

The fictional story as vehicle of lasting influence is well recognized in our world. As Abraham Lincoln said to Harriet Beecher Stowe, who wrote *Uncle Tom's Cabin*, "So you're the little lady who started the Civil War." There was some truth in his remark, although the other influences on that conflict make better stories. With 20-20 hindsight, we can see the influence of Bellamy's *Looking Backward* on 1930s socialism. We can see the influence of Huxley's *Brave New World* on today's attitudes toward population control and police states, or of Orwell's *1984* on the way we view utopias and dystopias. But none of these would have had any influence at all if contemporary readers had not been attracted to them for reasons that were primarily entertaining.

If you want a gold mine of science fiction material, pull the assumptions out of the current best-seller list. Turn those assumptions over, look at them from every angle you can imagine. Tear them apart. Put them back together. Put your new construction on another planet (or on this planet changed) and place believable human beings into the conflict situations thus created.

It isn't the ideas that make the story; it's what you do with them. Ideas are a dime a dozen. *Development of ideas—* that's where the diamonds are. The difference between dirt and ore is what you can get out of it.

The belief that the idea is the story persists, however. A bane of every writer's existence is the person who comes up to you and says: "Hey! I have this marvelous idea for a story! Now, if you'll just write it, I'll split whatever it makes with you."

My own response is to say: "I'm sorry, but I don't have

enough lifetimes to exploit all of the ideas I already have."

This doesn't always stop the more persistent. You can see in their eyes that they don't believe you. Regretfully, sometimes you have to be rude. Insist that the fountain of ideas write his own story. Refuse to listen. Flee.

So don't use my gold mine of science fiction material. Create your own. That's what it's all about, isn't it? But it might be helpful for you to see where we've already been, to learn the clichés, absorb the labels that communicate commonly understood concepts. *Robot*, as a word, entered the language at a particular place and time. There was no such thing as a *slidewalk* before Bob Heinlein gave it to us. Do you know how the mechanical amplifiers of human muscles came to be called *Waldos?* Where did the word *plasteel* originate?

As the best of the science fiction writers do, start looking at our present planet as a set of long-term influences, a system of resonances which can be read as bio-rhythms—the combined impact of moon, tides, sun, variations in atmospheric electricity, and so on. Did you know that the earth's tides change the amount of fluid in your body's cells? What would happen to "human psychology" on another planet with different tidal variations, different resonances in its atmospheric chemistry and electricity?

And if these ways of looking at our current condition don't work for you, invent your own ways of looking. But, to be sure you really are inventing, sample where imagination already has taken science fiction. Here are a few examples to show what I mean:

Brian Aldiss in *The Saliva Tree and Other Strange Growths* has extraterrestrials (aliens, eh?) visit a farm in turn-of-the-century England. The ETs make the farm blossom, intending to devour the entire animal population, including the humans. The viewpoint character exchanges letters with H. G. Wells.

Jack Vance in *The Dirdir*, which was the third in his *Planet of Adventure* series, has natives and humans of Ischai compete for dominance under conditions where his planet abounds with different species that complicate existence.

There are, to sample them, the Chasch breeds, the reptilian Wankh, and the predatory Dirdir, who hunt and eat humans. (See Aldiss, above.)

Mack Reynolds replays human history in *Space Barbarians*. The ingredients will seem familiar, although the settings are not. He exploits a highly technological society, vigorous and uncaring about who or what brings a profit, which clashes with a primitive society in a social and economic stasis. The outcome is not necessarily surprising, but the way there is entertaining and informative.

Through such stories wend certain assumptions. The legal owners of real estate, including a planet, are the beings who occupy it. Humans tend to shake down into hierarchies which resemble tribal organization. Science is good. Science is evil. Other planets have to be at least vaguely earthlike. (Otherwise humans can't live on them.) The alternative: adapt humans to the planet. (That's what evolution did, anyway, didn't it?) Time is linear and flowing—an analogue river. Mankind is headed toward some form of apotheosis (having fallen from paradise, humans will once more become godlike). Magic is merely science misunderstood.

And those observations just touch a few of the high points.

To come full circle, let's go back to myths. Myth here is used in its classical sense: a traditional or legendary story usually concerning events which transform human into superhuman, if only briefly. Science fiction is, in part, a myth-creative format. Since the creation of myths is a day-to-day process solidified and codified for an era by the surviving dramatic works of the time (thus becoming traditional and legendary), we have in science fiction a window on an ancient process. Through this window we can see the codified myths upon which humans of our time place their greatest faith: science, progress, the triumph of intellect. These are rooted in Platonic absolutes: "Somewhere there is a single law which will explain everything."

And, summated: Science can show us the future.

Lest you be led into believing such things absolutely,

take a brief look backward. The scientists of Franklin D. Roosevelt's Brain Trust, asked to predict "the course of technological development" from 1933 through 1958, said not one word about transistors, atomic power, jet engines or antibiotics.

Writing in 1967, Herman Kahn and Anthony Wiener for their book *The Year 2000* assumed a world system with a continuing increased rate of energy consumption spreading into the underdeveloped nations and culminating in such things as "moderately priced robots doing most of the housework..." plus "next-day delivery of mail" anywhere in the United States.

From a science fiction viewpoint, they made the depressingly common mistake of writing about *the* future instead of concerning themselves with a future based on current premises. They failed to examine many of their assumptions.

Given this kind of mass-energy bias, you can understand why David Lilienthal would assume that he could export his Tennessee Valley Authority, with all of its extensive relocations and disruptions of existing people and systems, taking the TVA bodily to South Vietnam. It wasn't that he disregarded the social facts of Southeast Asia—the survival importance of community vitality and the profoundly maintained ancestor worship which requires that communities remain close to ancestral burial grounds—no, Lilienthal just didn't even consider that such elements existed. He made the Henry Higgins mistake: "Why can't the South Vietnamese be more like Americans?"

"Just you wite, 'Enery 'Iggins! Just you wite!"

With the bad track record of such prestigious planners, it's no wonder that the current world bias is pessimistic. The world picture has grown so black that a President of France can warn us that "the great curves which describe the future in our times all lead to catastrophe."

Thank you, Mr. President.

But science fiction continues to plug along with its stories about futures in which there are surviving humans. Those humans may not live in a 1960-projected future of enormous skyscrapers linked by loops and curves of highways far above the surface, a future of individual one-man flying machines and plastic bubbles over everything from a backyard garden to New York City. It may not even be the kind of future we were predicting in the 1890s—with trips to the moon and women doctors of philosophy, a bicycle in every garage, fast railroad trains linking every major population center and propeller-driven gas balloons. It may be none of these.

There will be humans in these fictional creations, though. You'll recognize them from the descriptions: bipedal, two arms with hands, head on top with nose below the mouth and . . .

What price a glimpse of tomorrow?

Poetry

Poetry, that traditional bane of little boys who'd rather be out playing baseball, is booming. And for some reason, it's gaining among those same boys, now that they're growing up.

On campuses, in coffee houses and, to a degree, on Montgomery Street, you hear it said that poetry is a cool thing.

So where is the dividing line between the reluctant gradeschooler forced to memorize Thanatopsis and the sensitive human turned on by Dylan? What alchemy produces a poem and a poet? Why does a writer choose poetry over prose? What are the unique qualities which identify the poet and his work?

To find answers to these questions, Adrienne Marcus, a San Rafael poet (her work appears in *Borestone Mountain Poetry Awards 1968* volume) and College of Marin writing instructor, has surveyed poets from California to England for *California Living*. The results of her research carry fascinating overtones because they touch that problem which has modern psychiatry chasing its tail—the search for identity.

Oddly, there appears to be no standard lifestyle or physical type for a poet, Mrs. Marcus reports. Longshoremen, priests, hippies, housewives, advertising executives, physicians, even vice presidents of insurance companies, write poetry. Poets can be as ruggedly masculine as Howard Nemerov or as feminine as Anne Sexton.

They do, however, see our world in various ways that differ from the visions of non-poets.

William Stafford of Lake Oswego, Oregon, whose *Traveling Through the Dark* won the National Book Award, put it this way:

> The world happens twice: once the way we see it as; second, it legends itself, deep, the way it is. I write because I keep searching for that second happening, that deep legending of our lives.

Josephine Miles, who teaches at the University of California, Berkeley, leans on listening and interacting. The poet, she explains, needs "a natural bent for rhythm in relation to language. Then—the development of something to say. The first is so basic that when valuable ideas come along they naturally take on, for the poet, the patterns of rhythm and measure."

Brother Antoninus at Saint Albert's College, the Dominican House of Studies, Oakland, demonstrates that same fascination with language. There is, he believes, a "language-making faculty" in man which must seek out "its most primitive and unspoiled exercise . . . to be awestruck, or sobered, or shocked, or exalted. Language is female, the passive. It births the spirit. It is through her that I continually surprise myself."

"You have to like language," says Mrs. Marcus. "You have to hang around words a lot, as the man said. Listening —that's a necessary qualification. Writing, too—that's necessary, any kind of writing you can do. Don't knock newspaper work, advertising, scripts, anything. It's all language and can teach."

She sums it up with a line from one of her poems, *Becoming Thirty:* ". . . I am diseased with choice words, an endless weight of syllables."

Apparently, we have arrived at an identifying characteristic of the poet—deep involvement with the significance and rhythms of language.

James Dickey worked for an advertising agency; Dylan Thomas wrote scripts, memoirs, anything; Stephen Crane wrote for a newspaper. Mrs. Marcus considers herself lucky to have studied with Mark Linenthal, James Schevill, Herb Wilner and William Dickey, and has written many newspaper stories and articles.

All, she says, agree the embryo poet must write and read.

"You have to read all the poetry you can lay your hands on," she says. "You might have to try writing like someone else. Eventually, if you're strong enough, you'll have your own voice."

Marianne Moore, writing from New York, turns to Cicero for instruction and a reason to write poetry: "To delight, to instruct, to stir you to feelings you have not had . . ."

Brother Antoninus says of the poetic state: "In its travail of mutation it registers the heat between the polarities of all value—good and evil, positive and negative."

"I don't know that studying and working with poetry really changes anything," says Mrs. Marcus, "but it does make me more aware of my relationship to my surroundings. There are so many events every day in our lives . . . All the defenses have to go when you welcome a listener into your private landscape. It's a way of living with myself and the world. I can re-create, touch things, and sometimes, understand."

Margaret Albanese, another San Rafael poet, echoes this. She explains that she has found poetry "a lifelong habit, a way of recognizing and dealing with fragmentation, a ritual of defiance or acceptance of everyday terror, beauty, chaos, love, death—in other words, of the miraculous."

We venture another identifying mark for the poet: A person intensely aware of the movements in life all around him, alert to their underlying mystical nature, and determined that these things are important to interpret with individuality and style . . . in "your own voice."

"Anything that matters enough to a poet can be his subject matter," says Mrs. Marcus. "Sometimes it starts with a dream, with a few words overheard in a crowd. A reaction takes place, a gathering of words which is like a gathering of people. Everything interacts and goes on interacting. I think of Auden's observation that poems are never finished, they are merely abandoned. It always amazes me when words work. Once your eyes are opened, you find poetry all around you."

Says British poet Tony Connor: "The idea that if you're writing poetry you're not writing prose (and vice versa) lingers in our world. It's probably worth stressing once more that the two extremes are 'Poetry' and 'Non-Poetry,' and that at moments of great intensity, prose naturally rises, heightens into poetry. Every great novel bears witness to this. Think of Lawrence's *Rainbow* or the prose account of the death of Falstaff in *Henry V*."

Intensity. Drama. When does it cease being a recitative chore and begin igniting the mind? When is it poetry, even to the child in front of the class?

"Little by little, something occurs," Mrs. Marcus says. "It's almost electrical, a current that flows from the page to the reader, from the reader to the audience. You feel a sense of place, that you have been welcomed into a revelation."

In that moment, you have been transported into the translucent world of language where sounds become a captivating dance of symbols.

That dance is called a poem. The poet is a choreographer of words.

The Origins of *Dune*

There is no question that the Dune series has generated far more interest and acclaim than anything else Frank has written. It is worthwhile to read the following pieces for this reason alone. They provide insights into some of the roots of one of the most celebrated of all science fiction works.

They also illuminate directly one of Frank's most powerful and unconventional ideas—that the heroes who are the stock-in-trade not only of science fiction but of a great deal of popular literature can lead us into a dangerous way of thinking. While we need the models that heroes provide, our faith in them can undercut faith in ourselves, and can eat away at the self-reliance we need to cope with the real world.

Many readers of the Dune series have complained that Paul Atreides, the hero of the first novel, is tarnished in the second, and by the third, is made to seem an ineffectual failure. They share the puzzlement of John Campbell, the legendary science fiction editor, who had first published Dune but refused the sequel, Dune Messiah, and wonder at the apparent changes in Herbert's vision.

The pieces included in this section show unequivocally that the master plan of the initial Dune trilogy was largely in place from the beginning. (Volumes following Children of Dune in the series were conceived later.)

The first piece, "Dangers of the Superhero," is based on two separate reminiscences, one written for liner notes on Frank's first Caedmon recording of passages from Dune (The Banquet Scene), and the second to accompany the publication of John Schoenherr's Dune illustrations in Omni magazine. It lays out Frank's theory about the danger of superheroes and messiahs.

The second piece, "The Sparks Have Flown," covers the history of the Dune *trilogy from a somewhat different angle. It is based on two interviews, one by Professor Willis McNelly of California State University at Fullerton in 1968, and one which I did with Frank in New York about nine years later. These interviews touch on a wide range of subjects related to the origin of various aspects of* Dune.

In McNelly's interview, Frank points out that he loaded Dune *with hints that were not developed in the story, but which he hoped readers would find so interesting that they would continue to flesh them out in their own imagination. Probably the surest sign that Frank succeeded at this is* The Dune Encyclopedia, *a collection of imaginative extensions to the history, ecology, and philosophy of* Dune, *contributed by readers and edited by McNelly.*

"The Campbell Correspondence" is a fascinating exchange of letters between John Campbell and Frank Herbert. In his initial acceptance of the manuscript of Dune, *Campbell puts his finger right on what he considers a weakness in the plotting of the* Dune *trilogy. In fact, as Frank replies, the weakness is an essential part of the plot, to be revealed in the sequel.*

The final piece, the liner notes to Frank's second record for Caedmon, Sandworms of Dune, *gives some additional background on the shamanistic significance of the sandworms and spice.*

The sandworms are an essential part of the fascination of Dune. *These great predators make the surface of Frank's imaginary planet Arrakis deadly to those who cannot learn to move with its dangerous rhythms. At the same time, they are the source of the hallucinogenic, life-extending spice that gives the planet its unique value. And ultimately, they are the source of victory in the battle for control over the planet, since they open the desert to those brave enough to ride them.*

The name given to the sandworm by the natives of Arrakis is maker. *The title of this book,* The Maker of Dune, *pays homage both to this great imaginative creation and to the act of creative imagination itself. Though* Dune *is based on many well-conceived concepts, ultimately it gains its power from an imagination that is not controlled by the author, but summoned, and ridden like the great worm from the sands.*

Dangers
of the Superhero

When you look back at a work you've done and seek to define its essential motivations, the intervening years have a way of refining the original intent. We go on learning, even about ourselves.

Where *Dune* is concerned, I'd like to show the original spark, but that's now a conflagration. What I can do is take you through the chronology, show you the stepping stones that were the thoughts in my mind at the time.

Dune began with a concept whose mostly unfleshed images took shape across about six years of research and one and one-half years of writing. It was all in my head until it appeared on paper as I typed it.

How did it begin?

I conceived of a long novel, the whole trilogy as one book about the messianic convulsions that periodically overtake us. Demagogues, fanatics, con-game artists, the innocent and the not-so-innocent bystanders—all were to have a part in the drama. This grows from my theory that superheroes are disastrous for humankind, that even if we find a real hero (whatever that may be), eventually fallible mortals take over the power structure that always comes into being around such a leader. What better way to destroy a civilization, a society, or a race than to set people into the wild oscillations which follow their turning over their judgment and decision-making faculties to a superhero?

It's the systems themselves that I see as dangerous. Systematic is a deadly word. Systems originate with human creators, with people who employ them. Systems take over and grind on and on. They are like a flood tide that picks up everything in its path.

How do they originate?

Personal observation has convinced me that in the power arena of politics/economics, and in the logical consequence, war, people tend to give over every decision-making capacity to any leader who can wrap himself in the myth fabric of the society. Hitler did it. Churchill did it. Franklin D. Roosevelt did it. Lenin did it.

My favorite examples are John F. Kennedy and George Patton. Both fitted themselves into the flamboyant Camelot pattern, consciously assuming a bigger-than-life appearance. But the most casual observation reveals that neither was bigger than life. Both had our common human ailment—clay feet.

This, then, was one of my themes: *Don't give over all of your critical faculties to people in power, no matter how admirable those people may appear.* Beneath the hero's facade, you will find a human being who makes human mistakes. Enormous problems arise when human mistakes are made on the grand scale available to a superhero.

And sometimes you run into another problem.

It is demonstrable that power structures tend to attract people who want power for the sake of power and that a significant proportion of such people are sufficiently imbalanced they could be called insane.

That was the beginning: heroes are painful, superheroes involve too many of us in disaster.

All of this, however, encapsulates the stuff of high drama, of entertainment—and I'm in the entertainment business first. It's all right to include a pot of message, but that's not the key ingredient of wide readership. Yes, there are analogs in *Dune* of today's events—corruption and bribery in the highest places, whole police forces lost to organized crime, regulatory agencies taken over by the people they are supposed to regulate. The scarce water of *Dune* is an exact analog of oil scarcity. CHOAM is OPEC.

But that was only the beginning.

While this concept was still fresh in my mind, I went to

Florence, Oregon, to do a magazine article about a U.S. Department of Argriculture project there. The USDA was seeking ways to control coastal (and other) sand dunes. I already had written several pieces about ecological matters, but my superhero concept filled me with a concern that ecology might be the next banner for the demagogues and would-be heroes, for the power seekers and others ready to find an adrenaline high in the launching of a new crusade.

Our society, after all, operates on guilt, which often serves only to obscure the real workings and to prevent obvious solutions. An adrenaline high can be just as addictive as any other kind of high.

Ecology encompasses a real concern, however, and the Florence project fed my interest in how we inflict ourselves upon our planet. I could begin to see the shape of a global problem, no part of it separated from any other—social ecology, political ecology, economic ecology...

It's an open-ended list which has never closed.

Even after all of the research and writing, I find fresh nuances, things in religions, in psychoanalytic theories, in linguistics, economics, philosophy, in theories of history, geology, anthropology, plant research, soil chemistry, in the metalanguages or pheromones. A new field of study rises out of this like a spirit rising from a witch's caldron: *the psychology of planetary societies*.

Out of all this came a profound re-evaluation of my original concepts. At the beginning, I was just as ready as anyone to fall into step, to seek out the guilty and punish the sinners, even to become a leader. Nothing, I felt, would give me more gratification than riding the steed of yellow journalism into crusade, doing *the book* which would right the old wrongs.

At the start, I believed what the history books taught me—that we were what evolution had been seeking, that our society had achieved a pinnacle, that all humans are truly created equal.

Re-evaluation raised haunting questions. I now know that evolution or devolution never ends short of death, that no society has ever achieved an absolute pinnacle, that all humans are not created equal. In fact, I believe attempts to create some abstract equalization create a morass of injustices that rebound on the equalizers. Equal justice and equal opportunity are ideals we should seek, but we should recognize that humans administer the ideals and that humans do not have equal abilities.

Power is the trap, political power and the other kinds which congregate around it. And words are a vehicle of power. Language is like a tar pit which has accumulated the fossils of our past.

Re-evaluation taught me caution. I approached the problem with trepidation. Certainly, by the loosest of our standards, there were plenty of visible targets, plenty of the blind fanaticism and guilty opportunism at which to aim painful barbs.

But how did we get that way? What makes a Nixon? What part do the meek play in creating the powerful? If a leader cannot admit mistakes, those mistakes will be hidden. Who says our leaders must be perfect? Where do they learn this?

Enter the fugue. In music, the fugue is usually based on a single theme that is played many different ways. Sometimes there are free voices that do fanciful dances around the interplay. There can be secondary themes and contrasts in harmony, rhythm, and melody. From the moment a single voice introduces the primary theme, however, the whole is woven into a single fabric.

What were my instruments in this fugue? Images, conflicts, things that turn upon themselves and become something quite different, myth figures and strange creatures from the depths of our common heritage, products of our technological evolution, our desires and our fears . . .

As in an Escher lithograph, I involved myself with recurrent themes which turn to paradox. The central paradox concerns the human vision of time. What about Paul's *gift* of prescience—the Presbyterian fixation? For the Delphic Oracle to perform, it must tangle itself in a web of predestination. Yet predestination negates surprises and, in fact, sets up a mathematically enclosed universe whose limits are always inconsistent, always encountering the unprovable. It's like a koan, a Zen mind-breaker. It's like the Cretan Epimenides saying: "All Cretans are liars."

Each limiting, descriptive step you take drives your vision outward into a larger universe, which is contained in still a larger universe ad infinitum and in the smaller universes ad infinitum. No matter how finely you subdivide time and space, each tiny division contains infinity.

But this could imply that you can "cut across" linear time, open it like a ripe fruit, and *see* consequential connections. You could be prescient, predict accurately.

Predestination and paradox once more.

The flaw (I said) must lie in our methods of description, in languages, in social networks of meaning, in moral structures, and in philosophies and religions—all of which convey implicit limits where no limits exist. Paul-Muad'Dib, after all, says this *time after time*.

You want absolute prediction?

Then you want today only and you reject tomorrow. You are the ultimate conservative. You are trying to hold back movement in an infinitely changing universe.

The verb "to be" does make idiots of us all.

Of course, there are other themes and fugal interplays in *Dune* and throughout the trilogy. *Dune Messiah* performs a classic inversion of theme. *Children of Dune* expands the number of themes interplaying. I refuse, however, to provide further answers to this complex mixture. That, after all, fits the pattern of the fugue: you find your own solutions; don't look to me as your leader.

Caution is indeed indicated, but not the terror that prevents all movement. Hang loose. And when someone asks if you're starting a new cult, do what I do: run like hell.

The Sparks
Have Flown

Back in 1953, I was going to do an article (which I never finished) about the control of sand dunes. What many people don't realize is that the United States has pioneered in this, how to control the flow of sand dunes. There is a pilot project of the U.S. Forest Service in Florence, Oregon, which has been so successful that it has been visited and copied by experts from Chile, Israel, India, Pakistan, Great Britain, and several other countries. I became fascinated by sand dunes, because I'm always fascinated by the idea of something that is seen in miniature and then can be expanded to the macrocosm, or which, but for the difference in time, in the flow rate, and the entropy, is similar to other features that we wouldn't think were similar.

Sand dunes are like waves in a large body of water; they are just slower. And the people treating them as *fluid* learn to control them.

The whole idea fascinated me, so I started researching sand dunes, and of course from sand dunes it's a logical idea to go into a desert. Now, the way I accumulate data is that I start building file folders. Before long I saw I had far too much for an article and far too much for a short story. I didn't really know what I had. But I had an enormous amount of data, with avenues shooting off at all angles to gather more. I finally saw I had something enormously interesting going for me about the ecology of deserts, and it was, for a science fiction writer anyway, an easy step from that to think: what if I had an entire planet that was a desert?

During my studies of deserts, of course, and previous

studies of religions, I had seen that many religions began in a desert atmosphere. I decided to put the two together because I don't think that any one story should have any one thread.

I build on a layer technique, and of course putting in religion and religious ideas with ecological ideas you can play one against the other. And in studying sand dunes, you immediately get into not just the Arabian mystique but the Navaho mystique and the mystique of the Kalahari primitives and all. And you can't just stop with the people who are living in this type of environment: you have to go on to how the environment works on the people and how they work on their environment.

You could look at this thing on the Oregon coast quite simply, if you wanted to, and say, "Yes, the sand was covering the highway, and that's bad, so we plant certain grasses, and that stops the sand from moving, and that's good." And that's the end of it. But if you start going into the mechanics of how the United States Forest Service set up this project, and all of the internal politics that were involved, then you would probably have a story there, a "mainstream" type of story. But I got off on a different kick because of the science fiction angle and the emphasis on ecology.

It's been my belief for a long time that man inflicts himself on his environment. In Western culture, we tend to think that we can overcome nature by mechanical means; we accumulate enough data and we subdue it. This is a one-pointed vision of man, because if you really start looking at man, Western man, you'll see that you could cut him right down the middle and he's blind on that backside.

This is the point my wife, Bev, made earlier, talking about the death of the planetary ecologist in *Dune* being a very touching spot. A lot of the story swung around this: it was very important that the planet killed the ecologist. He knew what was happening to him and understood it and was technically capable of controlling it. The very fact that Kynes, who is the Western man, in my original construction of the book, sees all of these things happening to him as mechanical things doesn't subtract from the fact that he is still a part of this system. He'd lived out of rhythm with it and he got in the trough of the wave and it tumbled down on him.

Ecology, as somebody said—and I use this in *Dune* (I'd like to attribute this, but I don't recall where I encountered it—I did read over two hundred books as background for this novel)—ecology is the science of understanding consequences.* Just as it is today.

We play the game today with counters called money and we talk about laws of supply and demand and so on. There is a law of supply and demand as long as you only have one form of exchange, but once you start getting other media of exchange, such as force, then the law of supply and demand gets different beats on it, different rhythms.

Western man has assumed that all you need for any problem is enough force, and that there is no problem which won't submit to this approach, even the problem of our own ignorance. This assumption, you see, throws it out the window right there, because it is an asinine assumption, and the basic fallacy of Western man's approach to living. Now, I'm not saying that we should immediately drop this and adopt a Vedanta way of thinking. We need what I would call a science of wisdom.

The moral norm, as I try to show in *Dune*, is something imposed upon people by their environment. Ethical law takes a step in another direction, and it says that I, the thinking animal, see the logical consequences of these moral actions and maybe I'd better modify the moral law slightly by a higher ethical law. *Dune* shows the conflict between absolutes and the necessity of the moment. You might say it is an exercise in showing up the fallacy of absolutism.

At any rate, pretty soon I realized that I had the place, and the characters, and the thrust, for a monumental story, with a lot of action, people, and evolutionary processes displayed.

Anyway, I wrote the last chapter of *Dune*, and I had the evolutionary outline of what had to happen. And it kept getting bigger—of necessity, there were all kinds of things hap-

---

*This quote comes from Paul Sears's book on ecology, *Where There Is Life:* "The highest function of ecology is the understanding of consequences."

pening. At one point, I wrote a letter to my agent in New York, Lurton Blassingname, and I suggested that I might have a million-word novel.

I finally just took out my ideas about how long it "should" be. I started building from the back. Where does it have to go? So parts of *Children of Dune* and *Dune Messiah* were already written before I completed *Dune*. And the last chapter of *Dune* was written in almost its final form. There were a few subtle changes, but not many.

This was the first book where I really started carefully applying my ideas about the building of a rhythm within a story. Do you know how you choose a word in a given poem to control the beat of the poem? By changing the phraseology, placement of words, you can change that rhythm; you can slow it down, you can speed it up. Well, there is an analogous thing in prose. I think this point is quite easily defensible. Length of sentence, modifying clauses, variety of sentence structure—all these things control the pace of controlled reading.

I work orally, because I think language was spoken long before it was written, and I think that unconsciously we still accept it as an oral transmission. I controlled the pace, so I have several rhythms built into the story deliberately. First, I use poetry as part of the process of writing, of loading the prose. In a sense, I use poetry the way a batter coming up to the plate swings three bats. If I want a passage to be evocative, I will write it as poetry.

Then I conceal the poetry in the prose, in the paragraphing. I work on the beat, to fit the total rhythm of what I'm doing. I'm very conscious of the rhythmic structure of a novel. Any form of poetry is grist for my mill. I've done haiku and sonnets. I'm very fond of the lyric poetry that came from southeast France and northwest Italy in the Eleventh, Twelfth, and Thirteenth centuries. They are some of the most beautiful lyrics ever written, with a beat in them peculiar to the language of the time and which English really cannot duplicate.

This [belief in the importance of oral language] is also why I based the terminology in *Dune* on colloquial Arabic.

I used linguistic rules, psycho-linguistic rules, and an elision process to change it, because there's time passing, but I wanted to hold it close enough to the present, colloquial Arabic—which is the language that survives. The two surviving kinds of language you get are church languages, and idiomatic.

That changing mechanism we use for communication, that oral tool—it's a very powerful instrument, it has its own inertial forces in it, it's mind-shaping as well as being used by mind, and it's a beautiful thing, it's a lovely thing. I'm in love with language. I'm *in love* with language. If you are going to convey to a reader, and you want to give him the solid impression that he is not here and now, but that something of here and now has been carried to that faraway place and time, and it is desert, what better way to say to our culture that this is so—and not to say it not overtly, but covertly—than to give him the language of that place?

There is also a long-term rhythm in *Dune*. There is a coital rhythm all the way through the story—a very slow pace, increasing all the way through. When you get to the ending, I chopped the rhythm at a nonbreaking point, so that the person reading skids out of the story, trailing bits of it with him.

On this I know I was successful, because people come to me and say they want more. The stories that are remembered are the ones that strike sparks from your mind, one way or another. It's like a grinding wheel. They touch you and sparks fly.

Now we all have stories with which we go on after we finish reading them. I deliberately did this in *Dune*. I want the person to go on and construct for himself all of these marvelous flights of fantasy and imagination. For example, you haven't had the Spacing Guild explained completely—just enough so that you know of its existence. Now with lots of people, they've *got* to complete this. So they build it up in their own minds. Now this is right out of the story. The sparks have flown.

This is also true of the Bene Gesserit. Their whole mystique and so on is relatively unexplained.

I was at Sonoma State last month, talking to a class there, and the question that seemed to attract the most attention from the class was the Bene Gesserit's use of "the Voice." There seemed to be a lot of agreement with the point of view that it's impossible to do this. And so I said, *we do it all the time*.

It's amazing to me that anybody could even begin to question this as a fact of our existence. And they couldn't see it. So I said, Well, I'll give you an example. I'm going to describe a man to you. You know this man. And I'm going to give you a task of controlling him by voice after I've described him and after you recognize him. I said, This is a man who was in World War I as a sergeant; he came home from World War I to his small town in the Midwest, married his childhood sweetheart and went into his father's business; he raised two children, whom he doesn't understand—and who don't understand him—he joined the VFW and the legion, went on every picnic, every convention, lived by the double standard (he thought). Now on the telephone, strictly by voice, I want you to make him mad.

It's the simplest thing in the world! Now I've drawn a gross caricature. But I'm saying that if you know the individual well enough, if you know the subtleties of his strengths and weaknesses, merely by the way you cast your voice, by the words you select—you can control him. Now if you can do it in a gross way, obviously with refinements you can do it in much more subtle fashion. And it's done all the time in politics.

It's a well-recognized thing in semantics. Hayakawa uses this example: you're talking, you've met somebody for the first time, maybe at a business meeting in a convention, and you get acquainted. You exchange views, and at the end of it you say, "We must get together for lunch sometime." Now, in one case, the fellow will call you the next week or you'll call him and you *will* get together for lunch. He knows he's supposed to call you and make this luncheon date. In another case, you use this same phrase, and he knows that this is "Good-bye, I don't care to talk to you anymore." But it's the same phrase.

At the same time, I've always been amused by the statement or by the label of psychological warfare. There can be no such thing as psychological warfare—if you develop a psychological weapon sufficiently that it is destructive to anyone, it is also destructive to you. It is like a sword without a handle, and if you grab it hard enough to wield it, you're going to cut yourself.

The Bene Gesserit see this. You see how they keep themselves in the background? They want a user of power they can control.

Another point: *Dune* is an exposition of the point that man himself is going to change. We have changed, but our changes—the actual basic change—is a gradual climb. I don't see this as progress, I see it as a sort of entropy and as a growth of complexity. But this is such a slow process—it takes thousands upon thousands of years.

After I finished *Dune*, I felt kind of drained. I mailed it off, and Campbell* raved about it, but he couldn't run it as an extended serial, so he had to cut it into two books.**

And then I went out and did some other things while I was thinking about the sequel. I'd just been very deep into a book that drained me. And I knew to make the others fit, I was going to have to do it again.

I had to take some time off. It was kind of a psychological R-and-R period. I did some more research, but there wasn't really a way of delaying the process. I knew I had to have some more material. I went on building my file folders, but I knew in my guts that *Dune Messiah* was going to be the hardest of them all to write.

To understand this, let's look at another element in how the *Dune* trilogy was conceived. *Dune* was set up to imprint on you the reader, a superhero. I wanted you so totally involved with that superhero in all of his really fine qualities. And then I wanted to show what happens, in a natural, evo-

*John W. Campbell, Jr., the editor of *Analog*, in which *Dune* had first been published in serial form.
**Dune* was originally published in *Analog* as two books, *Dune World* and *The Prophet of Dune*.

The Campbell Correspondence

June 3, 1963

Dear Frank:

Congratulations! You are now the father of a fifteen-year-old superman!

But I betcha aren't gonna like it . . .

This is a grand yarn; I like it, and I'm going to buy it. But I have some comments that may make you want to make a slight change in the ending.

As the father—and/or stepfather!—of several literary supermen, I've learned something about their care and upbringing. They're very recalcitrant. Also hard to live with.

You can't think like a superman. You can't imagine his motivations. He's altruistic—and superman. Which means he will sacrifice the highest good you can imagine, for the sake of something you couldn't understand even if he explained it to you. He is gentle—which, when properly defined, means that he is kindly, but absolutely ruthless. Like the man who loves horses, and sorrowfully shoots the stallion with a broken leg. I doubt that the stallion would approve of that action.

No human being can write about the thoughts, philosophy, motivations, or evaluations of a superman.

There are two ways that supermen have been handled successfully in science fiction; method 1 is that van Vogt used in *Slan* . . . and is what you've got here, so far. You don't talk about the superman, don't try to portray the superman, but show a superboy, who hasn't yet developed his powers out and beyond your ability to conceive of them. Method 2 is that used by Norvel W. Page in "But Without Horns" in the old *Unknown*. The superman never appears on stage at all—you encounter only people who have met him, and the results of actions he's taken. You never meet him, and never do understand what his motivations are.

If *Dune* is to be the first of three, and you're planning on using Paul in the future ones . . . oh, man! You've set yourself one hell of a problem!

You might make the next one somewhat more plottable if you didn't give Paul quite so much of the super-duper.

You'd have someone exceedingly hard to defeat, and yet having certain definite limitations, if you gave him just one talent, the ability of transtemporal clairvoyance.

Now that could work like this: a man remembers the past he has experienced, but nobody knows how that's done. Suppose it's done by a faculty that any remembering entity actually has, of being able to "see" across time, and perceive the actual original event. When you "remember" going to the beach for a swim last summer, you perceive-across-time the actual event.

Now this time-scanning would, inherently, allow you to perceive anything anywhen anywhere. Which would simply drive you completely nuts. Data is useless, unless you can organize and relate it. Unlimited access to unlimited data would require infinite time to scan it all! And until you've scanned nearly all of it, you wouldn't know what data went with what.

So normal people use as an index-mark, as a guideline, the "I was there" factor in using their transtemporal clairvoyance. You can remember what you heard, saw, felt, tasted, thought, and your mood.

Once in a while, somebody slips a bit . . . and gets somebody else's "I was there" guideline—if he can remember anyone else's memories—he would be very hard to defeat.

Notice: if I could remember what you remembered, I would, in effect, have telepathy! I would not know what you are now thinking, but I would be able to "remember" what you were thinking a millisecond ago . . . which amounts to the same thing.

If, before he can "remember" someone else's memories, he must identify their "I-track"—if it is essential that he first have a take-off point of direct contact—then the only way an enemy could keep Paul from knowing his plans would be to make sure Paul never encountered him. To find the I-track of one individual among the n-billion people in the galaxy would be impossible without a contact point.

If you wind up this yarn with Paul acquiring that talent, all the present explanations can come out of it, i.e., he can remember back along Baron Harkonnen's line, Yeuh's, Kynes's, the Fremen he encountered, etc., to get the whole present background.

BUT . . . he doesn't have so much precognition that you can't build a workable plot for the next yarn.

You know the trouble with time-travel stories; if the guy has a time-travel machine, and the villain kidnaps the heroine, there's no sweat. The hero doesn't chase the villain; he looks annoyed, steps into the time machine, goes back thirty seconds before the villain's villainy, and tells the heroine, "Hey, honey—that stupid louse, Rudolph the Villain, is about to kidnap you. He's making a nuisance of himself, isn't he? Let's go somewhere else."

Give your hero precognition that works, and it's sort of like old-fashioned Presbyterian Predestination. There's no use trying, because he already knows what has to come. And everybody else is stuck with it, whether they like it or not.

However, with all the data-sources he gets with everybody's memories . . . he still doesn't know the future. He knows what they think the future is, and what he thinks it'll be . . . but not what it will be.

Incidentally, I find that the following is a useful analogy describing the process of Time. Imagine an immensely tall glass cylinder filled with water. The bottom of the thing is sitting in a tank of liquid air; naturally the water in the bottom is frozen solid, and as heat drains out to the liquid air, the surface of crystallization advances steadily up the column of water. The interface between still-liquid water and solidified ice is the instant Now; the frozen ice is the Past, and the free liquid water is the Future.

Now, when a substance crystallizes, there are inter-molecular forces at work that reach out from the already-solid crystal to drag in and align free molecules of the liquid, forcing each new molecule added to the crystal to fall into a precise alignment with the already-crystallized mole-cules. The interface, in other words, is not a no-thickness geometrical surface—it's a volume. Liquid well away from the interface is really pretty free, but liquid molecules near the interface are already subjected to alignment forces, and are being dragged into place.

Moreover, some crystals manage to grow faster than others; there will be spikes of crystal reaching out well ahead of the slower-growing mass.

If you watch the way crystals grow—epsom salts crys-tallizing when a solution is poured out on a pane of glass, for instance—it gives a remarkable mental picture of how align-ment forces reach out from the past through the instant-Now, and into the Future...and yet do not completely determine the future, because there are liquid zones among the out-reaching crystal forces.

One other item that makes supermen such nasty people to live with, when they're fifteen-year-old supermen: they are adolescent demi-gods—and personally, I can't imagine any-thing more horrible. An adolescent, no matter how intelli-gent, is not wise; he's only smart. Furthermore, adolescents have the most ghastly horrible tendency to be sure they have The Answers to all the world's problems, and it is only the stupid conservatism of the old fogies that makes them reject it.

And having all the knowledge in the world means noth-ing—because all knowledge is filtered through the individ-ual's attitudes and beliefs.

Can you imagine a sincere, dedicated, enormously intel-ligent, practically omniscient teenager...with the typical teenage tendency to be Sure He's Right about matters that only adult experience can make understandable?

Hitler was Sure He Was Right. So was Torquemada.

The ordinary, everyday adolescent is something of a problem to live with. A real genius-grade adolescent is much worse to live with, because he's just as certain he has the proper, logical, and righteous answers figured out, and being extremely smart, is very difficult to unconvince.

Want to try it with Paul—when he's decided, at age sixteen, How the Galaxy Should be Rearranged And Right Away Quick?

God preserve us! No one else would be able to!

Regards,

John W. Campbell
Editor

* * *

June 8, 1963

Dear John:

Sincere thanks for the two-edged congratulations.

As for liking the new parenthood . . . let me put my reaction this way: the blessing appears not only to be mixed, but more on the order of a parfait that tangled with Mr. Waring's blender. Out of the resultant mass, however, I still can distinguish two ingredients—a sense of gratification that this long labor has been favored by someone whose judgment I admire . . . and a sort of small-mouse feeling in the face of the mountain of work I can see ahead.

Perhaps it's naiveté, but I'm flattered by the length of your letter. I have editing chores on my own in addition to writing, and I know what happens to your time. (On second thought, what *does* happen to your time?)

So—to the subject of Time . . .

Your analogy of an advancing surface of crystallization touched a particular chord of interest in me. With your permission, I may adapt it (or part of it) to my needs.

First, though, here's how I see the Time and plot problem for a sequel to Dune:

You will recall that Paul has a vision of Time as the surface of a gauze kerchief undulating in the wind. As far as it goes, this is accurate, but immature. It's the child-vision. Clarification is yet to come and he isn't going to like what he sees.

Think now of a coracle, a chip floating on a stormy sea. The man of vision is in the coracle. When it rises to a crest, he can see around him (provided he has his eyes open at the moment and it's light enough to see—in other words, provided conditions are right). And what does he see? He sees the peaks of many waves. He sees troughs and flanks of his own wave complex. Troughs of subsequent waves are increasingly hidden from him.

Considered one way, your surface of crystallization is similar to this stormy-sea concept. If you could photograph that surface on movie film at one frame per minute and view it at 16 fps, the surface would heave and undulate in a similar manner as it advanced. (It's the idea of an *advancing* surface that catches my interest.)

Now consider Time as a system with its own form of obedience to its own form of entropy. What disrupts it? What causes Time storms? Among other things, a man of vision with his eyes open in good light and on the crest of the wave can cause Time storms. If you see that-which-is-not, that's hallucination. If you see that-which-is-not-yet, you give the not-yet a feedback circuit for which it is not-yet prepared. You set up a channel for convection currents across regions delicately susceptible to the slightest deflection.

(Think of the region *beyond* your surface of crystallization. Within this region, there's another barrier area within which the molecular tip-over toward one crystallizing system or another becomes extremely delicate.)

Prescience, then, shakes down to this:

Man of vision opens his inner eyes. He may find it dark all around him. He may find himself in the trough of the wave . . . in which case he sees only the flanks of adjoining waves towering over him and a limited curve of his own trough. He may find himself on a crest in good light . . . in which case he QUICK looks all around.

Vision ends.

The Time he "saw" may maintain itself in similar motions for a period, but it is in motion, it is changing. And the very action of his *looking* has accelerated and twisted and distorted the directions of change. (Do you think John the Baptist could predict all the outcomes of his prophecies?) Add the further complication that there are many men of vision with varying degrees of aptitude.

Most philosophies of Time I've encountered contain an unwritten convention that this "thing" is something ponderous (read juggernaut) and requires monstrous, universe-swaying forces to deflect it to any recognizable degree. Once set in motion, they say, Time tends to be *orderly* in its direction.

Obviously, there is in mankind a profound desire for a universe which is orderly and logical. But the desire for a thing should be a clue to actualities. Local areas of order exist, but beyond is chaos. Time in the larger sense is a disorderly harridan. (I'll digress on this a bit later.)

We can still see the thumb upraised in the Roman arena, yes. Its effects are all around us if we have the eyes for it, but we *are* looking backward here, not forward. While we're looking backward, then, what of the Natufian herdsman who carved himself a whistle from a twig to while away his hours on a hillside? Is there a line between him and a Greek herdsman playing the pan pipes near Athens . . . and between *that* herdsman and Bach? What of the sidelines, then, twisting away to . . . where?

And what of the Chellean nomad crossing the site of the future Gursu-Babylon? Does the stone he accidentally kicks aside influence the future location of a temple? If this isn't enough complication, consider the negative side—the down-turned thumb, the uncarved whistle, the unkicked stone . . . what if . . . what if . . . what if . . . what if . . .

What if a wandering cow had distracted the Natufian gentleman and he'd left the whistle-building to another herdsman in another culture? The line might still wind its way to Bach, but over other hills and dales, and a person gifted with both views would hear a difference—perhaps a profound difference.

We've narrowed our focus here down to a two-value system (on-off, yes-no), however. What we have in actuality is a multivalued, extended-spectrum system—magnificent degrees and permutations of variability. The Time surface is in a constant state of flux. It's only when we look backward and isolate a line *out of context* that we perceive any degree of order. And if we take this order and project it into the future, the distance during which it will continue to hold true is distinctly limited. (Couldn't you visualize certain possible changes in conditions which would make some of our laws of physics inoperable?)

The Time surface is in a constant state of flux—one of your crystal extrusions may project for ten million years ahead of the surround-surface in one cross-section *instant* only to be lopped off in the next. (There's a fascinating side consideration here if we continue viewing this as "crystal." It *exists* one instant and *is-not* in the next instant. What happens to its components, if you give them substance? Do they enter the surrounding solution? If so, where?)

Let's isolate that cross-section (see above) idea for a moment. This is the abstraction process, the taking-out-of-context, the stopping, the isolation. You limit your knowledge of a subject when you do this with any flowing process. To understand a flowing process, you have to get in with it, flow with it. This is the larger meaning within the gestalten concept.

I promised a certain digression earlier (one among many), and this appears to be the moment for it. Time, the disorderly harridan . . . We are, of course, considering chaos

versus order. Within this, there is always the unspoken judgment—one thing is "right" and the opposite is "wrong." So
let's look at the *logical* projection of completely orderly Time
and a universe of absolute logic. Aren't we saying here that
it's possible to "know" everything? Then doesn't this mean
that the system of "knowing" will one day enclose itself? And
isn't that a sort of prison?

For my part, I can conceive of infinite systems. I find
this reassuring—the chaos reassuring. It means there are no
walls, no limits, no boundaries except those that man himself
creates. Magnificent degrees and permutations of variability.

Now, of course, we build walls and erect barriers and
enclosed systems and we isolate and cut cross-sections to
study them. But if we ever forget that these are bubbles
which *we* are blowing, we're lost. If we ever lose sight of the
possibility that a wall we've erected may someday have to be
torn down, then we've bricked our*selves* in with the amontil-
lado and we can yell "For the love of God, Montressor!" all
we like. There'll be nobody listening outside who gives a fat
damn.

We seem to have wandered somewhat off the Time
track, but now you know some of the background which
flows over into my stories and which I'm pouring right now
into a sequel to *Dune*. You may understand now, also, why
time-travel stories have always been somewhat disappointing
to me. They may have excellent plotting, wonderful linearity, tremendous sense of direction . . . but little or no elbow
room.

Before winding this up, I'd like to take one more side
trip in time through the concept of "how long." The length of
an operation, of course, depends on the viewpoint and the
field of operations.

Through a combination of circumstances too tedious to
detail here, I found myself one morning a split second from
death (by impending accident). During a period of time that
could not possibly have been more than 1/25th of a second, I
calmly considered at least eight distinct solutions, examining
them in great detail, calling on memory aspects that wan-

dered through a number of cross-references that could only be referred to as enormous. Out of this and still within this shutter-blink of Time, I decided upon a solution that had its main inspiration in a circus trick I had seen just once, and I altered that circus trick to suit my needs. The solution worked *precisely* as I had visualized it. I could cover at least ten of these single-space pages with elements that went into that solution and still not exhaust them.

Obviously, there are certain conditions under which our view of Time may be compressed to the point where, for all practical purposes, the process is instantaneous. (Consider the hours-long dream that occurs between the ringing of the alarm and the hand reaching out to shut the damn thing off.)

Another way of looking at this is to say that the Time it takes for a given event (a vision, for example) may be almost interminable for one person (the one with the vision) but practically instantaneous to an outside observer.

We can postulate, also, that External Time (in the larger sense) has different speeds and currents for different viewpoints, that not only is the course within a given locale variable but also the local-speed-effect varies.

These ideas, then, form some of the boundaries (manmade) of Paul's prescience. He's in a situation where he must learn new ground rules. (There are rules, but he has to learn a shifting frame of reference to recognize them.) He's within the coracle. While on that word, I might add that I've been using the title "Muad'Dib" for the first draft of the sequel. I think, though, that this would be a better title: C ORACLE.

If I tell you any more now, I'll be giving away the sequel. It goes without saying, though, that your comments will be received with great interest and open mind. Tell me if what I've said here meets your plot objections. If not, I'm perfectly willing to find some common ground for ending the first story that will hold up in subsequent ones.

Warmest regards,

Frank Herbert

P.S.: I quite understand that what I've been discussing here is the subjective relationship between real time and time dilation. But this strikes me as a subject which deserves much greater exploration—especially where it regards what we commonly refer to as "the speed of thought."

Sandworms of Dune

Even while he is saying flattering things about my books, John Leonard of *The New York Times* warns that someday my "head is going to fall off" because it contains so many "feverish inventions... extraterrestrial theories of justice... moral sinews... *and* splendid entertainments."

Lest Mr. Leonard's dire prediction come true, I will unburden my head here and now of some of that load—namely the myth construction which went into the material in this recording.

The elements of any mythology must grow from something profoundly moving, something which threatens to overwhelm any consciousness which tries to confront the primal mystery. Yet, after the primal confrontation, the roots of this threat must appear as familiar and necessary as your own flesh.

For this, I give you the sandworms of Dune.

They are the mindless guardians of the terrible treasure. They live in the deeps and when they surface they threaten all who come upon them. To those who must live daily with such monsters, however, the sandworms are the familiar "Old Man of the Desert."

In the lair of this mystery, you learn to walk in a *different* way. You assume a new awareness. Still, this terrifying presence supports your life. The sandworms are the ultimate source of Dune's wealth (their bodies give up the melange-spice which extends lifespans) and they also produce most of Dune's oxygen (created in the monstrous chemical dissipation of heat which is produced by the friction of their passage).

The dragon who carries the "pearl of great price" in its mouth—this is a mythological equivalent of Dune's sandworms. When you watch the dragon dancers at a Chinese New Year celebration, you participate in a similar mystery to that of Dune's Fremen.

Here is Erebus, the son of Chaos and brother of Night. It is darkness personified in the passage of Hades. Yet, Erebus is also the father of Aether (the clear air) and of Hemera (day). Incest is clearly stated because the mother of these familiar children is the sister, Night. Another matter stated with equal clarity is that women remain the keepers of the dark mysteries and that men invade such matters at their own peril.

Thus, the sandworms of Dune and the trials of the male protagonists.

The death of a sandworm contributes the substance which arms consciousness for the transcendence of time. This is true whether it occurs in the sanctuary of a sietch cavern or by the natural process of the open desert.

To use such a substance, you pay the great price. You no longer live in the protective and gregarious midst of your own kind. Now, you are the shaman, alone and forced to master your own madness. You have grasped the tail of the ultimate tiger.

To fulfill its role, the sandworm is one vector in a circular process. Before its metamorphosis, it is the sandtrout, the leathery creature which encapsulates and withholds Dune's other treasure—water. Thus, the conditions which support it in its new form—it creates the waterless desert.

And what is poison to the sandworm?

Water.

In each instance, the elements of the mystery are intimately related: sandtrout/water, sandworm/spice.

The high value of the geriatric spice rests in its life extension for the users. This, naturally, sets the stage for life-threatening conflicts.

I am saying here that the extension of human lifespan cannot be an unmitigated blessing. Every such acquisition requires its new consciousness. And a new consciousness assumes that you will confront dangerous unknowns—you will go into the deeps.

It's an old, old story. Every *terra incognita* has its own rules which you must learn if you wish to survive. When you remain on familiar turf, you know where to walk; you recognize the dangerous creatures which share your world. The poisonous snakes have been identified and there are antitoxins. In some respects, this is pure myth, but your mythology does incorporate lessons of survival.

If you enter new terrain, however, you are the pioneer, the explorer *and you are expendable*. That is your function when you go into the deeps.

It's no wonder that our ancestors both admired and feared the ones who dared the perils of inner exploration— whether that exploration was ignited by peyote or amanita muscaria or by trials of pain and self-induced trance. And it's no wonder that such fears remain with us today. Our mythology is not all that different from the bushman's.

These elements remain so deeply rooted in Western culture that to profess even a casual understanding and belief in them is often enough to invite emotional reactions—anything from derision to physical attack. That's why I always point out that I don't necessarily believe in such things; I just write about them.

There! My head feels much lighter.

Frank Herbert
Port Townsend, Wash.
November 11, 1977

Possible
Futures

Of all the questions that are asked of science fiction writers, few are more distressing than "What do you expect to happen in the next (five, ten, fifty, one hundred) years?"

Contrary to popular opinion, very few science fiction writers are in the business of prediction. And with a few notable exceptions, they are not very good at it. Their business is to look at some aspect of the present, and to ask "What if?"

Here are a few of Frank's "what if?" sessions. The first, "Undersea Riches for Everybody," was written in the early 1950s, when he was researching his first novel. Under Pressure, *a futuristic look at undersea warfare that predicted, among other things, a global oil shortage. This piece was bought by* Colliers, *but never published, since the magazine folded before its scheduled publication. On the one hand, the piece seems a little dated, with little of the power of Frank's later writing. On the other, the points it makes are as true as ever they were . . . and are still waiting for fulfillment. At the time the article was written, it seemed inevitable that ocean-floor development was one of the new frontiers that would open up in succeeding decades. So much for prediction!*

"Man's Future in Space" is filled with optimistic comments written on the occasion of the first moon landing.

The third piece, "2068 A.D.," was written while Frank was the features editor of California Living, *the magazine section of the* San Francisco Examiner. *It combines the predictions of twenty science fiction writers from the San Francisco Bay Area.*

"The Sky Is Going to Fall" gives a much more guarded view of the future. It was written only five years later, and offers conditional hope for a future that must begin to consider renewable resources and the quality of life rather than a gung ho conquest of the environment by science and technology.

Undersea Riches
for Everybody

People would think it mighty peculiar if, when the Kentucky Derby starting bell rang, the horses remained at the post, their jockeys chatting about the weather and the foreign situation.

But nobody appears to think it strange at all that most Americans are sitting on their hands after the start of the greatest race in history: the scramble for riches under the sea.

If you've seen a few Western movies and didn't skip too many history classes, you probably have a mental picture of a homestead rush: settlers waiting on the prairie for the marshal to fire his .44, horses neighing, buggies creaking, excited talk.

Ahead of those settlers was land for the taking—rich land. Maybe you've said, "Those were the good old days!"

Well, brace yourself. If you're in one of the U.S. Coastal states, go down to the ocean beach, wait for low tide and walk out to that mark where the waves spend their last effort upon the sand.

You'll be standing on the starting line for our modern-day land rush.

We have an empire to develop. It dwarfs the total of all the homestead areas in our past; it is more important to our future than the Louisiana Purchase was in its day.

Our new empire is the continental shelf.

Off U.S. shores, that shelf is equal in size to the combined states of Maine, New York, Delaware, West Virginia, Florida, Pennsylvania, Kentucky, Texas, California and Washington: almost 750,000 square miles.

Beyond the surf which pounds our coasts are riches that make Pizarro's roomful of Inca gold appear like a stack of pennies in comparison. The Spaniards and every visitor to our shores since have sailed over more wealth than they found on land.

Why, then, have we been so deaf to the starting bell? Perhaps it's because our hearing has been deadened by too much political oratory. That gusher on the Potomac focused attention on offshore oil and gas. But petroleum is only a small fraction of the wealth beneath the sea. Just one of the ocean industries—bottom fisheries—far outstrips the fuel potential.

The steel in tomorrow's kitchen knives and family cars all will be made with manganese from submerged lands. We're already supplying a large part of this metal from the ocean. Black oxide of manganese forms a thick ebony crust over much of the sea bottom. One submarine mountain twenty miles long and ten miles wide in the Central Pacific holds fifty million tons of the stuff—ten times the present annual world production.

The bromine in that photograph you took at the picnic last July Fourth was recovered from ocean brine.

The iodine you painted on Junior's injured knee came from marine kelp.

Most of the world's population still uses sea salt at the table, recovering it today the same way they did in Biblical times.

Welsh coal miners hear the pounding surf of the Irish Sea above their heads. They work in shafts driven under the continental shelf from the shore.

But these items are only a fraction of the potential. All the main mineral elements of the world have been discovered in the ocean. Here is a partial list of what we already know is out there beneath the water: gold, silver, copper, iron, precious stones, silica, phosphate, vanadium, platinum, sulphur, uranium and radioactive trace elements, pottery clays, rock salt, building stone, peat, marl, chalk, shell, sponges, lead, sodium sulphate—and sand for everything from window glass to concrete.

How important is all of this to you? Read what one of the nation's foremost economists told a Senate committee last year:

> Any country which refuses to develop its ocean resources is going to fall by the wayside. Those resources are represented by a great range of mineral wealth and by an almost incredible variety of animal and plant life. Within a century, a country which refuses to use these resources will decline to a sixth-rate nation.

That is the opinion of Dr. Harold F. Clark, professor in charge of educational economics at Columbia University.

Dr. Clark believes England is in financial trouble today not because she lacks resources, but because she did not have the imagination to use her resources from the sea.

He told the senators that Australia, which has one of the largest continental shelf areas, "will almost certainly be one of the greatest powers in the world."

"If one does not understand why," he said, "then one does not understand what has happened in regard to the economic resources of the ocean."

Enough oratorical half truths and misinformation about the continental shelf have been gushered into the American atmosphere that it's a wonder anyone understands what has just happened in this country.

The plain truth is that the "states' rights" and "federal rights" champions have concluded a six-year political civil war. During those six years, development of the U.S. continental shelf remained practically at a standstill.

It's time we looked beyond the petroleum "political herring" because another fact emerged from the congressional debates: ninety-nine percent of the wealth in the U.S. continental shelf is still potential. And you have just as good a chance at it as the next fellow!

If you're the cautious type, perhaps you'd better buy some stock in one of the blue-chip companies moving into the submerged lands. Pull up your easy chair and keep an eye on the financial pages of your newspaper.

But if you have pioneering blood, you can join the men who are following a different course. Their ranks are thin; you'll have plenty of room.

These men are spending time to become familiar with continental shelf geology, a subject not too much different from upland geology. That's one of the fascinating things about the continental shelf: The stuff it's made of is similar to what is encountered every day on shore. But there's a difference; it's the difference, you might say, between observing a car in a showroom and seeing it assembled in the factory.

Geology is in action under the ocean. Here is the birthplace of sediment which one day will go into the stone front of a building or the dishes on your table. That sediment is being laid down constantly; while you read this it accumulates.

But knowledge of geology won't be all you'll need. The new type of prospector calls for special equipment: an aqualung, swim fins, crowbar (for prying off geological specimens), a good sharp knife. These are bare essentials.

If you set your sights on this region, here's a word of advice: check up on the laws for the locality you're going to cover. Rigid conservation practices are enforced on most of the states. If you use dynamite, there'll be a limit on the size of shot you can set off. If you put in pilings, you won't be permitted to abandon them before you cut them off below the mud line. If you erect a navigational hazard, the Coast Guard will step in and enforce its rules. As far as the law is concerned, your construction will be "a ship at sea."

Weather will assume new importance. In the Gulf, the June-November hurricane season requires a watchful eye on forecasts, and a radio to keep posted on weather changes.

You'll be confronted by a long list of new problems peculiar to the sea: that bane of all divers—the bends; corrosion and electrolysis that will eat away metal like some malignant ocean creature; dangerous sea life; limited visibility under water; swift submarine currents.

This new kind of prospecting calls for all of the imagination and ingenuity which made our nation the richest in the world, plus the vision to see that the goal is worth the effort.

The burro made it possible to invade the Western desert. The aqualung is the key to the submerged lands. It makes you a "fish" in depths to about two hundred feet. Unlike the solitary western "desert rat," however, you'd be wise to take on a partner equipped with another aqualung. Underwater, you'll be in a new and sometimes dangerous world, one on which we have very sketchy information.

We actually know more about the movements of distant stars than we do about the movements of ocean currents; we know more about the geography of "our side" of the moon than we do about the geography of undersea lands.

What's it like out there on the continental shelf? Let's take a look in Davy Jones's Locker, bring ourselves up to date on the little we do know. Man may have inherited the earth, but three-fourths of the earth's area is ocean. (Just one of the oceans, the Pacific, is larger than all the dry land regions combined!)

Now add to the ocean area another dimension, the vertical. The marine world suddenly shows up with three hundred times as much inhabitable space as dry land and fresh water regions together! This is a basic reason why the oceans are so vital to our future.

The floor of the ocean basins—an average of two and one half miles beneath the surface—is actually the dominant level of the earth. The continents stand about three miles above that floor, with the great volume of the oceans lapping high on their sides.

This zone where waves and currents cut into the flanks of the land is the continental shelf. The edge is where the gentle slope of the shelf suddenly dives off into the depths at a steep angle. This borderland—the real rim of the continent—is in water an average of 70 fathoms deep (six feet to the fathom: 420 feet).

Here in the waters beyond the white surf is a strange world where green twilight prevails at high noon. In one region will be barren rocks, or sand swept by strong currents. Another area will be an ocean garden: hairlike colonies of plant cells, pendulant leaf structures, slashed draperies of seaweed, crimson algae filaments, pastures of ocean reeds.

This is the earth's greatest "factory," where the mingling of mineral and animal sediment never stops. This is the "trap" for everything the waters sweep from the land, and for everything the surface currents give up to the depths.

When you go prospecting in this region, you'll have to draw many of your own maps, chart your own underwater canyons and plains. This is the real "terra incognita" of the earth.

As recently as 1934, writers were telling us of the "flat tableland beneath the sea." They were about as accurate as the grandees who sneered at Columbus. Erosion and upheavals of the earth's crust have carved beneath the ocean as dramatically as they have above it.

Slashing through the continental shelf are submarine canyons, steep-sided as railway cuts, strangely reminiscent of erosion gullies. Their cause is one of the great marine mysteries. Perhaps someone reading these words will one day pause in his underwater prospecting to observe a new phenomenon—and solve the mystery.

The United States' underwater empire reaches its widest—about 240 miles—off the Gulf of Maine, and its narrowest—less than 50 yards—off the southern Atlantic edge of Florida. Beyond Key West in the Gulf of Mexico it stretches out 150 miles, seldom deeper than 40 fathoms. The chicken-track pattern of the Mississippi Delta reaches almost to the shelf edge. Westward of the Delta is more shoal water (less than 35 fathoms) swinging wide along the curve of Texas.

On the West Coast, the shelf off California shifts from less than a mile out to 40 miles. It becomes progressively narrower and steeper as it reaches the rocky headlands of Oregon and Washington.

The warm waters of the Gulf of Mexico will be a prospectors' paradise. In this undersea land—roughly equal to the combined areas of New York and Kansas—washings from the land have been packed to depths of greater than 20,000 feet. The region is known as a geosyncline, a word meaning a hammock-shaped sediment trap beneath the sea. A line along the center of this "hammock" would de-

scribe a great sweeping curve, hung at one end from the vol-
canic peninsula of Yucatan.

Just north of Yucatan the bottom drops off into eerie
darkness of the Sigsbee Deep, some four miles straight down.
Oil seepage has been bubbling to the surface near the Sigsbee
Deep for as long as man has sailed these waters. Indian leg-
ends tell about the "blood of the water demon." Surface scum
oil blackened the hulls of Spanish galleons.

Along the entire Gulf of Mexico, the shoreside geological formations dip toward the sea. Offshore they are bowed
downward by the weight of sediment into the bowl of the
geosyncline. Farther at sea these formations rise close to the
surface.

Within thirty years, the experts believe we'll be taking
petroleum and other minerals from federal lands at the rim of
the continental shelf. But you'll see none of the sticklike drilling derricks which now dot our southern coast. The entire
operation—search and drilling—will be carried on underwater. At least four submersible drilling barges already are in
the race for the undersea wealth: steel behemoths of almost
3,700 tons which borrow at least half their features from sub-
marines. The barges are designed to go on the ocean surface
to a drilling site, then sink to the bottom for the actual work.

With a little imagination, we can project these barges
into tomorrow, see what they logically must become. Let's
peel back a small corner of the curtain which hides the future:

Focus your attention on a young man, aged somewhere
between twenty-five and thirty-five years. He could be the
son you send off to class each weekday morning of the school
year. We'll call him project chief. He rides a lurching bucket
seat in a monster of metal, quartz, and plastic. With him are
perhaps ten crewmen. They sit amid a maze of control bars
and dials.

The chief's glance goes to a quartz porthole through
which he can see the shimmering world of sea life brought
into vivid outline by searchlights. In the cold green twilight
of ninety fathoms the project chief is monarch, pilot of a
machine named, let's say, after the scorpion's deep-sea rela-
tive, *King Crab*.

The machine tips to the right, grinds downward into an ocean canyon. In the *King Crab*'s control room is the sound of pumps, humming electric motors, voices reading instrument data, squeaks and thumps, the muted grumbling of metal treads.

Two wavy blue lines merge on a screen in front of the project chief. He turns to his men: "The map says this is it. Drop a bore."

Anchor columns sink into the mud. Diamond cores go into the bottom muck and are lifted for examination. The humming engines quicken. Giant scoops open. Hydraulic cutters tear at the sea floor, send it coursing in a muddy flow across placer tables in the "factory" compartment. The tables begin to shake and quiver as the mud is flushed off them and returned to the sea. Soon the catch-riffles gleam with yellow. The chief bends forward, retrieves a nugget, scrapes the black manganese from part of it.

"Survey hit it on the nose," he says. "This is the richest dirt I've ever seen. That river must've been piling the stuff in here for a million years."

"Man, I'm thinking about that bonus!" says a crewman.

Those words of the future fit the picture today. There's a bonus waiting for us under the sea. Long after the oil and gas are exhausted, we'll be feeding ourselves, clothing ourselves and building our homes with products from this new frontier. The vision of the furious rush of human activity that's sure to intrude into our coastal waters tempts one to make a comparison.

Around 330 B.C. Alexander the Great was lowered to the bottom of the Mediterranean in a glass barrel. When his men hauled him back aboard their war galley, Alexander described the undersea world: a place of "rude fishes, and strange wonders which defy the imagination."

What might Alexander say if he could slip into an aqualung and swim beneath the waters off the U.S. coast a few summers from now? Perhaps he would say that the "rude fishes" had better move over; their cousin, Man, is coming back to claim his own.

Man's Future in Space

Measured against what is about to happen, the *Apollo* modules are our horse and buggy in space—primitive, but a reality of our time, which will open the door on a very different tomorrow.

If you ask "Should we be in space?" you ask a nonsense question.

We are in space.

We will be in space.

Mankind will become a creature of space.

About the only thing that could prevent this would be the total destruction of Earth, at present our only space platform. But our inexorable movement into space changes even that problem. The political reality of a humankind dispersed throughout the solar system presents a far different picture from that which we face as I write this—all of our eggs in one basket. No politico-economic system now being practiced on Earth can evade awareness of that fact. Not if the proponents of that politico-economic system wish their system to survive.

Which begs the question of communism versus capitalism.

Neither system will survive as we know it in space. Communism, which creates an all-powerful bureaucratic aristocracy, cannot survive without high walls around its population. There are no walls in space. Managed capitalism (which is really what we are talking about in the United States) cannot survive unless it controls the lines of energy and materials. No such controls are possible in space.

What we will see can be compared to what mankind faced on hostile frontiers throughout history—a kind of co-operation-by-necessity, an inescapable mutual interdependence for survival. You help your neighbor raise his barn because tomorrow you may need his help.

Our situation at present displays many similarities to conditions faced at the beginning of the steam age. The questions and pronouncements of that historical period give you a sense of *déjà vu*:

"If God had intended man to go sixty miles an hour..."

"The destruction of the family by these insensate machines cannot be tolerated!" (A Welsh minister in 1841)

"The displacement of population brought about by these unholy devices are such as no civilized people can permit." (A speech in the British Commons, 1838)

The real questions of those times were, as they are today, ones of politics and economics, not of science and engineering. The questions of politics and economics are always addressed after the fact. Science and engineering go about their business much like a force of nature.

With hindsight, these are the things we know today about the steam age: steam allowed us to do things we could not do before—such as pumping water from deep mines, milling hard metals, and moving heavy objects rapidly over long distances or short ones.

Steam also raised enormous political and economic issues that have not yet been resolved because we moved from steam into other energies that did much the same things but with more sophistication.

Reading the history of those times you can see the currents of these times. Many new people rose to positions of great power. Old power centers either adapted to the new conditions or they dissolved. Tremendous leverage gravitated to those who could employ creative imagination to control the new knowledge.

The political issues inherent in this are obvious. The

forces of conservatism (which in this sense really defines the status quo) will fight to maintain their present privileges— even if this means delaying our movement into space. In this arena of "pure-power politics" there is no escaping the fact that whoever controls space controls Earth. But the control of the space around Earth does not carry with it control of space beyond such a sphere. That is too simplistic a viewpoint. The movement outward will continue because it represents also a movement of escape from restrictions—no matter how you define restrictions.

What then can we predict about the aftermath of the *Apollo 11* landing and our other tentative outreachings into the airless void that surrounds our lonely space platform?

In the field of politics:

- People will move beyond the immediate control of any central government just as they did in the westward migrations across the American plains, and the northwestward migrations of the Germanic tribes into what are now Norway, Sweden, and Denmark.

- Some of the migrations into space will never be brought back into a central fold.

- Just as those Germanic tribes set a pattern for individual freedom and representative government, which helped to shape the British (and the U.S.) systems, the new migrations will once again reform social and governmental structures.

In the field of economics (which can never be separated from politics):

- New products will appear just because they can be manufactured only in the high vacuum of space.

- Familiar products will be manufactured in space at less cost and higher quality because of available abundant energy and the vacuum. This is especially true in electronics, metallurgy, and precision milling of metals.

- Cheaper energy in space will open enormous new areas for human habitation—although there still is some question whether electrical energy generated in space can be transmitted back to Earth without unacceptable damage to the planet's atmospheric shielding.

In the fields of medicine and genetics:

- Cheap cryogenic storage of whole people and "spare parts" will make profound changes in attitudes toward life and survival.

- Many medicines will be manufactured cheaper and of higher quality in space because of easily available sterile conditions and isolation facilities.

- Experiments with dangerous disease cultures will occur in safer isolation and, therefore, will become more common, leading to new achievements in disease control.

- Exposure of human reproductive cells to the heavier radiation loads of space will ignite a much greater mutation rate—most of which will be lethal or sterile. But those who survive with improved space adaptation characteristics will insure a wide divergence from what we now consider to be the human norm. Our descendants in space may look nothing at all like Earthbound humans.

At this moment, there is really no such thing as a space industry in terms of what we can expect to see by the year 2000. As the economic advantages of this outward movement become clearer to existing industry, as new inventions spread the base of "who can operate in space," that outward movement will become explosive. Then we will see a true space industry. Finally, something should be said about pure science. There is no doubt that off-planet scientific observations will add enormously to our store of practical knowledge; every advance of pure science in the past has had this effect. We can only guess at some of the consequences.

But there will be new materials made possible because of what we learn in space. And a more sophisticated understanding of astronomy and other spacial relationships may generate new ways of moving humans and/or materials across the void.

2068 A.D.

A bold look 100 years
into an exciting future

Imagine you're a latter-day Buck Rogers. You've just been awakened in a strange apartment by a voice coming from an instrument like a block of crystal without visible works. The voice says: "Morng, paddies! Sbrighday, nth of July 2068."

You sit bolt upright.

Did he say July 2068? 2068!

Words swim in the crystal block which is about eight inches square. Despite abbreviated writing, you make out that the words instruct you on how to set this "resonator" for morning call.

Outside the window (or what looks like a window, although it has controls reminiscent of a TV) is indeed mid-summer, 2068. You've had a one-hundred-year nap and there's a new city to explore. Let's explore it together. Your guides are Bay Area science fiction writers, circa 1968, whose predictions are combined here.

Please try to keep your good temper. It's true that the machinery and way of life in 2068 appear frighteningly strange. But imagine your grandfather's judgment of your 1968—"You don't wear enough clothes for decency! You don't need all that speed!"

Let's take the tour, first. . . .

THE BAY

Filling the Shoals With Garbage—Conservation versus Population

Potato Patch Shoals and the Great Bar's south shoals which claimed so many lives and ships are no more, covered

142

by fill that has created a New Golden Gate far outside the old one. But the sheltered waters of the New Bay are at least as large as in 1968, thanks to a 1967 invention by the Japanese, Kunitoshi Tezuka (who also invented the device which turns old auto bodies into lumps of metal). He solved San Francisco's garbage problem while adding about ten percent to The City's real estate. Garbage of the twenty-first century is compressed into impermeable twenty-ton blocks, barged to the shallows and sunk to create new land.

Fill can be seen also on the east shore where the shallows out to about the three-fathom line have been filled from the Richmond terminals on the north to San Jose on the south. El Cerrito Hill sits far inland; Alameda's port area and Government Island are many times their 1968 size.

The 1968 conservationist may rage at this, but the trend precedes 1968. All of your guides on this tour through time, despite frequently expressed hopes that men won't destroy their environment, tempered their predictions with pessimism based on mankind's past performance. Some natural wonders have been preserved for 2068, but not until much had been lost. The twenty-first-century conservationist, raging at the excesses of the past brought on largely by population pressures, has a special word (unprintable) of contempt for twentieth-century families with more than three children. He considers it a major victory that the lost Bay shrimp have been restocked and are thriving, and that population control is a major conservation plank of the new age.

TRANSPORTATION
Atomic Shuttleships from Space and High Speed Cargo Sailboats

You've noticed that the skimmer-copter taking us on this tour burns ammonia, not petroleum. Its exhaust is nitrogen and water vapor—fitting to the general ecological awareness that's belatedly cleaning up Earth's air and water. (And a comment on the way you squandered petroleum.)

Those aren't just big airplanes. They're atomic-powered shuttleships, each bringing about 1000 commuters from

Space Station San Francisco. The station's orbit holds it permanently above The City—about 300 miles above. Residents there think of themselves as San Franciscans. Their trip down to the space complex east of Mount Diablo (note the homing beacon tower atop Diablo's peak) and the fast skimmer-copter run to The City are a bore—strictly routine.

Waters of old Bay and new appear at times almost covered with commercial and sports craft which must hold to definite lanes. Most Bay traffic is pleasure boats, many patterned after giant cargo sailing vessels whose sails are enormously tall metal surfaces and rotating vanes. Hulls ride on bubble foils which compress into ski surfaces at speed. Sport sailboats top forty knots; cargo vessels do a more conservative thirty under sail. Most liquid cargo is towed in collapsible barges by atomic submarine tugs.

There's a fast passenger ferry system and every bridge has at least one parallel underwater tube, even that new long span from Marin over Angel Island and Alcatraz. What isn't apparent is that these bridges carry only commercial traffic. You'd need a special pass to take a private vehicle over them or on one of the "freeways"—all of which are reserved for commercial use. The "car" of 2068 is equally at home on land, water, or in the air. Its only roadbeds and landing pads are created in minutes by cheap spray-on soil stabilizers.

Most of the Bay's pleasure craft dock on the San Francisco side which has few commercial installations. (The east shore is little else but commercial, except for Old Berkeley, all of which has been taken over by the University of California, one gigantic building under a transparent roof, all sections linked by fast slidewalks.)

SAN FRANCISCO
A Gigantic Vacation Complex Dotted with Ethnic Villages

Old San Francisco has given unbridled vent to its love of the past and to period restorations. In some areas it looks as though Golden Gate Park had overflowed everything with scores of wildly different villages and isolated superbuildings poking up through a maze of landscaping and quaint old sky-scrapers. Cleared of most industrial activity, The City has become a gigantic vacation complex with hyper-ethnic archi-tecture in such divisions as Little Muscovy, Chinatown, Congo Center, Vikingstad, Zensville (the former Japanese Cultural Center at its core), Roma-Roma, Vienna West and the restored Barbary Coast. A Disneyized Emperor Norton walks the streets and the current uproar involves the alleged introduction on The Coast of android (mechanical humanoid) prostitutes.

San Francisco's waterfront is almost unrecognizable by 1968 eyes. Behind the pleasure boat moorings, copies of famous coastal towns from all over the world crowd the shores. A white-walled Italian fishing village stands hard by a Moro coastal community from the Philippines (occupying the frontage once taken by Fishermens Wharf).

You're delighted to see familiar cable cars, but delight is tempered when you learn more details. They run on tracks and they sound like their ancient counterparts, but they're self-powered and the sound issues from synchronized record-ings.

You note the tall towers on the land covering the Great Bar. These towers are topped by singing flames (another 1967 development which converts flame into an extremely high fidelity speaker). The flames relay music and public ser-vice announcements to resonators of the surrounding area.

Beneath the south tower, our pilot points out, is the Center for the Study of Mutations, a research establishment into drug- and radiation-induced genetic changes of humans.

A giant center for the performing arts has been built around the San Francisco Opera House. The Opera House and many other historic buildings were restored and im-proved after destruction in the quake of 2021. This quake ignited the research which resulted in lubrication of the San Andreas Fault by pumping silicone along its entire length. There are no more tembors, only a gradual slipping mea-sured in a few feet per century.

THE MEGALOPOLIS
Land Shafts, Undersea Housing, View "Windows" of Far Places

As our skimmer-copter lifts for a long view, you're suddenly struck by the magnitude of urban development. Population pressure has transformed the Bay Area into one gigantic megalopolis extending from Monterey-Hollister-Modesto to Ukiah and out under the ocean. Tubes link the mainland with underwater housing on the continental shelf. Many subdivisions are housed beneath retractable canopies. Others are contained in enormous condominiums above and beneath the land surface. Residential construction of the past fifty years has turned more and more to the region under land and sea. Land shafts driving down thousands of feet enclose self-contained communities with shops and services in walking distance along speedy sidewalks.

View windows underground are wall-size, three-dimensional "holographic" TV screens. View rental is big business. You can have Victoria Falls, Niagara, Yosemite, Mount Rainier, Fuji, Lake Louise, the pyramids of Giza, the Amazon jungle, the Taj Mahal (restored) or even London's streets. Residences along the waterfront boast underwater rooms with view windows open to the sea.

Power is delivered by low-cost atomic units and solar batteries. (As a by-product, the portability of these energy sources brought decentralization of industry and made desalinized sea water the major source of potable water. Like a row of falling dominoes, this doomed the giant dams except for those still built as flood control.)

HOW PEOPLE LIVE
Baroque Costumes, Sonic Baths, and Sharply Controlled Computers

Dramatic as these changes appear, the really striking changes of the twenty-first century are organizational—in the ways people live as individuals and societies. This is a hedonistic, laissez faire age, the age of the eight-hour week. It allows for wide differences of opinion, judgments and ways of life. Prominent in 2068 history books is the account of the violence at the turn of the century when people revolted against computer control. Computer-stored data (growing out of the old National Data Center) had been used to harass and persecute those whose views didn't conform with those of the majority. In the bloody revolt, most computers were destroyed, their data erased. This new age's laws reflect jealous guarding of personal privacy.

Computers remain, though, and are vital. They assist in the conquest of disease and injury. Children learn to use them in the first few grades. They're your library, your instructor (home programming of TV classes). They run your apartment, directing such chores as garbage disposal, dishwashing, cooking, lighting control, air conditioning and heating, tuning and changing of view-screen windows. They record and store personal information (anniversaries, birthdays, business appointments, financial data), take phone calls, accept mail (via scrambler telescreen circuits) and make your routine mathematical computations (including figuring your income tax, a chore requiring milliseconds).

Many baroque touches mark everyday life: elaborate costuming for work and to announce such things as political preference; jeweled housekeys, shaved and painted designs on heads, garments such as orange togas patterned with artificial crystals, net tights and doublets hand-embroidered by students in design at Berkeley.

You can have fresh plover eggs for breakfast, walrus steaks, orange juice piped from Southern California. Communal kitchens are centers for revival of ancient cooking skills almost lost in the prepackaging era.

Baths are sonic, using no water, requiring seconds.

Music in your home comes from library tape banks.

Rats, mice, fleas and other pests have been eradicated from all living areas.

There's a National Department of Controlled Violence

(supervising controlled violence between consenting adults) to drain off the worst aspects of aggression.

And more—much more than we've dared predict—all taking up this new age's extended leisure time. Complications, troubles—these will come, too. And, of course, all of these predictions presuppose that our world won't become a sad smear of ashes on a desolate planet. In that event, the above tour is declared null and void. The few Bay Area survivors will have fled by 2068 into the hill pockets of Northern California. There, small tribal units, all suspicious of every stranger, will exist on roots and berries, knocking each other on the head with wooden clubs.

20 AUTHORS WHO HELPED

The twenty science fiction writers who helped formulate this tour of the future—and some of their more famous story titles—are:

Poul Anderson, Orinda—"Corridors of Time"; Karen Anderson (Mrs. Poul)—"The Piebald Hippogriff"; Peter S. Beagle, Santa Cruz—"A Fine and Private Place"; the late Anthony Boucher (William A.P. White—H.H. Holmes), Berkeley—"The Quest for St. Aquin"; Reg Bretnor, Berkeley—"Modern Science Fiction, Its Meaning and Its Future" (a critical symposium); John DeCles (Don Studebaker), Berkeley—"The Picture Window"; Miriam Allen DeFord, San Francisco—"Space, Time and Crime."

Philip K. Dick, San Rafael—"Man in The High Castle"; Dick Goodman (A. Marshall), Berkeley—"Brain Bank"; Ron Goulart, San Francisco—"The Sword Swallowers"; Robert Heinlein, Scotts Valley—"Stranger in a Strange Land"; Frank Herbert, Fairfax—"Dune"; C.C. MacApp, San Francisco—"Omha Abides."

J.F. (Mick) McComas, San Francisco—"Brave New Word" (McComas was founder and editor with Boucher of the *Magazine of Fantasy and Science Fiction*); Ray Nelson, El Cerrito—"Eight O'Clock in the Morning"; Emil Petaja, San Francisco—"Tramontane" (latest in a tetrology based on

Finnish myths); Edgar Hoffman Price, Redwood City—
doyen of Bay Area science fiction writers, began publishing
in 1924 in such magazines as Droll Stories and Weird Tales;
Thomas Scortia, Cupertino—"Shores of Knight"; Wilmar
H. Shiras, Oakland—"Children of the Atom"; Jack Vance,
Montclair—"Eyes of the Overworld."

The Sky Is Going to Fall

I think the sky is going to fall. I predict blackouts, more strikes, starvation, all kinds of urban violence. But on a positive note, I also think we are still a society of screwdriver mechanics. Our society is particularly rich in people who, faced with a problem, don't sit down and say, "We are doomed"; but instead ask, "How are we going to solve that?"

The number-one problem is the relationship between energy and world population. We are being handed some straw men in the argument over our headlong plunge into atomic fission as an energy source. The real argument against this is that it has the potential for destroying large areas of real estate upon which our descendants will have to depend. Somebody must speak up for them.

The truth is there are many other nonpolluting energy sources, more than enough to take up the immediate slack and give us the time to arrive at more inventive, longer-range solutions.

We have not yet begun to explore the potential for a symbiotic relationship between large urban centers such as San Francisco, and the surrounding agricultural land. Most of the large cities in this world, with populations above 35,000, produce sufficient waste products to fertilize and maintain extremely large areas of agricultural land.

I predict you are going to see within the next 100 years, gigantic agri-businesses, large areas of agricultural land which depend upon waste we now throw away for fuel to drive machinery and fertilizer to keep them producing.

Our present cities were designed by the automobile, and

it's obvious they don't work. Our resources are going to have to be tapped to run our vehicles. And we are going to have to think about a completely redesigned-from-the-ground-up idea of what constitutes a city, setting cities up so we use and re-use products presently discarded, and also so they are both physically and psychologically supportive of the individual.

We'll have to put housing closer to jobs. We could put a steel mill next to a dwelling now, and you wouldn't know it was there. We have that capability.

There are several ways already advanced, Habitat in Montreal for instance, of putting enormous numbers of people into relatively small areas, in such a way that they are not constantly aware of a crush situation—neither seeing their neighbors, nor smelling them nor hearing them.

People once more need to feel needed and useful in what they do. One of the most efficient sources of energy in the world is still the human being. It is not true that machines can do everything better. For the most part, they are boringly repetitive even when they are most efficiently muscular.

Several things are going to happen, I think.

One is that the long-range economic rewards of making employees feel useful and necessary in the creation of human-supportive products will grow increasingly obvious to industry.

On the other hand, I see a resurgence in the next one hundred years of what can only be called cottage industries when many commonly used products are going to become art forms.

For instance, I can see a small cottage industry manufacturing an electric toaster which would be beautiful to the eye, simplicity itself to use and maintain, and would not need repair for sixty to one hundred years.

The pressure is on, in an area where our society really excels: imaginative creativity. For example, a couple of us have been exploring the re-design of the windmill. I am going to build one you would not have to shut down in a hurricane, it won't require exclusive, useless tower structures, and it will have a lot of push at zero revolutions with relatively low wind.

Our present hydro-electric system could be expanded enormously by setting up wind-operated pumping systems which would bring water back uphill behind existing dams, so it could run down through the turbines once more.

This nation was founded on a decent concern for the respect of all posterity. Unless we change our "don't give a damn" attitude, our descendants are going to plow up our cemeteries for anything they can use, including the bronze from caskets and our bones to make their china. The history books of such a future will curse these generations and the world will be less because of what we did.

The basic conflict is between how the individual sees what is needed for his immediate survival and what the race requires if anyone is to survive.

An
Understanding
of
Consequences

More than any other science fiction writer, Frank Herbert has come to be associated with ecology. This is no surprise, since the ecological framework of Dune *is not just a detailed work of the imagination but an elegant exposition of fundamental ecological principles.*

However, Frank always insisted he was not a "hot-gospel ecologist," and argued that one of the points of Dune *is that any science can be misused.*

The pieces that follow illustrate Frank's own application of the dictum of Paul Sears that was echoed in Dune *by the planetologist Liet-Kynes: "The highest function of ecology is the understanding of consequences." These pieces examine this principle, and thereby the whole subject of ecology, in sometimes unexpected ways.*

In one of our conversations, Frank pointed out:

If I'd been born in my grandfather's time, I'd have made my grandfather's mistakes. There's no doubt of it. *I just don't want to make my grandfather's mistakes today.* And if we can stretch our awareness across just that much time then we have started the stretching process.

Our chief ecological problem appears to be that we get inertial processes going that are very difficult to stop. And a lot of those inertial processes are based on decisions that become irrevocable. People say "I'm not gonna change." And we could change.

The first piece in this section, a brief selection from a conversation Frank and I had in 1983, was sparked by my remark that ecology is often confused with environmentalism, while in fact, environmentalism often leaves out the fact that people, too, can be a legitimate part of an ecosystem.

As Frank points out in the next selection (his introduction to Saving Worlds, *an anthology of ecologically oriented science fiction), ecology is itself a subject full of contradictions. It can be a tool of demagoguery and shortsightedness instead of a vehicle of insight into the interrelationships of man and his environment. The true ecologist must always be sensitive to what he is leaving out, must be alert to the possibility of error, and must remember to inquire about his own motivations, or else "ecology" is just one more way that man can "inflict himself on his environment."*

This of course was one of the themes of the Dune *series. For all that a precise knowledge of the planet's ecology is needed in order to set the transformation from desert to paradise in motion, in the long run, the indigenous fauna of the planet is wiped out when the transformation goes too far.*

Because human power is limited, sometimes the path to a desired end is not the most direct path. For example, Frank points out that the Sierra Club is probably responsible for the clear-cutting of redwoods in California. Because they led the lumber companies to believe that logging might be banned completely from some areas, those companies hurried to do their work before any legislation was passed. Extremism, in Frank's view, always tends to create what it opposes.

Frank gives concrete attention to specific environmental issues in the two pieces on air pollution which he wrote for the San Francisco Examiner, *"We're Losing the Smog War" and "Lying to Ourselves About Air." While the problem has not progressed as alarmingly as Frank warned back in 1968, air pollution remains with us.*

Of all the pieces in this section, "Ships" (also written for the Examiner*) has the least to do with ecology, but the most to do with the understanding of consequences. When we think about the quality of life we want for our children, we must think not just of the advances science and technology will bring us (as in the earlier article about life in "2068 A.D."), we must think of what we want to preserve, and what steps we must take to do it.*

In reading this article, I am reminded of a story told in Co-Evolution Quarterly, *Stewart Brand's magazine spinoff of the* Whole Earth Catalog. *Some years ago, the massive roof beams of one of the halls at Oxford University were discovered to be riddled with dry rot and in need of replacement. The university administrators were at a loss when they heard that beams of that size were simply not available anymore—nor were there trees of sufficient girth to make such beams. It was at this point that an elderly caretaker learned of the problem, and pointed out that the University had planted a stand of trees for just this purpose over a hundred years before.*

That's understanding of consequences.

The final piece in this section, "Doll Factory, Gun Factory," brings the questions of ecology full circle, to the question with which this collection opened: How can man best adapt to his dynamic, dangerous environment? I like his answer, and I think you will, too.

Natural Man, Natural Predator

Occasionally, I'm identified as an ecologist. People don't realize that I'm not a hot-gospel ecologist, saying lock it all up and throw the key away. Ecology has become, rather deservedly, a dirty word. Because it has been picked up by a lot of demagogues and a lot of people who are not looking at all of the necessities of their time.

I can document that the Sierra Club was one of the strong influences in the clear cutting of redwoods in California. They mounted a very powerful lobby in Sacramento which was aimed at locking up those forests. The minute they mounted this lobby, timber owners and loggers in northern California just went in and cut the redwoods because they were afraid they'd never be able to cut them. It happened virtually overnight. The environmental lobbyists just did not think ahead.

We saw it recently, in the Everglades. People wanted to go in and save the deer. The thing that the people who wanted to save the deer are not seeing, is that man has put himself in the position of being the only predator that is thinning the herds. We don't allow the other predators; we've killed off the cougar. There was a function of the predator that is no longer being fulfilled, and we, through mistaken sympathy with the wildlife, are not fulfilling that function.

I have really never been a sports hunter, but I grew up on part of this peninsula south of here during rather hard times. After the hunting season, we'd go out at night and jacklight. The earliest hunting experience I remember was when I was eight years old. My uncle Louie had a box about a foot square that held a car battery with two handles on it, and on top of it was a car headlight that you could turn. My job was to sit there with that thing between my knees above an abandoned orchard where we often hunted, and aim it at the deer that they pointed to. My uncle would tap me on the shoulder, I'd hit the switch, the light would go on, the deer would look at us, and *pow* over my head and there was the meat.

That wasn't sports hunting—the animal never had a chance. And I never could see the sport in hunting anyway. If you need the meat, if you're hungry—there it is. Go get it.

We went out after the season because we didn't want to get killed by the sportsmen banging away half drunk through the woods. We went out to jacklight them because we could be very selective.

Our preference was a barren doe. Barren does eat almost twice as much as any other deer in the herd and are big—a steer, a female steer. They are good to get out of the herd. But we didn't shoot them because it was good to get them out of the herd, we shot them because they were big. One bullet would kill them and they had the best meat. Through experience, we knew this.

Introduction to
Saving Worlds

One smoggy, eye-smarting day not too long ago, we awoke to find ourselves as a species in something like a tent revival meeting with the hot gospel of ecology blasting at us from all sides. The *preachers* with the loudest voices were saying:

"Come into the fold or you will experience hell on earth followed by a painful extinction."

Right up there with the loudest was our little band of science fiction writers, a hardy, resourceful and imaginative lot, saying:

"Here are a few of the possible hells, a few of the possible ends, and some colorful alternatives."

Our batting average has been frighteningly high.

Big Brother is watching you.

Have you checked the pills in your Malthusian belt lately, madam?

If your ego has been folded, stapled and mutilated, please be patient. Management has not yet developed a computer program to deal with all contingencies.

It makes me feel good all over when I realize that war is peace.

Keep in mind as you read this new collection of ecological projections that what the human imagination can dream, the human flesh can create. This will be true as long as we have a place to stand and the second law of thermodynamics continues in force. There will be stranger things than we foretell here.

When I think of ecology, I often recall the story about the man who was told he had one week to live unless he invested his life savings in a complex treatment which offered him a fifty-fifty chance of extending his life by only one year.

That's the hot gospel and you'd better believe it.

We say it here as we've said it before: the human species has reached the point where a single individual can control enough energy to obliterate us all. We have no assurances that such energy will remain in the hands of individuals whose good sense will steer us away from the bang or the whimper.

We *did* send chemical weed killers to Southeast Asia in tankers of sufficiently large capacity that the destruction of just one of them could have destroyed the oxygen regenerative capacity of the Pacific Ocean. And that's just one example.

The concept of "fail-safe" does not have a fail-safe built into it.

Power is the name of the game. We are in a wild energy time. This power is an odd thing. The militant says, "Power to the people." The governor says, "Send in the National Guard." The tactical squads are alerted. The newspaper editor tells his staff, "Play it cool; we don't want to contribute to the hysteria."

There also are those great bundles of accumulated energy which we call wealth—money. (The United States has almost no research funds invested in studies aimed at a world without war. The implications and consequences of this gap appear obvious.)

All of these power areas are correct in their internal assessments. Power often is what determines the short-term course in a society. And there obviously are many powers influencing humans. This makes it very easy for us to get sucked into the vortices where we are just reacting, where ultimately we feel we must do anything at all to influence others. This is the pot of message which a great many science fiction writers stir when they use the ecological theme. They do have an influence, too.

There's a striking thing about these power vortices, though. You see it time and again. A center of influence appears—a leader. A succession of leaders may make the scene.

It's as though they were drawn into a vacuum of genuine concern whose reality cannot be denied. Don't minimize the concerns. They are real and they focus on problems whose solutions are difficult. But the demand is for simple solutions framed in absolute terms. Here's where the demagogue makes his appeal. "Follow me! I have the answer!" And you want to believe because the simple statement of the problem carries the ring of truth.

Thus—the hot gospel. Thus Occam's razor cuts us up once more.

The vacuums of leadership continue to accumulate around the genuine problems, however. People come into the vacuum, exert power and, in the current idiom, they go on their ego trips. Invariably, these leaders run or drift away. They cut out. They go to Cuba or Algeria, to a commune in the country or a ranch on the Pedernales. They do this partly because they have behaved in a fashion best calculated to achieve this end. Since the abandonment of (or expulsion from) the power center is a predictable consequence of the leaders' activities, you can suspect it follows naturally on the use of power.

The leader goes on his trip, leaves and the vacuum remains. But its shape changes. It's as though the leader took the power with him. His movement starts to die of its own political machinations, sickened by lack of understanding and accumulating disorganization—by a choice of goals which don't really fit the situation.

Then it's everybody go on to the next cause.

There are indications that ecology, as a concern for the future of our species, is following this course.

The problems which aroused concern, however, are still with us. It's only the pattern of a "movement" which has beguiled us. The important thing to recognize is that ecology as a phenomenon reflects a genuine underlying malaise. The boil is a symptom of infection. It's when we confine ourselves to the surface symptoms that we guarantee more and more lethal eruptions.

This is the essence of the ecological message.

We are engaged in a planetwide crisis of the human species which is shared by all. We are well beyond the point of no return in technological developments which exert greater and greater influence upon individuals, often with shockingly destructive consequences which are amplified by war.

At this moment of crisis, we are being sold the hot gospel that our survival decisions must be made within the either/or arena of guilt-innocence. The moral cowardice of this insistence is blocked out by most of our species even while the increasingly strident screams which this insistence provokes trap us in ever more destructive confrontations.

It's the old schoolyard routine where someone inevitably demands that you "cry uncle."

In a typically either/or trap, many latter-day ecologists offer us the alternatives of austerity ("Kick the science habit, baby!") and/or poverty (spending our life savings for another year of dubious survival) or of a despairing decline into extinction. This trap is bound around with "cry uncle" walls of guilt-innocence.

"Who made the decisions which got us into this fix? The only thing wrong with this country is its politicians!"

"We'll straighten things out when we get rid of (Nixon, Johnson, Laird, Wallace, etc.)."

Who are the bad guys?

Nowhere is it suggested that lethal decisions may have been products of their contexts.

Richard Nixon did *not* invent the system of consensus reality within which he made his choices.

The same is true of rebels who feel that the only answer is to plant explosives in a bank.

Or of those who insist we must invent a better machine.

People who say, "The only answer is . . ." demonstrate little more than the tightness, the confining restrictions of the either/or arena within which they insist we must make our decisions.

Few focus on the size of the arena or upon the destructive assumptions which form its walls. Few observe that mankind is attuned to this planet and to tidal forces which resonate in and around it. The word "lunacy" did not enter our language by accident. One of those lunatic tidal forces appears to make us prefer small and comforting arenas, places which do not dwarf us by their immensity or by their dangerous unknowns. We prefer the tranquil pond to the perilous rapids.

But the science fiction writers and ecologists keep saying: "You're already into the rapids, buddy. What're you going to do now?"

And the onslaught of science-technology keeps reminding us that even if we accumulate ten billion years of human history, that will remain a microscopic event in the face of infinity.

Such reminders and their echoes of fatalism tend to fill each of us with despairing anger. In the throes of subjective turmoil, itself partly a product of current contexts, we are told we must raise our ecological sights, raise our awareness, attempt new heights of objectivity. We are told we must do this in a relativistic universe where the best operational answers we can achieve are only probable, not absolute, that we can never test the reliability of our system by requiring it to agree with another system.

All of this continues despite the accumulating evidence that no corner of human endeavor escapes the clouding, the fuddlement and mistaken assumptions of previous contexts. And nowhere does this show up more strongly than in the education which we call science.

Psychologist L. Johnson Abercrombie in *The Anatomy of Judgment* tells us how science students, learning to read X-ray plates, demonstrate an inability to distinguish between what is shown on the plate and what they believe to be shown. When confronted with proof of the extent to which preconceptions influence their judgments, the initial reaction of these students tends to be surprise and anger.

Surprise and anger.

Throughout our lives these emotions represent a dominant tendency through which we interpret the brute facts of experience in a relativistic, changing universe. Having been taught from infancy by countless implicit lessons to expect a universe of perfect cause and effect amid absolute objects, we react predictably when told: "It ain't so, Joe."

Here may be a major area where ecological science fiction raises the reader's hackles. Many people tell me they read such science fiction "with terrified fascination," suggesting the reaction of a chicken confronted by a snake.

One view of history says men will undergo violent contortions, will even die, to prove themselves "right"—to keep their pet beliefs intact. Another view says terror may attract humans like a magnet, drawing them into the very situation they fear most. Science fiction has been playing with these themes at least since Plato's day.

By the questions asked, by the alternatives displayed for your consideration, such science fiction represents a metaphor of history and sometimes becomes a preview of reality.

Those of us who are looking now at contexts, rather than at *blameworthy* individuals, are beginning to ask a new question: How do we deal with lag times for out-of-date contexts when such contexts represent power and identity to entrenched blocs of our fellow humans?

There may be an implicit answer in the very framework of the question, and it's possible you can see this answer in every story between the covers of this book. Here's one way of putting it: we stop condemning our fellow humans. (My God! That sounds like "Judge not, lest ye be judged.")

If we learn one thing from observing the life around us, it's that hierarchies exist and that mistakes occur within the multiplex niches of those hierarchies. To approach the study of these circular relationships only to find the guilty and the innocent represents a form of nonsense, an old context whose assumptions don't work. That context breaks down. It doesn't march.

The lesson of *infinity* as applied to hierarchies says there always exists another level beyond the ones we can see. There are more niches in heaven and hell than we have dreamed of in our philosophies, even in the philosophies of ecological science fiction.

Survival decisions (and that's at the core of ecological concern) require us to refuse to be confined in the systems which our ancestors gave us. The geneticist observes that we are continually breaking out of the old genetic framework.

This appears to be equally true of those abstract frameworks which we call consensus reality.

The mechanic in us argues: "If the gear doesn't work, replace it or design a new one."

The ecologist says: "Now you have to learn about systems."

By understanding system relationships, the ways the parts operate together and how those relationships link us to the infinite universe around us, we enter the real realm of science, including the realm of science fiction. One of the things this art form has been saying to us all along is: "Increase your grasp on probabilities."

Look at your own hand. Isn't that a metaphor standing for how we seek to influence our universe? Think of the limits in that flesh and how we construct amplifiers (waldoes) to overcome those limits, only to find new limits beyond those we had perceived.

The message of this metaphor and of ecology is that we need to stop asking why and start asking how. Behavior is observable and can be dealt with operationally. We can analyze behavior for its probabilities. Infinity merely warns us that because one event regularly precedes another we are not necessarily dealing with cause and effect. The crowing rooster does not cause the sun to rise.

The lesson of hierarchies-over-infinity tells us the probabilities are high that any assemblage of specialized data will indicate larger and more fundamental events in our universe.

Any assemblage.

Short-term cause and effect, that ancient illusion of a universe reduced to the hand of god, is out. That's not the current style. Now we are a world-band of humans seeking a perilous course through a relativistic universe where new conditions constantly assault our sense of balance. An enormous amount of evidence has accumulated around the concept that this is an impermanent universe composed of impermanent bits. An intellect educated to demand otherwise tends to make reactive decisions to this evidence in a pattern of surprise and anger followed by despair and rejection.

Herein may be the essential *new thing* with which ecological awareness has armed us. We appear to be reacting within lethal systems of resonance (vibration) which make it highly probable that we soon will destroy this planet and every living thing on it—unless we dampen the system.

We have more than enough data to describe existing conditions. We understand our moment of surprise and anger. The ecologist is telling us to recognize now that we have limited ourselves to microscopic arenas of either/or within which we cannot solve our problems.

The species knows its travail. This shines through every bit of ecological science fiction I have ever read. The implicit observation within this accumulated artistry appears this way to me—that all of the individual cells, sharing the common condition, must share in the solution. A full description of all those defensive, disconnected, short-term responses we have been making to our problems is also a full description of how we maintain our problems. Behavior cannot be separated from biology with any hope of understanding the system they share. You cannot cure the hand and leave the body sick. Indeed, that approach makes the sickness worse.

It's not so much our addiction to science which is killing us, but how we make our connections. War, as the foremost ecological disaster of any age, merely reflects the general state of man's affairs at that time. It represents a choice of how to use our energy. Our problems appear to arise not from the use of energy, but from destructive by-products of how we choose to use our energy. Discarded by-products are polluting both our physical and our psychological environment. Misused human talents and the toxic effluent of unburned fuels—both are choking us.

We know some things about the consequences of not facing such problems—no matter how large the problems may appear. Facing problems represents positive action. It counters the deadly debilitating force which follows our surprise and anger. It counteracts frustration. By this we revitalize the decision-making abilities. Facing the probability of species extinction, an implicit message of ecology, has shocked many humans into various forms of despair which appear to be a kind of blind acceptance. They say: "We are caught in the contradictory systems which give us improved means to produce deteriorating life styles."

The signposts on our mutual road to disaster stand tall and unavoidable. The seamless web of our world has come apart at the seams and we didn't know it had. And the ecologist and science fiction writer are merely saying: "Hey! Look there!"

In this moment of despair, I am suggesting we re-examine the road system. Let's look at the dynamics of the energy flow through our system. Let's examine the connections, the seams. I'm not suggesting we abandon any present social system for another. In my view, communism-socialism and capitalism have such similar energy-flow systems that a visitor from Arcturus might find it difficult to tell them apart. The hierarchies are interchangeable. The motives are interchangeable. The methods of self-justification and enforced compliance are overwhelmingly alike.

In each, the individual is the ultimate cog, abandoned in his solitary despair. Yet the species remains at the mercy of this individual. He can decide to exstinguish all of us. He is acquiring the use of greater and greater energy with each passing instant. Just as we cannot separate behavior from biology, we cannot separate the individual from the species and hope to learn what is required of us in this moment of crisis.

Our new condition demands that we understand a new and larger arena of either/or, a new set of choices which balance the needs of any individual against the needs of the species. Each must be served. The energy requirements of this arena are enormous. The need to waste nothing is pre-eminent. The responsibility to our descendants that we keep the system working cannot be evaded.

We are surfboard riders on an infinite sea and the waves around us have changed. This is the lesson of ecological science fiction: *Regain our balance and teach our young how to balance.*

We're Losing
the Smog War

While researching this story I kept thinking about the two men who fall off the Empire State Building. One screams all the way down; the other silently admires the changing view. At the fortieth floor, Silent looks at Screamer and asks: "Why're you screaming? We're all right this far."

You'd better decide whether you're Silent or Screamer. We may have time to pop the parachute, but time's running out faster than you think and . . . there are complications.

For some four months, I've been struggling through the air pollution maze. At times, I found myself surrounded by nightmare mountains of papers, books, magazines—confusing and conflicting data, scare stories and avuncular pats on the head. A solution must be in that maze somewhere, I thought, but I probably was just too stupid to see it.

Frustrated, I went outside one day for a bouquet of diesel exhaust from a city bus. The date was September 25 when the official air pollution reading for Burlingame reached .37—well into the danger zone for human health. Suddenly, I saw the obvious answer: anyone forced to breathe that kind of aerial sewage knows all he needs to know about air pollution.

As an angry secretary at the State Public Health Department in Berkeley put it that day: "No matter how you look at it, smog's depressing."

If she's reading this, let me say to her that the true depression probably goes beyond her wildest fears. We are dealing here with what I choose to call a Warfarin Effect. Warfarin is a rat poison. Rats are difficult to poison because food that kills one is avoided by the others. Warfarin is effective because it takes several visits before the poison claims its victim. The way it kills is particularly appropriate to this comparison. It's an anti-coagulant. The rat often drowns as blood fills its lungs.

Match this effect with emphysema, the fastest growing cause of human deaths in the United States. Emphysema, a deadly breakdown of lung function, is up 300% in California since 1955. It's pushing lung cancer into a back seat. Lung cancer, which has undergone a thirty-fold increase in this nation since 1900, shouldn't be ignored, though.

Air pollution is implicated in both these tragic examples of runaway statistics. But emphysema gives us a dramatic foundation on which to make our case. Not only humans, but animals living in our polluted cities are dying of this disease in increasing numbers.

Cigarette smoking obviously accounts for much of the lung cancer. Among urban smokers, lung cancer is eleven times more frequent than among rural nonsmokers.

But animals don't smoke.

We've executed many a criminal on less evidence than we have against air pollution. It's implicated in a long list of diseases, deadly, debilitating and deforming—gastric cancer, stillbirths and birth deformities, a speed up in the aging process, chronic bronchitis, a dramatically lowered resistance to virus infections, lowering of the fertility rate.

"It's no longer possible to say there's no firm evidence linking air pollution to health hazards," says Vernon G. MacKenzie, deputy director of the U.S. Public Health Service Bureau of Disease Prevention. "The evidence is there if you look."

Officers of London's Air Pollution Research Unit say: "We have abundant evidence that the sharp peaks of mortality and hospital morbidity that we see on our charts are caused by air pollution of some kind, rather than just by unusual weather conditions."

According to San Francisco's Dr. Roger H. L. Wilson, National Secretary for the Council of Public Health and Air

Pollution of the American College of Chest Physicians, the cumulative burden on human life from using the sky as a sewer is growing too fast for scientists to catalog.

"We are increasing production of inhalable, volatile materials," he said. "Parathion poisoning is becoming more common. Even worse, we've found it diagnosed as pneumonia. The human eating and drinking of insecticides increases at a measurable rate. And the base areas we've used as smog-free for our studies are growing rarer.

"We see the curious phenomenon of only a very small increase per year in pollution at the centers of our cities, but in the outskirts where we're paving over, ripping out trees, driving freeways through open country, the air that used to be relatively fresh and clean grows fouler at a terrifying rate."

No matter where you look for air pollution in today's world, you find it—on the slopes of Hawaii's Mauna Loa, at the bottom of a Death Valley mine, at the North Pole or South Pole. The city experience forecasts what we can expect. Just inhaling the air of our more polluted localities is equivalent to smoking two packs of cigarettes a day.

When urban air acquires too many pollutants, city dwellers die—not just a few, but by the hundreds and the thousands. London documented four thousand excess deaths during a single air pollution episode in 1952. Four years later, another thousand London residents died in a similar episode. New York city medical studies reveal a similar story.

Immediate deaths aren't the only casualties. The 1948 Donora, Pa., episode, one of the most infamous examples of a community being poisoned by aerial sewage, was investigated ten years later by the U.S. Public Health Service. They found survivors of the Donora episode had a higher sickness rate, were more susceptible to air pollution, and they died at an earlier age than the average for all U.S. townspeople.

The Donora experience tells us that many of the adverse health effects of such pollution are chronic or cumulative, that they are not detectable either early or easily—the Warfarin Effect.

Dr. Arie J. Haagen-Smit, the world famed Caltech biochemist, chairman of California's Air Resources Board, compares the fight for clean air to a war.

"Our first target is to make the air breathable," he says. "It's not breathable now. This is war. In a war, it's best to strike at weak points—one weak point at a time. We don't dare diffuse our attacks; we're not that strong yet.

"But if only one thousand cars are refused by potential buyers because of our warnings, that makes a lot of waves. We've put the industry on notice that we aren't completely powerless. The auto people are beginning to understand that this isn't all nonsense."

Haagen-Smit, directing his forces in attacks on motor vehicle emissions of hydrocarbons, carbon monoxide and nitrogen oxides, now points an accusing finger at the lead alkyls added to gasolines at two to four grams a gallon to increase octane ratings and reduce engine knock.

"Almost all gasolines are leaded," he says. "It's emitted in very fine particles which the industry would like us to believe are harmless. In the last few decades, levels of lead in our food, water and air have been rising so steadily that there's increasing worry about it in the scientific-medical community.

"Lead is a body burden which settles in our bones. It's a poison. And there's absolutely no reason for it to be in the gasoline, no reason at all."

Haagen-Smit's concentration on motor vehicles as the major poisoners comes from the fact that 60 to 75% of the aerial sewage we breathe can be traced to this source. Total motor vehicle emission of all pollutants approaches 150 million tons a year for the nation.

Harry F. Barr, vice president in engineering for General Motors, is one of the more outspoken defenders of the auto industry. Let's listen as he makes an official statement before the Senate Commerce Committee:

"GM engineers and scientists have been doing basic research on auto pollutants since the late 1940s and developing the results into practical hardware.

"Our research demonstrates to us that we will be able to

achieve very low pollution levels with the internal combustion engine—levels that are consistent with known ambient air quality objectives. While our research offers great promise, much development work remains to be done.

"The upward trend in automotive pollutants was halted in California in 1961 with the advent of crankcase emission control. The crankcase device was applied nationally in 1963. With the additional application of exhaust emission control systems beginning with the 1966 models in California, and nationally with 1968 models, a downward trend in automotive pollutants is being established despite the increasing car population."

The industry may be able to "achieve" low pollution levels in control of these sources, but you'll note Barr says nothing about maintaining them. We'll discuss this aspect in more detail presently. First, let's understand that the crankcase device was not applied nationally in 1963 to all cars, and the exhaust control system still is not being applied nationally to all cars.

There was no halt in the upward trend of automotive pollutants in 1961, and there still is no such halt.

Public officials from the highest to the lowest say the entire effort of our pollution control establishment may be just barely enough to maintain a dangerous status quo.

Then again, it may not.

An employee of the Bay Area Air Pollution Control District told me flatly that by 1980 at the latest, San Francisco's air will be right back where it was in 1965—and downhill from there on. That's if we meet ideal control standards, a thing we've never done.

One of the nastiest facts about the growth in the number of motor vehicles (quadrupled since 1945) is that the more vehicles we put on our streets and highways, the more we drive each vehicle. That means we burn more gasoline per car as their numbers increase. When you add the mounting congestion this traffic inevitably brings, you get a consequent increase in the time each vehicle sits idling in traffic jams.

Idling is blue murder.

Your average car puts out many times more pollutants

while idling than it does while cruising at moderate speeds. Can laws requiring control devices and systems take care of this?

Let's ask ourselves how effective our laws are going to be when twenty thousand miles of driving on many cars is enough to make anti-pollution devices ineffective? Some 87 pct. failed in recent tests to meet California standards after that length of driving. According to the most recent State tests, 1966 autos exceeded hydrocarbon emission standards at about eight thousand miles. The 1967 cars went over our standards at about twelve thousand miles. First samples of 1968 cars, however, met the standards until fifty thousand miles.

Lest this lull you into a sense of complacency, let me warn you that many observers say our standards are too lenient.

"Even if by 1980, every car in the state is producing only half its present average pollution, motor vehicle pollution will be greater than it is now," says Los Angeles County Pollution Control Officer Louis Fuller.

Fuller is well aware that keeping to California standards requires regular, expensive and exacting maintenance. The hidden joker in such maintenance is a fact which hasn't received wide publicity—yet.

Controlling exhaust emissions on an internal combustion engine requires you to put up with a car which doesn't run as well as a pollution producer, not as efficient, and often with deliberately increased slippage in the automatic transmission.

Here's what garage mechanics, the men who'll really have to maintain the system, say about it:

Some 40% of our crankcase control devices are not up to standards and can be brought up to standards only at considerable expense to the owner. (This 40% figure agrees with the State's own assessment on faulty crankcase control.)

Said a mechanic at a State garage: "Candidly, my experience is that almost 90% of the exhaust emission systems don't hold up in everyday driving."

The problem is this: only three or four degrees of difference in timing on a car's ignition can improve performing enormously, but it sends pollutants soaring "right off the scale."

"Advance the timing about two degrees on some of these 1968 engines and it feels like you've added one hundred horsepower," said another mechanic. "When you retard the timing to comply with factory directives (and with the law), your car puts out less pollution, but it runs like a staggering jackrabbit. Most shops don't comply with maintenance directives now. I don't expect they ever will unless we have an inspector behind every mechanic."

Factory bulletins contain these warnings about results of anti-pollution tuning: poorer gas mileage, lower power, rougher and faster idling, harder starting.

What will probably happen if we continue our present course?

We know from experience that wherever the selfish aims of enough people unite, the law fails. Don't minimize the pressures against strict controls and enforced compliance. The auto industry is putting itself into a position where it can say: "Well, the air would be clean if you'd only use our systems correctly."

Time after time with dreadful repetitiveness, I met the official or recognized expert who punctuated our conversation with: "Now, understand, I have to breathe this air, too, but . . ."

Often, this was the same person who, after explaining some dangerous aspect of air pollution, would add: "You'd better not say anything about that. We wouldn't want to alarm the public."

I heard statements to this effect from an employee of the Bay Area Air Pollution Control District, from an officer of the San Francisco County Medical Society, from public health officials, from State officials and from businessmen.

It's instructive to examine just one of these cases. For background, note that flower growers say Bay Area nurserymen have lost millions of dollars to air pollution.

According to Roy Hudson, San Francisco's assistant superintendent of parks: "Smog damage isn't unusual in Golden Gate Park. Nurserymen tell me it's growing worse yearly. Sensitive leaves are being damaged more and more frequently."

Among big losers have been growers of orchids and petunias. One, after admitting he's moving many of the more sensitive plants of his nursery to the cleaner air of Watsonville, added: "All of us (Bay Area nurserymen) are trying to suppress this. If we go out and tell what smog's doing to our plants, that's a good way of telling people not to buy our products."

He didn't want the flower-buying public to learn a fact most florists already know through experience and plant pathology reports from the University of California, Riverside. Polluted air can cause serious damage to plants without producing any immediately visible external effects.

Since the Bay Area is one of the world's largest flower-producing centers, his concern is understandable. What he proposes to do about it—move out and suppress the seriousness of air pollution—is not.

If he were alone in this attitude, there might be no problem. But almost every person who drives an automobile is in there with him to some degree. Your little addition to air pollution can't make much difference, can it? Besides, you live on San Francisco Bay where we get all that clean air right off the Pacific Ocean.

Lying to Ourselves About Air

The fragility of our position on this planet is little understood by most people. Population growth is straining many systems to the breaking point. We share a finite volume of air with a world population of some three and a half billion which is doubling every twenty to twenty-five years.

At a rate of fourteen to eighteen breaths a minute, each of us exhausts three hundred cubic feet of that air daily. We each use another five thousand cubic feet daily for all other purposes. The air begins as a gaseous mixture about one-fifth oxygen and four-fifths nitrogen, argon, traces of other gases, variable amounts of water vapor, plus all the aerial sewage we dump into it. After we've used it, the air is useless for breathing unless diluted with fresh air renewed by growing plants.

For every new car we put on the highways (at a rate of about 5% a year) we should be planting one hundred new trees to help renew the despoiled air. We remove at least one hundred trees per car, instead.

Well, you say, there's really so much air we don't have to worry. False. When you ask how much air there is on earth, you get nonsense statements such as "between five and six quadrillion tons." That tells you nothing.

Take an orange. Coat it with a thin layer of shellac. If you think of that orange as the earth, the thin coat of shellac represents our total air supply. The part readily available to us, however, is only about the bottom tenth of that thin layer. Most of the air we use is in the first two thousand feet of our atmosphere. We ordinarily breathe only the first seven feet. And the rate of interchange between successive layers of air slows remarkably the higher you go.

There are even greater limitations on the supply. Inversion layers in the atmosphere can put a cork on a relatively small air basin or blanket thousands of square miles. The U.S. Weather Bureau reports inversions bottling up our air one fourth of the time anywhere in the nation in all seasons. And this atmospheric plug is even more common over most cities and heavily built-up regions.

Think of a bathtub with a normal overflow. You know it's possible to run the water into the tub too fast for the overflow drain to handle it. When you do that, water floods the bathroom and if you don't catch it, the house floods.

It's plain that we're headed toward a flooded house.

New Jersey pollutes New York and, when the wind veers, New York pollutes New Jersey. U.S. smelters kill farm crops in Canada. Polluted air from San Francisco has been found at the farthest reaches of the Bay Area Air Pollution Control District.

Horrified Ojai Valley residents watch Los Angeles pollution spill through the mountain passes and fill up their entire valley. Livermore, with probably the worst smog problem in the Bay Area, suffers because it's "downstream" from the region's major pollution sources.

Farmers east of Los Angeles are moving to sue L.A. for pollution damage to crops. San Francisco, Oakland, Richmond and San Jose could face such action by Livermore.

There are alternatives.

What would you do, for example, if a barrier dropped in front of you some morning as you headed up the Bayshore Freeway or over the Golden Gate or Bay Bridge? The barrier sign would read something like this:

SMOG DANGER! NO AUTO TRAFFIC BEYOND THIS POINT UNTIL FURTHER NOTICE!

This solution already is being tried in Germany's Ruhr Valley. It's being considered in the British Midlands and has been talked of as a possible necessity on our own East Coast. Los Angeles could come to it and so could we.

In the face of all the evidence, do you think it incredible

that our "solutions" continue to limp along while officials try not to "alarm" the public? Do human societies ever remain indifferent to a real menace?

Silly questions.

You didn't keel over after taking a deep breath of polluted air, so what harm can it do to you?

Make no mistake, there's powerful opposition to pollution control, and it doesn't come from industry. We'll explore this presently, but first, a look at organized opposition.

Publicity releases and executive statements from the auto industry, from electric companies, the National Coal Association, the National Coal Policy Conference, the United Mine Workers, the American Petroleum Institute—all have announced opposition to controls on air quality. They take the general position that air pollution is such a complicated problem, almost nothing can be done about it—and there's more danger from overcontrol than from under control. Besides, we all know the problem has been with us for centuries. If Elizabethan England couldn't clean up its air, how can we be expected to do it?

The issue as many auto manufacturers see it is that any change in power plant—to external combustion steam engine, to turbine or electric with battery or fuel cells or any combination of these—must match the sophistication of present internal combustion engines.

Not so.

The issue is air which won't cripple or kill us. It's not whether our horseless carriage is a regression to, say, the level of 1956 in its power and sophistication.

Despite the opposition, some highly placed experts believe we must phase out the internal combustion engine between now and 1980, replacing it with any one or all of the above combinations.

Here's Health Education and Welfare Secretary John Gardner: "We need to look into the electric car, the turbine car and any other means of propulsion that's pollution free. Perhaps we need also to find other ways of moving people around. The day is coming when we may have to trade the convenience of the private auto for survival."

Says Dr. John R. Goldsmith, chief of Environmental Hazards Evaluation for the California Public Health Department: "There's no reason the wife should roll out the family road locomotive for a two mile trip to the store or to pick up the children. This could be done just as well by public transportation or small, non-polluting vehicles. Inclusion of such clean transportation should be mandatory in subdivision planning."

Behind the opposition, industry's reaction varies. Auto manufacturers are spending a small amount of money to study the possibility of converting to steam cars (Ford), to electric (GM) and turbine (Chrysler). They are spending much more to develop and sell the public on control devices or control systems for internal combustion engines.

There is, however, increased activity in cleaning up fuel for industry or converting to cleaner fuels. Sulphur dioxide is being extracted (at a profit) from oils and coals. Natural gas, a much cleaner fuel, is coming into more and more use for heat.

But proposals for dramatic conversions which everyone agrees would clean up our air still face tremendous inertia from auto and petroleum industries and from all their supporting arms. They form a common front demanding: "How can you link us with these deaths?" They point to our Pollution Control Establishment and say: "These people, your own experts, say we're moving toward an orderly solution."

The case is made that we're not moving toward an orderly solution. We've moving toward more confusion, disorder and increased poisons in our air.

But it's a human trait to defer to the cult of science. Authorities and Experts *must* know more than we do. It's their job.

It's also their job to stay in the office and maintain their own image of themselves. This image is hard to see through because it's most often sincere, based on a belief that "we're doing the only practical thing we can do." The men and women holding this belief while they gamble with our lives and with the lives of future generations are, for the most part,

honest. They also work daily with a number of truly dedicated people who are constantly frustrated and crying out:
"Nobody will listen!" This makes it extremely easy for the
"job holder" to rationalize delay tactics and to defend actions
in the name of "practical politics" and/or good business which
he knows to be dangerous to our survival.

The extent of the cynicism and frustration in the Pollution Control Establishment cannot be overestimated. Here
are people who truly know the danger and urgency; they are
told to solve it, and they are not given the power to solve it.

Dr. Goldsmith believes California has neither the laws
nor the agencies to cope with the mounting problem.

"There's a dangerous lack of central planning combined
with a lack of central control," he says. "We need a perspec-
tive on air pollution which is based more on the next breath
you inhale than on abstract, esoteric discussions."

Someone once said air pollution begins and ends with
politics. Haagen-Smit puts it this way: "The presence of air
pollution is inescapable evidence of bad judgment by politicians."

The consequences of political mismanagement at this
point are obvious—more slums, more riots, chronic traffic
congestion, mounting death toll from pollution-caused diseases. But this political arena is where we're going to win
Haagen-Smit's "war for clean air" or lose it. This is a political
environment where most of the public puts far more value on
the "right" to a car which can be driven anywhere anytime
than it puts on the right to breathe.

Haagen-Smit, a motorist as well as chairman of the State
Air Resources Board, learned from personal experience how
highly charged this problem is. Although the law didn't require it (he'd bought his car new before pollution control legislation), his engineers installed a crankcase device on his
twelve-year-old Plymouth.

After the installation, his car stalled five times on freeways. That's the kind of trouble you have with an older car
when you put the crankcase device on it.

"My natural inclination was to pull the damn thing out,"

he admits. "But you can't do that. I finally adjusted the carburetor myself to where my car no longer stalled. But I learned my lesson.

"This is no simple problem. It's costly to the individual and to the industry. But the longer we delay, the more it's going to cost. And half measures may be the most costly of all. We just have to get used to the idea that there's no way out of paying the price. No way out for any of us."

It's easy to see the pressures which guided his compliance. You can't have an official of the ARB going around polluting the air. But what about someone without his moral courage and deep concern? Ask yourself how many people in your circle of acquaintances might have "pulled the damn thing out"?

In the face of such pressures, will we be able to legislate the necessary morality? The legislature, after all, represents a common denominator of morality. No need here to review the numerous examples of legislative venality and corruption. We all know the only requirement for hamstringing legislation is sufficient public resentment and/or a few corrupt men in key places.

Is it hopeless, then?

Where do we seek a solution when such people as Dr. Mario Menesini, the nationally recognized ecologist at U.C., Davis, turns away from most of the adult population and concentrates his efforts on teaching the next generation how to build a balanced environment?

"Unless you want to send your child to school in a gas mask, you must begin a love affair with our environment," Menesini pleads.

It looks bad, especially when you know that most of the knowledgeable "insiders" agree there's a point where the problem becomes economically uncontrollable. What do you do when even the cheapest solution may bankrupt half the population?

But do we really need statistics, epidemiological studies and the gobbledygook of science to solve it while we still can? It's obvious, isn't it, that a certain "statistical percentage" of our present population has been written off by the "practical" solutions now being tried? The expendable are those most susceptible to poisonous air—the very young, the very old, those with asthma, emphysema and other lung ailments, a great many smokers, people with heart ailments....

It's equally obvious that, since this is a problem created by masses of people, then masses of people must be involved in the solution. All of us must recognize the deadly nature of the trap we're in, and we must climb out of it together.

The Russians are proud of the fact that they've removed 90% of the solid particle pollution from Moscow's air. Sweden, with a crash program for pollution control, may be on the verge of going to all-electric mass transportation. The British are converting their "black area" (polluted) heating to non-polluting fuels.

These are actions ignited by an alarmed populace.

And there's your answer.

The courageous few such as Haagen-Smit, Goldsmith, Wilson and Menesini need your united support. They need you alarmed and bringing political pressure where it will be felt. They also need you individually acting to clean your own air.

The State Department of Public Health is again reviewing its data and consulting other agencies to determine what standards and what target dates will be announced next. They are doing this with the announced purpose of tightening standards, seeking stringent penalties and developing careful inspection procedures.

These actions will be no more effective than the support you give them. If public indifference and apathy continue, expect more delays. That's the pattern of the past.

Effective pollution control will remain a myth until you take your part in the war and make it clear you'll accept no more nonsense. We all have to come to full realization that there no longer is any "away" where we can throw things.

And don't let anyone tell you the issue is anything except survival. We are dealing with a basic resource, perhaps *the* most basic resource. It has fundamental limits directly involved with all life—including your own. No dollar value can be placed on such an issue. It goes far beyond considerations of comfort or individual and industry-wide interest.

If someone warns that we may stop progress by acting too fast, point out that progress is a dubious concept chiefly valuable for hiding us from the terrors of an uncertain future.

"How is the patient doing, doctor?"

"He's progressing."

The problem is every bit as bad as I've described. It grows larger every year. Soon it will encompass the entire world.

If we remain individually committed to our own personal advancement and selfish desires, if we refuse to share the common effort our survival requires, the consequences are sure to take your breath away.

Ships

Where are the iron men now that the wooden ships need them?

Rusting away . . . on the beach . . . dwindling . . .

And the tragedy is this: the lack of trained men could send several historic Bay Area ships to rotten row after about fifteen years. The same problem already is causing trouble at the world's largest marine museum, Mystic Seaport, Mystic, Connecticut.

Endangered in the Bay are the square-rigged *Balclutha* and the ships of the San Francisco Maritime State Historical Park at the foot of Hyde Street—the *C.A. Thayer*, an 1895 three-masted lumber schooner; the steam schooner *Wapama*, another veteran of lumber trade in Mendocino's dogholes; the *Eureka*, last walking-beam ferry to operate in the United States, a side-wheeler which ran from Tiburon, Sausalito, and Oakland to San Francisco for some seventy years; and the *Alma*, a scow schooner which carried hay and grain on the Bay at the turn of the century.

The looming crisis involves shipwrights trained in building and maintaining large wooden vessels. Every year, fewer such men answer the roll call.

And they're not being replaced.

According to the Shipwrights, Boatbuilders, Millmen and Loftmen Union, Local 1149, there's no apprentice program in the Bay Area training men to handle the big timbers and planks for this construction—and they know of no such program in the entire nation. Even the Navy isn't training wooden ship shipwrights—hasn't been for twenty-five years.

The last shipwright trained in wooden ships at the Bremerton Navy Yard retired six years ago.

Wooden ships weren't built to last forever. They require periodic hull maintenance to combat marine worms and plants. Each time ships of this size and vintage are dry-docked, it becomes increasingly difficult to find shipwrights for them. On this summer's overhaul of the 205-foot *Wapama*, Bethelehem Shipyards "drafted" an old timer in his seventies, taking him from a pile driver crew to help spile (scribe) sixteen bottom planks.

Mystic Seaport has the same problem, only more of it.

Mystic's director, Waldo Johnston, responsible for more than one hundred ships and boats, wants to start his own training program. He recently brought two expert ship joiners from Ireland, hoping to train them as shipwrights, and he'd like to get more men out of the Old World tradition of fine craftmanship.

Johnston combed the East Coast this year for deck caulkers—found one, just one.

There're still some wooden ship shipwrights in Nova Scotia and a few in Maine, he said, but he expects to "run out" of them in about ten years.

Bethelehem's shipwright foreman, Bill McKay, who is fifty, has three men trained in wooden ships. All are over sixty.

"It'll be a lost art in about fifteen years," McKay said. "Economically there isn't enough of this work to warrant training and keeping people on the job."

Shipwrights trained in smaller wooden vessels conceivably could be called in for the bigger jobs when needed. The differences are ones of degree, not of kind. But fewer and fewer small boats are being built of wood along the old lines. Metals, plastics and plywood are taking over. Different materials permit radical new designs. Trimarans, basically plywood and fiberglass, are coming up fast on the outside. At best, this source of trained men might provide a few years' grace period, the experts believe.

As one put it: "Some modern boat builders don't know a

keel rabbet from a bunny rabbit and couldn't care less. The materials they use don't require the old methods."

The vanishing wooden ship shipwright focuses the problem because his role is a key one. He's responsible for the lines, placement of bulkheads—for the shape of the ship. But he's just one part of a larger problem, all played on the same sour note.

Building the old wooden ships required more than shipwrights.

Jack Dickerhoff, rigging boss at the Hyde Street pier, is fifty-nine. He's an artist with cable and rope. His splices and cordage work bear that fine look of the old time craftsman. California has no replacement for him when he retires— probably at sixty-five. More than that, where do you find men who can duplicate an 1890s brass door latch and lock when it falls apart on a stateroom door?

The Hyde Park pier has stored away two dozen crook knees, ship knees cut from natural forks of trees, but has no source of supply when they're gone. Mystic Seaport, faced with a similar problem, is thinking of starting its own reforestation program for the special woods.

Finding the right wood in the right size is a critical problem. A fir plank four inches by eighteen inches by seventy feet was taken out of the *Wapama* when she was drydocked this summer. It had to be replaced with two thirty-five-footers. These had to be specially ordered from an Oregon mill months in advance. Then they were treated with creosote under pressure and aged on the park's pier. All this takes knowledge which is fading away.

"We've looked for men to take over these jobs, looked far and wide," says Jace Hesemeyer, supervisor of California's ship park. "We haven't found any and really don't have the facilities to train new people."

Hesemeyer, born in Oakland and raised on the Oakland estuary, played as a boy on ships similar to the ones he now protects. He feels a deep and personal concern about the oncoming crisis.

"What I want to see is a living museum, training its own

replacements," he said. "I'd like a historical display modeled on Mystic Seaport, but even closer to the people—engines that move, sails that lift, young people allowed to get their hands on the working gear of the old ships and feel their history. We should have bars and restaurants on the pier suited to the period we're producing, shops making artifacts of the time—blacksmiths, shipwrights, rigging loft, sail loft, all open to public view."

This, he admits, is a dream.

Of more immediate concern is the dry rot recently discovered on frames and planks around the *Thayer*'s hawse pipes. Luckily, the damage is all above the water line, but repairs will require sister framing and scarfing—and men who understand these tasks.

Harry Dring, restoration and maintenance supervisor for the park, can rely on his own know-how and a trained crew to save the *Thayer* from the dry rot threat . . . this time.

"But none of us are spring chickens," Dring said. "The point is, there's no young people coming up behind us. What the devil—I started going to sea in 1938 . . . none of us lasts forever."

The fine old ships won't last forever, either, and this has to be faced.

"Forever is one damned long time," says Mystic's Johnston. "We'd be foolish to think we can make our ships last indefinitely in water."

His solution: house them.

Johnston has seriously considered bringing these marine relics ashore onto an artificial sea of ripple glass which would be underlighted. This would permit the real boat buffs to go below and see the underwater lines. Underlighting would prevent sightseers topside from seeing through the glass at the water line.

Johnston's plan, however, raises its own problems—beyond those of cost. If you dry out one of these large wooden ships and do it incorrectly, you can warp her badly, change her lines, even destroy her.

"It'd have to be done slowly, gently and with loving preparation," he said. "But it's feasible. After all, furniture kept under conditions of controlled humidity and out of the weather lasts hundreds of years. We ought to think of these ships as the furniture of all mankind."

Whether the ships become "mankind's furniture" or expendable relics may be decided in the next few years.

Hesemeyer and his fellow park employees at the Hyde Street pier watch the tourists throng to their display and hope for something "close to forever." Some of the tourists, they note with amusement, race down the pier "to catch the *Eureka* before she steams off to Sausalito." The old ferry does, indeed, look as though it's ready to go. The people who did the restoration work which created this illusion are keeping their fingers crossed. They hope the day will never come when sightseers have to race down the pier to the *Eureka* . . . before she sinks.

Doll Factory, Gun Factory

A fable for our times (about half past tomorrow). If you believe you recognize in this fable any dolls living or dead, you could be suffering from a warped reality.

Once upon a time there was a factory operated by dolls. The factory was called *Reality* and it was built in the land of *Possible* where improbable things often occurred. The factory manufactured guns and dolls, and it supposedly operated on a self-limiting principle. When there were too many dolls, the factory turned out more guns, which were intended to reduce the doll population.

An improbable thing happened, however. At the end of each supposedly self-limiting cycle, *Possible* found itself with more dolls *and* more guns than had existed before the start of the cycle.

This unexpected relationship between dolls and guns did not make itself immediately apparent to the factory's doll managers, who were a select group within the regular output of *Reality*. Even when some dolls began to suggest such a relationship, their speculations were made the object of laughter. Everyone knew *Reality* had been designed on a self-limiting loop of the Universal Continuum and that the factory's controls had been left in the hands of the dolls by the Original Builder.

It came to pass then that the dolls of *Possible* found *Reality* straining to its limits. The cycles turned faster and faster. The entire process developed odd wobbles and eccentricities. Parts of *Reality* often were attacked and sometimes damaged. The factory's managers took to shoring up their structure which, through long addition and revision, appeared rambling and haphazard. The repairs were sometimes makeshift and improbable. Everyone from the highest managerial circles to the lowliest laboring dolls felt beleaguered, the target of threats too large to be understood.

Possible's dolls began more and more to question self-limiting as a principle. Some sneered at doll control. Great blocs of dolls even openly denied that there had been an Original Builder. They substituted the Theory of the Grand Accident, sometimes called The Enormous Dichotomy.

All of this time, *Reality* seethed with questions about how to produce more guns and/or more dolls, or better dolls or better guns. Many splinter groups formed. Some argued for limiting guns, others for limiting dolls. An organizational schism developed within the factory. A large body of dolls revised an ancient concept called Deterrent Defense and named it now Sacred Security. Each splinter group developed its own factions. Many argued for such programs as speeding up the cycles or aiming for improbable goals of doll efficiency and gun efficiency. Gun to doll and doll to gun ratios were examined with fine attention to detail. Doll support and gun support became issues of the moment while the effects of such eccentric alternation reverberated throughout *Possible*.

A curious transformation began to occur in the dolls flowing from the factory. Some of the managers called it a manufacturing flaw and argued for new and better controls on doll production. Discontinuance of entire lines of dolls was proposed and some tried to carry out such programs, but the curious transformation continued. It assumed a major form called *Variants*. They were divided primarily into two categories: dolls intended for functions concerned mainly with doll quality and welfare began doing things which increased the production of guns; gun-oriented dolls began to deny the principles beneath their function. It frequently was difficult to tell a doll-doll from a gun-doll.

In all of *Possible* there now remained only a few small doll voices saying: "Let us re-examine the whole function of *Reality*. Perhaps we have been blinded to important parts of the system by our belief in improbable principles."

So few dolls paid attention to these warnings, however, that the mad cycles continued unabated—faster and faster, more and more eccentric. Finally, the whole system came crashing down in one last paroxysm of dolls and guns. *Reality* was left in ruins and *Possible*, stripped of all its dolls, reverted to a barren wilderness where chaotic improbabilities reigned supreme.

Moral: If you were built to prefer either dolls or guns, perhaps you were intended only for a limited function.

THE FUTURE THAT ISN'T

When I was quite young, long before I became perfect (a perfected thing), I began to suspect there must be flaws in my sense of reality. It seemed to my dim sense of confusion that *things* often blended, one into another, and the Law of the Excluded Middle merely opened up a void wherein anything was possible. But I had been produced to focus on objects (things) and not on systems (processes). This left so much unexplained that no thing behaved invariably as intended, provided that such a concept as *intention* could be entertained even for an instant.

What was even more important, I had somehow acquired an obvious predilection for excluding myself from all considerations about the world around me. A *thing?* Me? How awful!

This led naturally to a belief that I could be the sole exception to any rule which I detected. Rules were made for things, not for me, possessor of absolute free will.

In some odd fashion, all of the fellow humans I encountered appeared to have this same belief. Not a one of them seemed to suspect that our universe might be larger, more complex and subtle than our presumptive little *Laws* assumed. I reasoned that an unspoken (or unrecognized) assumption might be a signpost at the outer limits of where we humans ventured, but this *personal exclusion principle* confused me. It made it difficult to question the authenticity of any *Law* because the arguments kept returning to things which needed "no further explanation" and which "everybody" knew.

Except me—I didn't know.

This did litle more than make me feel stupid and force me into actions which were asinine, to say the least: either I agreed hypocritically that "sure, everybody knows that" or I just joined all the rest of my kind in refusing to examine such disturbing areas. After all, what were the assumption sign-posts set up for?

Thus, I was taught to believe utterly and unquestioningly in principles and even more so in First Principles, the ones from which there could be no exclusions (except me). It was a universe of absolutes which provided me with an infinite source of comforting reassurances. It said:

"All questions have answers."

However, with my core of confusion—an unprincipled attitude—I suspected a flaw in the fabric of the universe: a question, one at the very least, without any answer whatsoever.

Despite what my fellow humans, western variety, employed as consensus reality, my own set of local beliefs came to contain more and more naked kings. This was a series of very traumatic experiences.

The frustrations of these early traumas led me to formulate five assumptions for my own study of reality. Because I want many of the words which follow to be a shared exploration of possible futures (alternate realities) with emphasis on mankind's Utopian dreams, it seems only fair to begin the sharing with a brief statement of these assumptions.

Assumption I: There exists a kind of self-reflexive laugh reaction in humankind which often releases tensions and links us to that balance which we call sanity. (If I cannot laugh at myself, I risk turning the whole future and sanity business over to non-laughers.)

Assumption II: Many Academic/Scientific Futurists who supposedly are guiding our philosophic and technologic trip through Time have a monkey on their backs, a burden of memories and concepts which contain alternate, often mutually exclusive versions of reality. (A monkey on the back sometimes can be detected by its characteristic chattering.)

Assumption III: If we define Futurism as an exploration

beyond accepted limits, then the nature of limiting systems becomes the first object of exploration. (Some people who say they are talking about a future are only talking about their own self-imposed limits.)

Assumption IV: A prominent and commonly accepted reality matrix by which Futurism and Reality are interpreted suffers from false assumptions about control. The false assumptions can be described thusly: that manipulation can be absolute, and that power is not subject to relativistic influences.

Assumption V: Implications of Relativity Theory have not been applied to the ways humans relate to each other or to the ways humans relate to the universe. (We tend to project the future onto a screen whose subtitle says: "It's better to live in a box than to face up to infinity.")

Five assumptions represent a weak arsenal with which to go up against thousands of years of reality production. It's one thing to recognize that consensus reality (our ideas about common belief) includes errors. It's quite another thing to put on Don Quixote's armor, take up the Lance of the Five Assumptions, and charge forth to do battle with a dystopic universe. Rebellion can make you just as drunk as pot or alcohol, and there's no guarantee that recognition of error will direct you to a proper correction of that error.

A city planner once told me his job was to seek "a compromise between the impossible and the improbable."

This aphorism tied off a long harangue in which he had detailed his frustrations over trying to prevent a housing development on a flood plain which had been taken over by real estate speculators.

I asked him if he had even once looked at the problem from the point of view of the speculators, whose assumptions and the context defined by those assumptions had led them into this "anti-social" behavior. He dismissed my question as "politically naive."

Our *scientific* culture, like the Victorian-industrial culture before it, sets sharp limits on what it will accept as a reality experience. Step outside those limits and the influence they have on the kinds of futures the society says it will permit, and you get cut off.

There's obvious fallacy in the concept that you can deal with any problem as an isolated bit all of whose consequences can be anticipated and "controlled." But consensus reality, reinforced by conformity, language and conditioning, continually traps us into positions where we deny that awareness by our actions.

My five assumptions tell me there are no facts, only observational postulates in an endlessly regenerative mish-mash of predictions—some faulty, some accurate . . . for the time being. To *plan for the future*, to attempt guiding humankind into "the better life" which our Utopian dreams define, we are involving ourselves with the monitoring and manipulation of *change*. This means inevitably that we change our frame of reference, our consensus reality.

But all around us exist societies demanding fixed frames of reference. In a multi-level universe, there can be no absolute fixed frames of reference and thus no absolute consensus reality. A relativistic universe makes it impossible to test the reliability of any expert by requiring him to agree with another expert. Both can be correct—within their individual frames of reference.

The city planner and the real estate speculator are both correct. Richard Nixon and the Students for a Democratic Society are correct—each in his own context. Mao and Nixon are both right.

Comes now the *Futurist* and the *Ecologist*, each with his bag of expertise, each making new demands and asking new questions. Comes now the SDS (and other "radicals") accusing: "You won't give us a better world because you're bad."

Each is *right* and each is *wrong*.

The five assumptions suggest to me that we are making many pointless demands and are asking many meaningless questions. We often do this after developing an "expertise" within a frame of reference which has little or no relationship to the frame of reference within which the questions are asked or the demands are made.

It is as pointless for the SDS to ask Nixon "Why are you so bad?" as it is for Nixon to demand of the SDS "Why are you so crazy?" Each bedazzled by his own *rightness* and the other's *wrongness* fails to see a larger system whose dynamics have us all resonating.

The dolls are jumping. They are performing in response to a multitude of system-influences, most of which are only dimly understood by the performers. Advice comes from all sides, each bundle of pronouncements translated from a specialized expertise (local reality) which sets the whole system bouncing, often in unexpected ways. The leaders of each frame of reference guide that framework as though it were the only exception to all of the rules they have discovered. It appears to be an odd amplification of the *personal exclusion principle*.

It would seem that a Futurist concerned with our Utopian dreams needs to listen, to observe and to develop expertise to fit the problems, not the other way around. But that is not our dominant approach.

Let us pause a moment and advance a tentative postulate based on my Assumption V (and the Special Theory of Relativity).

Postulate I: When taken out of a larger system of dynamic relationships, all inertial frames of reference are equivalent.

According to this postulate, both Pakistan and India are equally right, and equally wrong. The same applies to Democrats and Republicans, to Left and Right, to Israel and the Arab states, to Irish Protestants and Irish Catholics. The latter would appear in this view still to be resonating to the Battle of the Boyne with consequences no less bloody than those of the original.

This postulate says any group seeking to defend its own reality (frame of reference) at the expense of another group's reality will be led into a circular argument and inevitably will try to prove its own *rightness* in terms of faith expressed as propositions whose most basic assumption can be translated this way:

"I believe this because I want to believe it (or because it is so beautiful, or so simple, or so obvious, etc.)."

In this light, the advocacy principle behind western law/ jurisprudence, insofar as it ignores the wild vibrations it may set up in larger systems, appears to suffer from a basic flaw.

From within the boundaries of any specialized viewpoint, these are outrageous statements. I can say to you they are based in part on mathematics *(we inevitably are led to prove any proposition in terms of unproven propositions)* or upon physics *(no absolute frame of reference can be demonstrated)*. Neither statement subtracts from that first flush of outrage. Indeed, *Postulate I* leads inexorably to an ever more outrageous postulate.

Postulate II: Logic that is sound for a finite system is not necessarily sound for an infinite system.

This asserts that no matter how tightly you construct a system of arguments and close up all of the holes in your globe of reality, an infinite universe predicts a larger system outside of yours which can negate everything you say.

There are no impenetrable boxes in an infinite universe.

I am saying to you that a Futurist, as the role is presently recognized, who functions on this planet in this universe, must act within the rigors of these postulates unless he can produce another frame of reference which demonstrates greater operational reliability.

At this point, I can involve myself blindly in the circular definition game. I can assemble arguments from philosophy (no man is an island), from psychology (all organisms are primarily motivated to control and modify their environment), from physics and mathematics (see above), etc. to defend my assumed wide-angle assault on accepted limiting frameworks. It should be obvious, however, that my assumptions and postulates already possess circular characteristics, are based on existing systems, and eventually go back to an unproven proposition which says:

"I believe this because I want to believe it."

What is it I believe?

I believe we are well into a period when technological developments exert greater and greater influence on the indi-

vidual human life, often with shockingly destructive consequences.

I believe we are engaged in a crisis of the human species
which is shared by all and that it is pointless to discuss Futurism or Utopian dreams without recognizing the nature of
this crisis.

I believe the explosive core of this crisis involves an en-
ergy-release cycle which is running wild. I see the fate of the
species inextricably tangled with the fate of the individual, if
for no other reason than that the individual is becoming a
releaser of greater and greater energy bundles.

Any number of my fellow humans have pointed to this
energy focus—the amount of energy one individual can re-
lease—and how this is increasing on an exponential curve
which is climbing at a wild-growth rate.

When you consider the destructive energy represented
in this curve, it gives you such comparisons as this: The murderers of Mary Stuart's husband, Darnley, had to fill a basement with explosives to assassinate the royal consort. Today,
they could carry the equivalent energy in a rather small
satchel. Furthermore, explosive materials are more readily
available in our age. If I were insane enough to wish to destroy a building, murdering a head of state, I could do it with
a device incorporating materials purchased from a corner
drugstore.

The amount of energy available for misuse is increasing
beyond the point where one person is able to wreck the
planet we all share. We have no guarantees that such energy
will remain in the hands of individuals who will not do this.

With human defined as "like me," I believe we suffer
from a world sickness whose most destructive symptom is a
denial of that likeness. This is an absurd sickness. It represents taking up arms against yourself in the name of taking up
arms against others.

In the face of all this, I believe that humankind need not
come to a cataclysmic end, that we can engage ourselves, as
a species, with infinity. I am aware of the growth-cycle arguments against this viewpoint. ("All organisms, including
societies and civilizations, go through a process of birth,

maturation and death.") I hear the chorus of cynical "cannots." I am also aware that the statement "I cannot" often is an unconscious substitute for "I will not." I am saying to all such doomscriers: The man who turns against himself or against his fellowman—either singly or as part of a massive effort—is running away from life, is admitting a defeat which his own actions help create.

A kind of moral cowardice can be sensed in wanting to believe only what comforts us. Thus, I give you no absolute assurances behind any of these beliefs. Indeed, in the universe I am describing, we are destined forever to find ourselves shocked to wakefulness on paths we do not recognize, in places where we do not want to be, in a universe which does not care about our distress, which has no anthropomorphic center from which even to notice us.

A basic distress shared by all of humankind and against which we have raised so many fragile defenses—that death may cancel us out—comes with the original package and remains with it. Despite all of our efforts to project anthropomorphic images onto this universe, it continually presents us with a view of chaos. In this view, we breast a gray void which conceals our uncertain future, uncertain except for one thing: that which we perceive here disappears into the void, and we interpret that disappearance as an ending.

To much of humankind, this represents a vision of ultimate despair. In this desperate moment of our species, with extinction real and imminent, there grows a suspicion that we may occupy the only island of life which has ever occurred. Indeed, the statistical arguments for extraterrestrial life remain unproven and smell of ad hoc constructions, a kind of collective whistling past the cemetery. We want to believe these arguments because they comfort us in our moment of despair. (In this light, science fiction appears more akin to religion than to escapist entertainment.)

In the typical dichotomous trap, we are offered the alternatives of belief (one of the old "tried and true" beliefs or any of the new ones which proliferate around us) or participation in profound despair.

But why should any human (any *life*) remain confined in

the arena of "either/or" when an infinite universe offers us its boundless playground? Who says we have only two choices? Another perception of *Infinity* says: "No cages or boxes— ever." What a joyful vision unfolds in this perception. Here appears a concept of *freedom* beyond any other dream.

How do we sensitize ourselves to such a *free* universe? How do you examine a system of which you are a part? What unconscious blinders narrow the vision of our questions?

Try these for a multi-dimensional leverage:

Postulate III: Any dichotomy confronts us ultimately with contradictions. (Unless we are prepared to be taught by and then abandon contradictions, the "yes-or-no" arena represents a trap.)

Postulate IV: All answers represent mirror images of the questions which produced them. (If we ask a question from a "go/no-go" assumption, we get both "go" *and* "no-go" answers. Both are inherent in the question and thus are inherent in the answers.)

Our questions tend to ignite awareness and to limit the kinds of answers we get. The *mirror* reflects a state of consciousness as well as the direction in which our attention is aimed.

These postulates indicate that a small bite may best be savored in terms of a whole meal. If I say to you that I am a transient visitor at an endless banquet, this can mean that I have heard an invitation and have accepted it. (The suggestions that more and more of humankind is hearing the invitation, but is unable to respond, has been advanced several times as a major element of the crisis in which the species finds itself.)

If we must be prepared to abandon answers to any question how do we rebuild our *Reality* factory and set it to producing operational frames of reference? Our aim could be defined this way: to develop ways of dealing with an infinite universe, ways which allow for nonlethal emergency changes of direction. The framework we're dealing with is the one upon which we hang our sense of reality. Remember that one of our preliminary requirements is that we not become explosively disoriented.

Here are a few questions just to begin our exercise in a multi-dimensional infinite universe. Try your own answers, being prepared to abandon any assumption (all answers provisional), noting limits and aims of any new questions which may be ignited in you by my questions and suggestions.

1. When frames of reference come into conflict, how do we compare and relate them while keeping survival avenues open for our species? (If we are mediating with methods which have always led to disasters in the past, why do we continue employing such methods?)

2. How do we distinguish between our technology, the world which influences it (and is influenced by it) and the universe outside this framework?

3. Do determinist concepts such as "progress" hide us from the terrors of an uncertain future while beguiling us with sugarplum visions which can visit us with bloody disasters?

4. How can we deal with lag times for out-of-date information, especially when such information represents power and identity to entrenched blocs of our fellow humans?

5. Does identifying a larger spectrum of influences upon myself and my fellows necessarily lead to a dampening of deadly resonances in our mutual system?

6. Isn't it odd that we've never mounted a full-scale investigation into whether pheromones (external hormones) interact between members of our species the way they interact within other animal species? (That $52 million spent last year in the United States for the purchase of vaginal deodorants does more than disturb my sense of reality.)

7. Is it enough to say "I am human and you are human," or is it closer to the mark to say "I am

animal and you are animal"? (How about "I am alive and you are alive"?)

8. Is it possible to demand absolute answers from an infinite universe?

9. If we are to be suspicious of even the *processes* by which we create our images of reality, where do we look for a stable horizon by which to keep our balance?

10. Is it sufficient to have each other, to be a world-band of humans in motion through a moving universe?

Enough of this question game.

The surfer, the swimmer and the skier should have a body-sense of what I am suggesting we require as a species-sense. Oddly enough, it also may help if you recall the last time you sat in a movie theater with your attention focused on the screen and its attendant sounds.

Jean Piaget, the famed co-director of the Institute of Educational Science in Geneva, Switzerland, sets the stage. Piaget, in *The Construction of Reality in the Child*, begins his discourse by stating flatly that "the budding intelligence constructs the external world." He says we not only furnish this composition with permanent objects in a spatial universe, but also construct "a world obeying the principle of causality," and that this stable external universe remains "distinct from the internal world."

He notes from his long observation and experimentation that the human develops an "object concept" which, "far from being innate or given ready-made in experience, is constructed little by little." Further, he observes that recognition of objects is "extended into belief in the permanence of the object itself."

Thank you, doctor. But out of what does the budding intelligence construct its external world of causal relationships and permanent objects?

Somewhere between my twentieth and thirtieth years, I

began to suspect I was on a railway trip, and instead of a conductor and engineer, my journey was under the direction of a movie projectionist. This projectionist with his little machine situated somewhere in my consciousness carried major influence over what I perceived as reality. If something disagreed with *projection-reality*, a filter dropped into place and I did not sense that disagreement. Nothing came through. But if something agreed with *projection-reality*, the spotlights came on, the music, the drama, the amplifiers. I became engrossed and all too willing to suspend my critical sense of disbelief.

Motion and illusion, that's all it was.

With this thought came a gigantic suspicion: perhaps even the motion was unreal. Who needs motion when he has a projectionist as talented as this? There was no trip at all, no waystops, no terminals—just that projectionist throwing his illusions upon the colossal screen which was my sense of reality.

"We are such stuff as dreams are made on. . . ."

There can be only a jury-rigged ad hoc response to this solipsist giggling in all philosophers' nightmares. Instead of throwing up our hands in rage and fear, however, let us ask what this bit of solipsism tells us. What can we learn from the inevitable store of illusion always beyond our transient reality?

Postulate V: There are questions which can never be answered. (The mathematician demonstrates that there are problems which can never be solved.)

Watch out for the play of the verb *to be* in my words, in the work of mathematicians, of physicists and other scientists. Every now and then, a bit of something extraordinary shows through the illusory screen. The causal absolutes don't quite filter out everything which might disturb our fixed sense of reality. There are shadows, *ombres chinoises*, figures out of context. It's like an audience arriving late for the show, stepping on our toes and casting their shadows on our screen in spite of the busy projectionist.

When I said *nothing* came through the filtering system, I should have added *most of the time*.

To be carries a heavy load of Piaget's objective, fixed,

causal absolutism into the "budding intelligence." That little indefinite article, *the*, aids mightily in this reality-building.

"*The* answer *is* . . ." (Supply your own ending.)

I am not suggesting you immediately discard all forms of *to be* and that you substitute *a* for *the* from this point onward. Filters can be useful when you understand how they operate. No movie cameraman has to wait for moonlight to produce a moonlight effect. He can use a blue filter. Most audiences understand this. It's one of the conventions we accept in this art form.

You ask yourself now: is he suggesting that the building of our consensus reality may be an *art form?* If so, what have we been experiencing, a theater of the macabre?

A look at the scenario for 1971 suggests something even worse than the macabre.

Ten Million Refugees Flee Pakistan

U.S. Escalates Air War in Southeast Asia

New Bomb Kills Every Living Thing Within 3,000 Feet

Belfast Bomb Kills Child

Napalm Survivors: A Legacy of the Maimed

Three Policemen Murdered

Palestinian Guerrillas Raid Village—10 Dead

Bangladesh Death Toll May Top Million

Israelis Level Arab Village

Prisoners Tortured to Death in Dacca

Starvation: Way of Life on American Indian Reservation

Who wrote this scenario?

You did. I did. Others among the 3.5 billion of our fellow humans on this ball of dirt did. Our ancestors contributed many of the lines. Some of the bits came from chaotic influences. Many oscillations can be identified as resonating through our species. We have influenced and been influenced. We have acted and been acted upon.

A physicist sees our universe as quantum-mechanical with energy locked in various frequency phenomena (and with energy available through manipulation of such phenomena). Human relationships can be seen as frequency phenomena. We have a wave nature.

There *is* a tide in the affairs of men.

We respond to wave-form influences; we perform strange dances to strange music. We occupy (and are occupied by) a multi-wave, multi-level system whose dynamics we do not understand. We interrelate with our system in transient ways, and the interlocked weight of transient influences can be variable.

Recognition of wave-type influences upon us, of the element of art form available to our reality, of the limiting impositions within language-genetic accident-social environment—this recognition brings with it a new freedom and independence.

Once I have recognized bad drama, lethal interrelationships, lines that don't play—once I am aware of these things as specific influences—I no longer am responsible for *any* of the scenarios produced by my ancestors or even for the scenarios I wrote yesterday. However, I remain responsible for putting new scenarios on the boards *which don't repeat old mistakes*.

The objective description of our universe rooted in the dogma of classic religions and political theories has broken down. We have been misled by stellar performances from fellow humans—from Solomon to Machiavelli to Nixon, from Hammurabi to St. Paul to Martin Luther to Paul VI, from Confucius to Aristotle to Descartes to Hegel to Freud to Skinner—by stellar performers remembered and unremembered and by a host of satellite performers within their influence.

We have been misled, with accent on *led*.

Leaders require followers, teachers require students,

knowers require the ignorant and vice versa ad infinitum. Every dichotomy needs actors (dolls?) who play their parts without question.

We play out the dichotomies to their inevitable contradictions, having chosen and accepted our parts, and when the condition of *conjugate variables* becomes inescapable, when the paired things interfere with each other, we scream "paradox" or give up to despair.

Like the good dolls of *Probable*, we play our parts just as we were designed to do within the orderly confines of *Reality*.

But those fleeing *refugees* and the *forces* from which they fled, the *pilots* and the *targets* in the air war, the maimed *survivors* of napalm and the *makers* of the napalm, the *bombardiers* and the *living things* killed by the new concussion bomb, the Belfast *bombers* and the dead *child*, the murdered *policemen* and the *murderers*, the *guerrillas* and the *10 dead* in the village, the tortured *prisoners* and the *torturers*, the starving American *Indians* and the *officials* of the Bureau of Indian Affairs—all are humans, not dolls. They are a form of animal life indigenous to this planet, to the best of our knowledge. They are highly susceptible to geocentric influences, profoundly dichotomized and polarized.

We possess an unlimited fund of euphemisms with which to filter out the observation that it is fellow humans upon whom we perform our resonating atrocities.

Many clues to the filter systems provided us by *Reality* remain in our symbols—in euphemisms, in verb constructions, in gestures and other actions, in unexamined assumptions behind some of our more commonly accepted terms.

Take the word *knowing* for example. Here's a remarkable filter. When I *know* a thing, I am efficiently insulated from any disturbing questions which might throw doubt upon my *position. Knowing* creates a "bound state" like a satellite tied to its parent body by mechanical forces. The operation of *knowing* can be seen in the ways we create specializations and other compartmentalizing techniques (such as education confined to pre-selected categories) which turn more and more of our destiny over to fewer and fewer experts.

Take the concept of *guilt*.

One of my black brothers recently accused me of oppressing him "for more than four hundred years." The accusation was based on the observable fact that my skin is white.

Now, I haven't been around for four hundred years, worse luck, but I have been around long enough to research this question farther back than four hundred years. I have news for my black brother. Whites have been oppressing blacks and blacks oppressing whites for a helluva lot longer than four hundred years.

And do my researches turn up a load of guilt for him!

The elite black troops brought into Spain by the Moors used to ride into a Spanish village, tie up all of the inhabitants, slaughter the children in front of their parents, rape all of the women, then wipe out the survivors by slow torture.

The trouble with this *knowledge* applied as a guilt-weapon is that a little additional research into ancestral probabilities reveals the disturbing item that my black brother and I each had ancestors on both sides of those atrocities.

If you can trace any ancestors back to the Mediterranean littoral (placing absolute confidence in the breeding habits of your great-grandmothers *and* their progenitors), then it is a high likelihood that you have a mixture of black, white, and semitic ancestry no matter the present shape of your nose or color of your skin. While you're tracing, don't forget that the Phoenicians traded far and wide from their Mediterranean bases, that the Hanseatic merchants brought back more than merchandise, and that some survivors of the Spanish Armada lived long enough in Ireland to leave genetic tracks.

Like good dolls, we're still playing the dichotomy games, choosing sides, resonating. One of our weapons-filters is *guilt*; another is *knowing*.

What do I really know?

What are the visible consequences of past "good works"? (How *did* we come by that pejorative label: "do-gooder"? What did someone say the road to hell was paved with?)

Isn't it possible for us to laugh at ourselves even a little bit when our own best efforts go awry? Having laughed at ourselves, isn't it then possible to answer the demands for change? Haven't we learned yet that extended "stability" represents a lethal form of existence?

In a *possible* universe with multi-level systems, influences of and consequences of our actions can be deceptive, and the scientist who says the simpler of available answers always is to be preferred may be misleading himself and us. Operational evidence which is not subject to continual monitoring and projection of consequences can lead us into lethal cul-de-sacs. Trying to control the future in absolute terms "for all time" tends to make *any* future at all less and less likely for humans. Absolutist logic based on determinism fails when confronted by Infinity.

A reading of our present condition indicates that our reality factory is profoundly out of step with our universe. Perhaps the human mind isn't well adapted (or conditioned, or aimed, or channeled, etc.) to view its own involvement in the systems which influence (resonate) it—including the system represented by the language with which I articulate such ideas. Perhaps our concept of knowing, of control and power, needs to be modified by a concept of mutual influences and fluid consequences. The ancient Greeks may have been correct when they spoke of humours. They meant *wet* or *flowing* by the term. It signified movement and change.

Let's try another postulate:

Postulate VI: Simplistic, stabilized, absolute, and fixed views of reality (frames of reference) always interfere with our view of the future.

Everything we do can be traced to microscopic events. The deeper we probe into that microscopic universe, the more and more difficulty we encounter in predicting the future of isolated phenomena. One of our problems in developing an Infinity Logic is the inescapable conclusion that, in an infinite framework, *we* are microscopic events. Our problem can be stated this way:

To develop sufficiently extended mass-time-energy frameworks it is necessary that we become macroscopic and thus subject to probability patterns.

When we come in big enough packages, you can predict our behavior.

We appear to occupy a potentially definable spectrum in an infinite system where the potential and the definitions change as we expand the limits of our view.

It is only in the macroscopic world that we have found future behavior of probability systems to be determined by their past. Only when we get a big enough view of the dynamics of a system have we been able to tell how it performs.

Then how is our reality factor out of step? We have stored data for centuries. We have accumulations of observations which span thousands of years. We are making our first toddler's steps toward world government. We have large associations and corporations.

But no one is putting it all together.

The creative genesis of new and larger frames of reference has been sidetracked while we devote greater and greater energy to specializations of narrower and narrower focus. Academic research is dominated by the "bit which I can encompass in my lifetime." Research in other areas is dominated by corporate security of various denominations from Merck & Co., Inc., to the State of France. Each seeks that transient myth, *the competitive edge*. And every competitive edge (based as they are on the inevitable contradictions of dichotomy) dissolves in disaster. The stirrup escalates cavalry until it encounters a see-saw standoff against armor and castles until these dissolve before logical developments along the gunpowder line until all are crushed by the energy within the atom.

Finally, no piece of real estate can be defended with absolute security. (There never was such a defense anyway.)

We have awakened to a new age in which chemical and bacteriological warfare put mass murder into the hands of small groups operating with a few thousand dollars from basement laboratories. There exists a sufficient number of psychotic frames of reference in our world to insure that such operations already are under way. And the high probabilities in technological research promise us even greater horrors for as long as we operate from a reality which assumes the absolute reliability of narrowing dichotomies as a way of life.

It appears that any path which continues to narrow our possibilities represents a lethal trap. The model of a humankind which threads its nervous way through an infinite maze can be the dominant aspect of our universe only for creatures with noses to the ground, following a simplistic track. Physics, mathematics and philosophy over the past two decades have shot this view of an either/or universe so full of contradictions that it now presents us with the appearance of a swiss cheese. No matter how you cut it, the slices contain holes.

In such a universe, specialists continue to stake out their exclusive slices (holes and all) from which to say: "You cannot discuss my specialty unless you come up the same track I did."

Attempts to create interdisciplinary bridges between existing specialties tend to stir up specialists the way a shovel stirs up an ant hill. Of the many U.S. university attempts to set up interdisciplinary systems over the past twelve years, the only doctoral level effort to survive, that at Syracuse in Humanities, remains under continuing attack. All of the others, beset by severely limiting restrictions and constant efforts to eliminate them, have produced little impact upon academia. Renewed interdisciplinary efforts in higher education, dating back some three years and aimed at extensive reforms with greater impact, must pass through an administrative gantlet which is essentially unchanged from twelve years ago.

(While you're contemplating this state of affairs, please note the dichotomies awaiting the unwary in *inter*disciplinary and in *bridge.*)

The behavior of many specialists at interdisciplinary conferences is particularly revealing. They tend to gravitate toward their own kind. They tend to show up only for the readings of those papers which "relate to my field." They tend to behave in microscopic ways against a macroscopic background. And every one of these actions can be defended with sound logic from a consistent frame of reference.

It is this very consistency and any frame of reference (reality) which it supports that I am holding up for questioning and suspicion. It isn't so much the either/or approach which traps us as it is the way we hold on to our *discoveries*.

On a human-crowded world where our own population represents a high energy system, the life expectancy of any consistent position can be expected to grow shorter and shorter. Quantum leaps in energy predict this. Remember that it is large numbers of events which give us probable results. It is with large enough numbers that we have developed a degree of accuracy in predicting the future. We may not be dolls, but we occupy the land of *Probable*. Our insurance statisticians tell us: "I can't say whether you're going to have an accident next year, but I can predict how many people of your age and income will have accidents."

The time has come for us to suspect simplistic dichotomies to which we have clung for long periods. (Crime prevention *has* created increases in crime; medicine *has* increased sickness, and religions of peace *have* fostered violence.) This is a time for courageous movement and a profound change in our attitude toward the *overview*, that it too represents process and movement.

We have more than enough data to describe existing conditions. We understand our problems all too well. It is time now to recognize that a full description of all those disconnected, short-term responses we are making to our problems is also a description of how we maintain our problems. Indeed, to make our problems worse, we need only continue present response patterns.

Our consensus reality is demonstrably unreal; it isn't working. We have not developed an operationally reliable logic for Infinity. We are afraid of Infinity in its rawest form because even to think about it takes us through a period when each of us is no longer here. In a sense, most humans peer outward through the overwhelming dichotomy of their own mortal existence and scream:

"If I have to go, I don't care who I take with me!"

A "budding intelligence" (after Piaget) constructs its external world of causal relationships and permanent objects through such a filtering system and out of a demand for the comforting reassurance that "I can stave off disaster."

Out of this narrowing view, I believe we have developed a world society which fulfills the essential requirements for a psychotic organism, including transference relationships (unconscious mutual support of destructive behavior) with those who say they are solving our problems.

Explosive disorientation describes a dominant condition already at work in our world, not from the actions of "guilty people," but from systems which we accept as our limits. We stumble from psychotic break to psychotic break within these unworkable systems, and each break is larger, more violent and more degrading than the one before it.

Thomas More, who put the word *Utopia* into our language by attaching that label to his literary *perfect island*, died of a disease called *man*. (He refused to agree with a psychotic tyrant and was executed.) We still are trying to play More's game by his rules and under conditions where the disease which killed him is even more virulent.

If I am to talk about *utopian futurism* (my avowed purpose here) then I must begin by explaining why I believe we have set up lethal systems of resonance which, if they continue undamped, make it highly probable that we soon will destroy this planet and every living thing on it. In the land of *Probable*, the resolution of this dichotomy is our primary problem because a failure to solve for extinction negates all other problems. Given the survival of our species as the issue at stake, if we then play idle word games around improbable consequences which ignore this stake, that clearly describes a symptom of the insane fragmentation which we have identified as schizophrenia.

My first requirement for a sane futurism begins with the simple statement: *I am not here to participate in the destruction of a world where I have (or hope to have) descendants*. When I raise my gaze to Infinity, I see that a species which incorporates consciousness need not be mortal, need not die.

From this beginning, simplicity evaporates. All of us may not be fertile, but *descendant* already has broad meaning and infinite implications.

If we are surfboard riders on an infinite sea, then when the waves change we adjust our balance. The most dangerous condition is that of imbalance. In the midst of infinite waves, we must gauge as many of them as we can detect and influence them for species survival wherever we can. For a species balancing in such a universe, unanswerable questions which perpetuate self-limiting systems represent lethal danger. We know how we blind ourselves—by fixed roles, by dropping filters over our senses and forgetting them, by locking ourselves into tighter and tighter orbits, by turning our gaze away from creative interaction with an infinite playground which offers itself for our most artistic expressions. The demand of this dichotomy is loud and clear. That human Phoenix Ezra Pound said it: "Make it new."

Do Not
Fold, Spindle,
or Mutilate

One of the things that gives Frank Herbert's work its greatest power is the honest caring for people that shines through. Though he may have written about strange places and stranger people, they are people still. And more than anything else, his work is about what it will take for people to make it over the long term.

The pieces contained in this section may seem at first to be an odd lot. But they have one thing in common: they are fundamentally about what it means to be human, to have hopes and fears, to care what happens to the rest of those we share this planet with.

The first piece, "The Tillers," is adapted from the script Frank wrote for a documentary film about the work of Roy Prosterman, a University of Washington professor working on land reform in Third World countries. Frank had participated with Roy Prosterman in a study of land reform in South Vietnam shortly before the end of the Vietnam War. A series of articles he wrote for the Seattle Post-Intelligencer on his return from Vietnam analyzed the details of Prosterman's proposals. This film attempted to capture the spirit.

I find the second piece, "Flying Saucers—Facts or Farce?" especially touching. This article was written for the San Francisco Examiner in 1963, not long after Frank had finished Dune. Here you see the other side of the man who railed against the danger of superheroes and messiahs—the man who could say that the belief that "men from outer space will step in on Earth 'before it's too late' ... partakes of the old messianic dream.... The dream may be out of touch with history, but it's a good dream.... Look beyond the wacky arguments to the motivation—that sense of brotherhood which is all that has ever saved humankind from going over the brink."

The third piece is woven from two solid days of conversation that Frank and I had in his home in Port Townsend in the spring of 1983. Our conversation ranged from education to government to religion, but ultimately, what we talked of is man's desire to perfect himself, what baggage holds him back, and what hope there is for that desire to be realized.

The section, and this book, closes with a series of prefatory notes that Frank wrote for an anthology to accompany a Today Show *special on Earth Week, 1970. While the contents of that anthology (New World or No World) have become dated—the posturings of politicians and academics riding a bandwagon—Frank's introductory remarks to the various segments of the show remain potent.*

The concern for ecology, and the role each of us has in saving or damning the world, that he expresses in these notes is ultimately the same concern for people that runs through all of his work.

Whether the subject is ecology, evolutionary psychology, or the excesses of messianic religion, this is one of Frank's basic messages: We as individuals must take action to create the future we would like to enjoy. And we must shape our institutions so that they do not take away our freedom to do so.

He expressed this feeling in a story that he wrote for the Seattle Post-Intelligencer *at about the same time as the notes for* New World or No World. *The story found the University of Washington guilty of being an educational factory, and summed up the reasons for student unrest with the line:*

I am an individual. Do not fold, spindle, or mutilate.

The Tillers
Political Dynamite

They are the tillers of the soil. They are four-fifths of the world's most oppressed people. They hold the key to any future mankind may have. In a very real way, they are the clients of Roy Prosterman, who teaches law at the University of Washington.

Prosterman says: "Man began his long journey to civilization on land much like theirs. Without the plowman to feed our leisure, there would be no civilization. But these tillers have been the first to suffer and the last to benefit from the civilization they support. Wars grind them into their own soil. Arrogant governments tax them into starvation. They die at the whims of weather, wild animals, pestilence . . . and of absentee land owners. Because most of these tillers do not own the soil which they work."

In the service of his clients, Roy Prosterman stands on the dry Barani land of Pakistan. Here, as elsewhere, he wants the tillers to stand with dignity on their own land. He wants an end to the dirty business of tenant farming, because he knows that landless peasants have formed the nucleus of every bloody revolution in this century.

While this continues, no man can sleep safely in his own home.

To learn about the landless peasants, you must go to where they toil. Prosterman is one of the world's foremost experts on land law—but before any law there is a reason for that law and this reason is in the hearts of people.

In Pakistan, that reasoning boils down to things easily understood. It's in water still laboriously raised by hand from an old well. It's in oxcarts and camel carts. It's in goats—the goats which turned the Near East into a desert are still busy here making desert at the rate of about a million acres every ten years.

Prosterman's research party goes into the field, into the Barani—which means simply "rain-fed." But that rain is often less than three inches a year. And the heat! On this day, the outside temperature in the shade stands at 114 degrees Fahrenheit. This valley of the Soan River often appears like a Biblical landscape, almost incapable of supporting life. Here, you can sense an essential truth: That the tiller's biggest problem often may be himself—that man may be the last animal on Earth to be tamed.

Whether it comes from an ancient Persian well or a modern drilled tubewell with electric pump, water is the key to survival here. Water makes the land blossom and the people content. It's no surprise that the sound of running water is required for Moslem meditation.

Prosterman will recommend that the Pakistan government drill a national grid of tubewells and manage the irrigation water to make the dry lands prosper.

Where the water flows richly after the monsoon rains as it does in another region of Pakistan, near Lahore, the tillers plant rice—by hand with cheap labor.

Less than a day's drive away, here in the Barani, they plow dry fields and build their villages of adobe mud.

The green revolution has increased the harvest dramatically. But it chiefly benefits the landowner, who does not live here in the hot, dry Barani.

To the landless peasant, the green revolution has been a disaster. Here in Pakistan, it moved the landowners to drive the tenants from the land. More then 100,000 former tenants have been displaced. The lucky few survive as cheap farm labor. Most of the others live (if you can call it living) in near starvation in the cities.

The benefits of a green revolution and plentiful water do not mean much to such people. They are things from the West, and suspect. And perhaps with good reason.

The Tarbella Dam will be the tallest earth-fill dam in the

world when it's completed. Because it will spill clear water into the downstream part of the Indus, it will increase erosion problems there. It will rob the downstream of silt fertilizer and will make necessary the use of artificial fertilizers in gigantic quantities. The dam will silt up in about sixty years, creating about 800,000 acres of Pakistan's deepest topsoil—a gigantic beaver meadow.

Meanwhile, this impounded water creates electricity and wealth. . . . It's the same story all over this region—water, wealth, land, political power—and landless peasants who are political dynamite.

Prosterman takes his investigative team to South Vietnam—by small plane over war-scarred countryside to a small landing field deep in the Mekong Delta.

They go from the field by jeep to a nearby village which knows the nightly terror of threat from the Vietcong. But this village, its people thronging to greet the honored visitors, is considered secure. Land Reform—a system giving ownership of the land to those who farm it, a system authored by Roy Prosterman—is a reality here. No longer do the Vietcong find easy recruiting among the landless, saying: "We gave you the land; give us your sons." The South Vietnamese know that the Hanoi government gave with one hand and took with the other. The North Vietnamese slaughtered almost 100,000 peasants taking back and collectivizing the land which they control. All of Vietnam know this.

Here, in South Vietnam, these are new landowners: almost a million people in this region alone who are settled on land to which they hold title.

Prosterman, returning to assess the Land Reform program which he fathered, finds himself a much-honored guest by peasants and government officials alike.

He goes from village to village—seeing the new signs of prosperity: motorbikes, stock . . . rich rice plantings in fields which no longer grow crops to be raided by Vietcong or a greedy government. In the ordinary events of an age-old way of life you sense the new feeling of security which ownership of land gives to these people.

Water is plentiful along the Mekong.

The South Vietnamese live with the river's reassuring presence. They use it as a major transportation avenue... and... they play in it....

These are the monsoon rains—gold from the sky.

The river and its byways are filled. There are fish to be netted... people and their crops to be ferried to market.... Prosterman and his team go through the countryside, reading the signs of prosperity and of security.... There are many questions to ask, answers to assess:

> How many can now afford fertilizer?
> Are you using the new miracle rice?
> Have any of you bought a bullock?
> How many have received title to your own land?

That precious title is the icon, the beautiful symbol of the new life... a tiller's proudest possession...

... and those titles come from this office in Saigon by the most modern computer printing techniques. Titles come spewing out of the printer at thousands an hour—the best of the present age enlisted to meet an age-old human demand: to live on your own land.

With these titles goes a highly streamlined system of delivery and investigation to prevent corruption. Absentee ownership of the land is dying out. You see it dying right here. And with that passing, you see the drying up of the fertile ground upon which revolutions have flourished.

The new times bring their new problems, of course. The streets of Saigon are as congested as those of any city in the world. To travel them is to encounter as much peril as in some battle zones. The stink of carbon monoxide and unburned oils is everywhere...

... except outside the city on the precious land. If people are to survive, if man is ever to complete that long journey into civilization, the rice must be planted, the crops must be harvested.

But the land remains incredibly fertile, renewed by high water every year... and man has been on this land for thousands of years, contending with absolute monarchs and the absolute terrors of a war which most of these people never wanted.

Consider Ba Ahm Lake, built by hand almost two-thousand years ago to water an emperor's elephants . . . and now its diked sides provide some protection for farm stock. The stock is sheltered here while less than a half mile beyond the dike, the remnants of a Vietcong force hides in a mangrove swamp. The Vietcong were driven off by a home guard of regional forces, not by the South Vietnamese Army, but by armed farmers defending their own land.

It reportedly was a shock to the Vietcong which once recruited about one-thousand men a month throughout this region, most of their recruits being volunteers from the families of landless peasants. . . .

Even when the land thrives and shows no war scars, the subtle signs remain. Prosterman's team, interviewing a woman beside her rice field, found that she must do all of the work which men once did. Her husband is away in the army. It is her own land though, and she speaks easily of satisfaction about that.

She is only one of the millions who no longer want any interference in their lives—from the North Vietnamese, from the United States Military . . . or from any other foreign power. All of the ideological arguments are boiled away in the crucible of an unwanted war.

As she plows her land, her whole body speaks of the only remaining argument, the oldest one of all: leave us alone to live our lives in our own way on our own land. If you do that, we will not cause trouble for you.

This is the argument of survival which Roy Prosterman of Seattle finds over and over again as he defends his clients . . .

The Tillers.

Flying Saucers: Facts or Farce?

Certainly the most durable dinnerware on the American scene is the flying saucer. It withstands the hottest derision, the coldest denials and survives being tossed out at high altitudes even by the U.S. Air Force.

Without chipping.

The saucer (or UFO for Unidentified Flying Object) is with us today virtually unchanged from the original models —which pulsated, behaved erratically in flight and befuddled all officialdom. A recent sighting over Woodside and Los Altos was described thusly: "A half-moon–shaped, pulsating object heading southward and leaving a vapor trail."

The Federal Aviation Agency's air route traffic control center showed nice taste in maintaining this as a "classic case." They confessed complete ignorance about it.

No state in the Union, no nation on the globe has escaped the saucer's visitation.

It left "luminous trails" over Kentucky in 1947, the year people began noticing the UFO on a large scale. It sent Moscow residents to their rooftops in 1948. They stared at "a speedy object in the eastern sky." (Could it have been a U-2?) It was chased over Hokkaido, Japan, in 1953 by the USAF, and was seen by copper miners in Rhodesia the following year. It was spied over Marseilles, France, in the fall of 1957, becoming involved there with "a bulbous cloud formation of very odd shape." It has even been photographed by the United States Coast Guard (over Salem, Mass., in 1952).

Northern California (we deliberately exclude everything

south of the Tehachapis) has appeared at times to be an assembly point for saucers.

All this is quite a record for something that probably doesn't exist. The word "probably" is used here to keep us from being picketed by saucerians, as some of the believers call themselves. It would not be very scientific, either, to throw out all possibility that "something is out there."

The truth of the matter is that we just don't know.

What we do know is that some of the most remarkable "statistics" and wacky arguments are used to bolster the saucerian case. And because I write science fiction, I'm a natural target for these people. I've heard all the stories. Just like science fiction editors, saucerians know all about "willing suspension of disbelief." Unlike these editors (and most of the writers), the saucerians somehow manage to keep themselves in permanent suspension.

Saucerians have their own lingo, too. It includes one of the most delightful words ever coined—"contactee." A "contactee" is a person who claims to have made contact with people from other planets. You haven't lived until you've been cornered by a "contactee." Here are some of the things I've heard them say:

"Forty percent of the sightings are unexplained! This proves they're people from space!" (As a matter of fact, the Air Force says only two percent of the sightings are unexplained, but what's thirty-eight percent among friends?)

"They tuned in on my mind from Venus." (This was before the Mariner space probe told us a few definite facts about Venus.)

"I saw this ship—oh, it was about 250 feet in diameter —and these people came out of it. They looked just like anyone else, just like you and me. They invited me inside and took me on a trip around the moon." (It was shortly after this that I grew a beard. We have to tell the humans from the spacemen somehow.)

"You say flying saucers are impossible? Well, they said television was impossible, too."

This is only a small sampling. All kinds of people have gotten into this act. I've even seen an UFO myself. We'll discuss that in a moment. First, you should meet some members of the cast.

There's Reingold Oscar Schmidt whose flying saucer was grounded in Alameda a couple of years ago. He was convicted of cheating an Oakland widow. She gave him $5,000 to invest in an Alaska gold mine and Sierra quartz deposit which he said he "spotted from a flying saucer."

And there's always George Adamski, author, lecturer, and high priest of UFO. Adamski, you may remember, claims to have been taken for a turn around the moon in 1959 by friendly men from Saturn.

Even the Red man has had his innings. Chief Standing Horse, an Ottawan from Oklahoma, told a recent Space Craft Convention in Berkeley about his 1960 trip with men from space. They went to the planets Mars, Venus, Clarion, and Orion. (Clarion and Orion, for you newcomers, are hidden from us on the other side of the moon.)

Chief Standing Horse has not been heard from since the recent space probe finding that Venus has a surface temperature hot enough to boil lead. (Adamski, however, has also a few words to add about Venus because he, too, claims a Venus contact. According to Adamski, the space probe made a mistake. If you're a "contactee" these things are simple.)

Saucers have, on occasion, skimmed through the political arena. Gabriel Green, candidate of the Amalgamated Flying Saucer Clubs of America, ran for President in 1960 because "I was asked to do so by a spaceman from Alpha Centauri." Gabe is from Los Angeles. (Where else?) He reports straight-faced—and that's the only way to fly—that spacemen from another planet took President Eisenhower for a ride and once identified themselves to Richard Nixon . . . but not to John F. Kennedy. Well, even spacemen can make mistakes.

We musn't exclude the common citizen from this cast, either. Common citizens, that's you and me. During the silly season of 1960, CC's of Red Bluff too numerous to mention reported a mysterious "thing" like a flying football. Officials decided it was a weather balloon.

The winter of 1959–60 saw a rash of sightings in the Bay area and other northern California regions—a red flying object over the Oakland-Fremont sector ("It shot upward at a fantastic speed and exploded into a white, vaporous cloud."), an object that discharged green, red and white flames over Modesto, a "strangely luminescent" craft that hovered over the Golden Gate, and "an object with silver discs and red lights attached" seen over Martinez.

The year before that, a CC reported a "winking, pulsating flying object" made a large circle one midnight over Golden Gate park.

In 1959 the pilot and co-pilot of a Pan American airliner outbound from San Francisco to Honolulu reported being "buzzed by a gargantuan flying object" which appeared as "one intensely bright light followed by four smaller lights."

It was shortly after this that the Air Force said it hoped the "flying saucer era" was a thing of the past. "We're becoming used to space," said Lt. Col. Lawrence T. Tacker, an AF information officer. "I think this will really signify the end of the so-called saucer era." He certainly didn't know his unbreakable china, did he?

My own sighting, just to wind up this CC bit, was in 1954 in the Sonoma Valley. There were six of us on a porch on the south side of the valley. We were trying out a new pair of binoculars by looking through them at the north side of the valley. It was evening, about an hour before sunset.

A patch of the opposite hillside on Hood Mountain, perhaps five miles away, suddenly sprouted a tall, red, conical object with silver portholes. We all swore nothing had been there just seconds before. Estimating from the size of the surrounding trees, the thing was about sixty feet tall. We all looked at it through the binoculars, studying it for about half an hour. As abruptly as it had appeared, the thing shimmered and was gone. Two of my companions swore it "flew off to the northeast." On that, I can't testify. I didn't see it because I was looking at the binoculars.

The next day, I drove over and investigated the area which wasn't difficult to pinpoint because of surrounding landscape features we had all noted through the binoculars. Nothing. No road there. No mysterious holes. No mysterious burned patch on the ground. Just nothing. Period.

Officials questioned included the Forest Service, the Air Force and sheriff's office. All maintained the classic tradition. They had no explanation.

Okay. What did we see? Honestly, I don't know, but this doesn't mean I consider my experience valid evidence that the little green men have landed. Like most such experiences it's merely inconclusive.

Let's get back to the cast of characters. Among the more respected commentators in this field are retired Marine Maj. Donald E. Keyhoe, director of the National Investigations Committee on Aerial Phenomena (he means saucers), who is a believer, and Dr. Donald H. Menzel, professor of astrophysics at Harvard, who's an infidel. Keyhoe is author of "Flying Saucers—Top Secret." Doctor Menzel's most recent work of debunkery is "The World of Flying Saucers."

Keyhoe is also one of the authors of a confidential report sent to Congress giving details of "verified sightings of UFO's and documented evidence of the censorship, suppression or distortion of them by the Air Force."

You pays your money and you takes your choice. You can join the sober believers who're backed by assorted scientists and military types (including jet pilot Senator Barry Goldwater) or you can join the sober unbelievers with their own coterie of tame experts, or you can join the fringe.

Or you can join one other group which is not to be dismissed lightly and where you may find the heart of the saucer phenomenon. This group is composed of those for whom belief in saucers is tantamount to religion. They attend lectures titled: "The Earth Satellite Program and Its Relation to the Christian Church." Their meetings have a revivalist air. The sincerity of most of these people is beyond question. You hear it in the tremolo of their voices and see it in the fixity of their stares as they present their arguments.

What does this group believe?

They believe men from outer space will step in on Earth "before it's too late," put a stop to the atomic bomb threat "by their superior powers," and enforce perpetual peace "for the good of the universe."

This is unassailable idealism.

It partakes of the old messianic dream. It's rooted in the fears to which all men are heir and, thus, deserves sympathy, not censure or laughter. The dream may be out of touch with history, but it's a good dream, and it doesn't appear to have been used to bilk gullible widows out of their savings. Never mind that we have a consistent record of slaughtering our messiahs. Look beyond the wacky arguments to the motivation—that sense of brotherhood which is all that has ever saved humankind from going over the brink.

Attend one of their meetings and listen between the lines.

You may even want to collect some of their literature and read it, or contribute to their cause. Frequently, you can make your contribution by purchasing items they have for sale at the door. A common item among these is a rubber stamp which you can use to imprint a four-word slogan on all your mail. It reads:

"FLYING SAUCERS ARE FRIENDLY."

Conversations in Port Townsend

The following piece is a distillation of two days of conversations Frank and I had in his home in Port Townsend, Washington, in the summer of 1983. In the course of these conversations, we discussed education, altered states of consciousness, and the stultifying effects of bureaucracy in religion and politics. We covered a great many topics, but all revolved around the issue of the positive side of the superhero mystique in science fiction.

While I have always been convinced by Frank's arguments about the danger of superheroes, like John Campbell (and I suspect, most of Dune's readers), I have also been tremendously drawn to the insight, preternatural abilities, and high aims of his heroes.

I don't believe that even Frank could have written so convincingly of these things if he hadn't been drawn to them also. His love for the potential he saw in people, both as individuals and as a species, was the inescapable base on which he built his warnings of how that potential can go awry.

One thing I see coming down on us like gangbusters is education. It's going to be taken out of the hands of the professional educators, primarily because there is enormous profit in it. Computers are opening the way to that.

The entrenched bureaucracy is going to be reduced to a kind of circuit riding—home testing. They will knock on the door and say "It's Wednesday, I'm here to test Johnny." And then that will be phased out also.

The path is already being cut. If a parent finds out, as they are finding out that certain lines of education and certain things that are valuable to know, can be taught better and more rapidly by home study and the computer (which challenges the child and is actually programmed to stay that challenge level ahead of the particular student) there is going to be parent pressure. The only thing the school will do from then on is babysit.

Babysitting is a major function of school, but you know that if a profit is to be made in this, then an alternative to the babysitting function will be discovered by the people who want to make profit out of it.

And the entrenched bureaucracy won't be able to do a thing about it because they will not be able to keep up with the effectiveness of the new system.

I think that more and more people are setting up their own individual human potential movements. And more and more people are finding the pitfalls of collecting your own little band of followers. You've got enough followers and they're going to project on you the thing that they demand—what they want, and what you may not necessarily want, as their chosen leader. The interplay between leaders and followers is not very well understood in our society. For example, I don't think many people have focused on the way John F. Kennedy deliberately set out to create that charismatic image and surrounded himself with the knights of the round table. And then, projecting that image on society, the society then projected back the expectations of certain kinds of behavior and certain kinds of decision-making which they absolutely demanded. There was no escaping them, and they also projected modes of behavior which he had to follow at that point. I think this did as much to kill him as anything. I think our society set him up. But he didn't realize, I don't think, at any point how the force of that would be projected onto him.

In *Dune*, Paul had an education and a training program which selected him out to make him better than what he otherwise might have been. At many levels. The thing that many people don't realize is that this is generally available to them.

Most modern education tends to put blinders on students and channelize them. They can be great in whatever field they are pointed into and let go. The real flaw is that we're not taking the individual and saying: you have a hand in your own education. You probably know more about what you need than anyone else. In fact, quite the contrary, we are saying that only the trained expert can tell you what you can do best. That's a flaw.

Lots of times, a person can be a genius only in the area of persistence, patience, of honing one talent or honing a small talent into a great one. Disraeli has always fascinated me in history; I've read everything I could get my hands on. His brilliance was channeled into what we call dilettante playboy activity today. He was really a dilettante as far as his own education was concerned until Wendell Lewis bought him a seat in Parliament. (He paid the voters to vote for him.) Then, Disraeli had found his milieu, and he started honing his ability. And he honed it and he honed it.

He was a politician in the right place at the right time, and he became a superb politician eventually. There was a place in his society which he fit and where he could excel. He was lucky. Does that mean that he was the best of his contemporaries for that job? Does it mean that no one else in his society could have been put in that position and honed to a finer tune? I don't think so. I think, undoubtedly, there were people in that society who never got into politics, who never thought of it, who never had the opportunity to think of it— who would have done the job far better than he did.

And this is a flaw in the social organization. The individual in our society requires more control over where he goes. He needs more influence on his own education, a wider spectrum of opportunities, things that he can be exposed to, and say "Oh, that would be a nice thing to do."

Am I talking about utopia? Of course not. I think the society which does not open up these avenues of human potential is going to self-destruct. Because parallel to all this we've opened Pandora's box of technological toys. Some of those toys are enormously destructive and cheap to come by. We're seeing only a small element of the destructive potential of that right now in what we refer to as terrorism. Technology is both a tool for helping humans and for destroying them. This is the paradox of our times which we're compelled to face.

One danger in most educational systems today is that the student dare not show that he is better than the teacher. I've had some dealings with how we react to the gifted student in the state of Washington. I'm on the governor's blue ribbon committee for dealing with this problem. My own observation is that the best chance the gifted student has right now is to stay mostly undercover — to adopt protective coloration. Because the real problem is that most teachers, if they're not trained to it, and haven't had some exposure to their own reactions, tend to be threatened by the really gifted student and to react against the student. This is while they give lip service to something else, a too extreme subservience to IQ.

Blacks have run into this. But they aren't alone. I sat in a meeting on this blue ribbon committee where we had a man who had been at Stanford for the revision of the Stanford Binet IQ test. He spent almost two hours of that meeting explaining to us the value of using the Stanford Binet to winkle out the gifted students in the Washington educational system. There were two of us on the committee, which was composed of nine people, who saw through this immediately. We tried to direct the attention of the committee into an area where we could be extremely valuable to gifted students. Spending the money that they had available for this sort of thing, to put through a special education program for teachers that might encounter gifted students. We have to educate teachers to deal with their own reactive feelings, because often the disruptive force is built into a gifted student, because he's striking out trying to find someplace to go. In my own experience at Centrum, the approximately ten percent of students that were sent to us by the high schools from around the state as gifted students who were actually gifted, were disruptive, to the point where I had to devise a system of getting the message to them that I understood. And then things went very well.

I was teaching writing—teaching the plumbing, because you really don't teach writing. It was more the care and feeding of editors, that sort of thing. And where you can go for the best supportive backing for what you choose to do. I gave them some very pragmatic tips on it.

But my point is, that the system, not just the bureaucratic educational system, but the whole system, is such that we tend to either divert or suppress not just the gifted, but anyone who really wants to take off on a particular talent and develop it. I don't see the survival of the species anywhere in that, and that tends to be my measurement criterium.

One of the very attractive strengths of our society, which brought boat loads and plane loads of people here, was the clear view that the individual had a better opportunity here of taking his talent and running with it. The individual, not the cog and the collective. This is really why the Berlin wall is there. No matter what arguments are given to it. Wherever we have laid an imprint of what is better in this society, we are more classless than any other society. But we're losing elements of that and I don't think it's to our good.

The individual has to be catered to in any strong society even if that individual will become a major leader and displace existing leaders. Of course, I'm directing my attention to one of the major factors in the suppression training. The gifted individual is a threat somewhere along the line. Job security is always there as a demand on the people in power.

So to get back to the thrust of the question, as a teacher, you have to make your own time available to some of those (not all—you can't) who can use it. And you have to do the thing which is hardest, for me anyway. You have to train yourself to listen at several levels. I say "train yourself" because I don't know of any major course in our society which teaches people to listen. It's difficult because your eyes are on the other person, your head is boiling with responses. The thing that helps me most is the recognition that every conversation is a kind of a jazz performance.

I developed a technique when I was teaching at the University of Washington. The technique went this way: I made the class the teachers for the next class coming in. They wrote the text book. I made them interchange the role of teaching each other as they went along. And I structured the class in such a way that if anyone in that class dragged his feet—he put more work on the others. I did it with malice aforethought, telling them I was doing it and why—I didn't hide a thing. I said, "I'm doing this because your contemporaries will put more pressures on you than I can. If you put more workload on your fellow students they're going to let you know right away."

I did this in several ways. One, I gave them projects that they could do together. If one person took it over and tried to do it alone, the others were so motivated by the other elements of the course that they wouldn't let him do it. But if any person in there didn't carry his own load, it became immediately apparent he wasn't going to the library doing the research, he wasn't doing part of the typing, he wasn't doing part of the duplicating.

In the classroom situation, I spread the reporting loads so it rotated through the group. There wasn't a big enough group that we missed anybody regularly. It was very noticeable in the total group as well as in the small groups of two, three, and four. Anyone that wasn't pulling his weight showed up immediately. Also, since the whole thing was parceled out, nobody had all of the elements. They had to bring back the little pieces of the total classroom problem. So they put them all together and saw the synergistic effect in the classroom setting. All of this was cumulative.

There was another phenomenon. I knew that if they were examining the myth-making propensity of human society and their own involvement in it, and how that myth-making was used as a screen through which to interpret reality, that there was going to be a certain reluctance to touch some areas which were sensitive to the individual. Further, each individual's sensitivity would vary through the classroom. And I knew that the pressure of the unfolding process would be cumulative; it would get stronger the closer we came to the end of the class. The last two or three classes were just going to be very tough, because at that point there's no avoiding the fact that on that day, say two weeks away, we don't meet again, that's the end of it.

I had anticipated some of this but nowhere near the extent of what happened. A two-hour class lasted six hours. I let it go because great stuff was coming out. I remember one young woman who always appeared in bib overalls, looking like female Farmer Brown, rather dowdy; at least a half hour of the class was taken up with her exposing her own motivations for this—that it was protective coloration. She didn't want to get out in the stream of other things that were happening—a thing that she knew would occur if she changed her personal dress and her personal habits. And that opened the floodgates. No one in the room was immune to this. It all started coming out. At the end of that six hours I had a roomful of people that really understood from personal experience how they contributed to myth-making and to a sense of reality—how they change reality out there in their own perceptions. So the class was a success. That was the theme.

Why does it set up those dynamics? I have a theory about this. I think that there is a form of very natural social conditioning that starts quite young, where we learn to be learners. And we become very sensitive to what those big people around us want, and so the first thing we learn is to regurgitate what they want. We learn how to respond, to bring back what they want because that wins all kinds of goodies and keeps the stick away. This sets up a kind of automatic role-playing device. You see it in primitive societies. Primitive societies become very sensitive to what the more sophisticated society demands of them. And they will regurgitate lies as long as they spot what they want as well. The teacher will telegraph what the teacher wants.

I think if you're aware of this you can watch for the role-playing signals that come up while people are playing student, while people are playing teacher. And then you sensitize people to how easy it is to fold in to different kinds of roles. And you can break through the pattern in the behavior. Lots of times you can do it simply by cutting across the placement situation that they expect. One of the things that I did in my classes at the university is that I insisted that nobody sit twice in the same place from class to class, myself included. We had to come up to that table, but we sat in a different relationship each time, so nobody got seated into the thing.

I do it in so-called lecture situations. It is not always possible because the lectures are designed by people who hate people, I think. But wherever possible, instead of getting up on the platform, the ideal situation is to come down there with a broadcast mike which you take with you right down on the floor with the people. Then I begin by addressing why I'm doing this.

Another thing I insist on is that when people ask a question, they give me their first name. I say, "You all know my name, but I don't know more than three or four of you—the people who brought me in. So at least give your first name." And so they have to get up and say "My name is George and what I'd like to know is . . ." and so forth.

There are a lot of tricks you can do to break down roleplaying blocks. These are only a few of the surface ones; the other ones relate to your own personal mannerisms. I have a friend, a psychologist, down in San Francisco, who is a notorious heavy-footed driver and has never had a speeding ticket. He brags about this. He gets stopped by a cop, and he leans back and exposes his throat. . . . He said he's got a lot of lectures from the cops, but he's never gotten a ticket. And he says they don't know what's happening to them. He says, "You think primitive behavior has no influence on this society?"

I don't think we've exhausted the possibilities the problems that are created around and within the search for excellence. And I take your question as meaning how do we open up more avenues for excellence in the world.

I think I'm doing something about it in the sense that I'm saying, "There's the train. It's coming, and here's how you can raise your consciousness. And here's how attractive it can be. Yes, you can be excellent in whatever you choose to do if you really choose that." I'm not some Pollyanna sitting here saying, "Yes, you can be the best of all persons in the best of all possible worlds." I'm just saying the doors are not closed to you. You may imagine that they have been, but it's partly a process of conditioning.

I don't think there's any simple one-shot answer. I've said time and again that any mechanic knows there are automotive problems you do not adjust by getting in there with a screwdriver and turning one screw. Because if you turn one, you've got to make other adjustments. The *system* has to be balanced. That gets back to the question of the baggage we carry with us.

I'm a little bit chary about the word *instinct*, although I use it. It's a grab-bag word that tends to be used without proper consideration. The term *racial memory* is more to the point. It suggests that we have an accumulation of all kinds of material, some of which may be useful, some of which may not be useful, and some of which may make demands upon us unconsciously or consciously. In other words, it a wider-spectrum label.

I think that there are techniques of education available to us for making ourselves more aware of what is going on around us. And this is only one aspect of lifting consciousness, whether it lifts us to hyperconsciousness or not.

Hyperconsciousness can be a full-on type of thing, when all senses are on, the neuroreactions are speeded to their physical limits—perhaps beyond expected physical limits—or it can be like a laser beam that avoids everything outside it and just goes for one shot to some object. And I see the term hyperconsciousness being used both ways. Perhaps we need a new word, or two new words, to separate them. But as long as we understand that differentiation, we can discuss it. If we are talking about the full-on thing, many people have experienced this. I think that in some instances it has been helped by drugs, but I don't think drugs are the answer, I think drugs tend to be self-delimiting. People who come to rely on them begin to lose consciousness. We see this quite dramatically.

There's another kind that I've spoken about and written of. I've experienced it, and I've talked to quite a few people who have experienced it. And that is the life-threatening situation, or something similar, where you're suddenly turned on to find the solution that will save you.

You find it frequently with automobile drivers. Suddenly they're in a tight spot and afterward realize that they went through many computations, considered many options, in a fraction of a second, as though the internal time clock slowed down or stretched out in relationship to the external time clock, which was demanding action. I think that's hyperconsciousness, too. All of this says that we have mental capabilities related to physical action ignition systems, which we don't use, normally. We go along petty pace.

I think it is directly related to the evolution of consciousness. I think that stress is an educator, and that stress can apply to an individual or to a species. I've a theory about war, for example. I think war tends to be both an individual and species stress.

At the same time, I think people can become addicted to adrenaline. This happens among terrorist groups, quite obviously. Secret societies trade on it. The adrenaline shot is seen as something very desirable after the fact. Otherwise, why would veterans of a war come back and focus only on the high times and how good it was? You've heard of it.

All of these things point to ways of training. The military uses it—they put people under very stressful situations to weld them into a body which is hyperconscious in a particular directable way. That says to me that we could be hyperconscious in a lot of ways and that the techniques for producing that action are there.

I don't think there is any single technique, I think we have a lot of them. Some of them are probably more productive than others and some of them are probably more dangerous than others.

I would think hypnosis has some application. Hypnosis tends to be a channeling technique where many things are pushed out of the immediate sensory awareness and the individual is aimed in some direction to do something, to react in a certain way. The fact that the human mental/nervous system can do it also says to me that here is something else that can be applied to teaching people how to live better with themselves, how to be able to react at a higher level when needed.

Ultimately, I would hope I was saying something in my books not just about hyperconsciousness, but about sanity. I have a fluid definition of it, which is that sanity is the ability to balance under stress, or to balance whatever the conditions are, and to bounce when knocked down. That little Japanese toy eight times down, nine times up. That fits my definition of sanity.

But furthermore, if you create a language, a way of dealing with something, you've actually increased consciousness. If you recognize that language is a changeable system and it has to be subjected to cut and fit, then you come back somewhere near Korzybski's insight (which I think was dramatically important for humankind as a whole and has never been picked up to the extent it ought to be). If language has no fixed reference, but only immediately applicable reference, which must be tested each time against the predictive capacity, then you're not going to be upset when the world doesn't behave as you thought it should. You learn to say that the observational system that we call language needs correction there. I think that is a requisite for raised consciousness.

I'm saying something else, too, that I think is equally, perhaps even more important. You can learn as much or more from your mistakes, from where the thing doesn't fit, as you can from your successes. Successes tend to blind us to the inaccuracies of our predictive system. Success will spoil Rock Hunter.

I think it's very true, for example, that a writer can write his own psychoanalysis. It all comes out. I've warned young writers about this, and told them to accept it rather than try to hold back on stuff. Everything has to hang out, the good and the bad, the acceptable and the unacceptable, because what's unacceptable today may be acceptable tomorrow and vice versa. You cannot, while you're writing, try to worry about that. On reflection over what you've written, you get a lot out of it. If you put a lot into it, you get even more out of it. I also think that as you write, and gain these insights into yourself and others and into motivational processes surrounding you, you can raise your own consciousness. This happens naturally in the process.

You also find yourself looking at your world in a very different way from that which you did before this all began. It's a different world. The trees may still be trees and the rivers rivers and mountains mountains, but they have different shapes afterward. It's a thing that is very difficult to explain without having been experienced, because people will think you're talking about some mystical experience, some form of *satori*, and you're not.

The closest I've ever come to it is to observe something that happens a lot with science fiction writers. We seem to stretch time in a different way than most people do. During the period of writing a story I'm living in that time, with the instruments of the imagination that are put into the story. They are in many respects dramatically different from what we find around us right now. After finishing the story, you pull out and come back to these primitive times.

The word primitive has a peculiar meaning to a lot of science fiction writers. If you look at it in our own historical terms, and look back only one hundred years, let's say, a lot of that looks primitive to us right now. You go back two hundred years and it's even more primitive, right? If you have stretched your mind out, for the story's purpose, twenty thousand, a hundred thousand years into man's future, and then come back to these times you would look at these times the way you might look if you were suddenly pushed back into Shakespeare's time.

I don't know if it's proper to call that way of looking at things hyperconsciousness, but it certainly is a different consciousness. Your yardsticks are different.

I've also experienced the stress reaction, in which the flow of time was changed dramatically, and I've considered several dozen options in what could not have been more than a fractional part of a second. I made a choice based on considering all of these options and survived. I had a choice one time, in less than a second, whether to hit the throttle on an automobile and crash through a bridge barrier and leap a hole in the bridge, or to hit the clay bank on the left, or to go off into the trees down a deep gorge on the right, or to hit my brakes and skid into the hole in the bridge. The warning was a two-by-four laid at an angle ten feet away from the bridge as you came around the corner.

I had experience at that bridge, and I remembered that it had a crown at each end—it was an arc. I was doing about forty-five–fifty miles an hour, so I hit the throttle and I leaped it. I leaped a twelve-foot hole. Twelve four-by-twelve boards had been taken out of the bridge. And the crew went off to get breakfast while I was heading for the ferry on Vachon Island.

This time-compression phenomenon is so well recorded that although a lot of scientists pooh-pooh it because they cannot duplicate it on demand, I think it has to be accepted.

I'm saying evolution doesn't stop. Don't imply that there is a fixed and final goal for consciousness. It's like blowing up a balloon, as you increase the space within it, you also increase the interface with where it can go.

Religion can be both an amplifier and a suppressant of consciousness, as we well know. And it has to be looked at from a lot of directions, as all elements of our universe have to be looked at. One direction is that major religions are organized. Organized religions have a managerial bureaucracy aspect to them—with all of the usefulness and depressing things that come about power positions. (I really do think that they attract the nuts!) And I don't think religions are immune from this because they are so obviously potent in dealing with human problems.

This doesn't mean that I am anti-religion. I just think we should watch it very cautiously. Then it doesn't develop dangerous fanatics. Also I don't think we ought to ignore religion as a part of human history and developmental influence.

It struck me quite often how similar are some aspects of various religions. It seems to indicate that somewhere along the line, if you dig deeply enough into what can be lumped under the spiritual aspects of human existence, you come out with very similar results. This is especially down at the level of the person who is trying to do what we were discussing earlier—improve himself.

I had to give the commencement address at Seattle University last year—a Catholic university. It was probably the shortest commencement address they ever had. They applauded longer than I spoke. (I knew they were applauding the shortness of it.) It summed up the strength of the golden rule. If only one person in our world follows that golden rule, it's a better world. So the argument that I don't follow it because George and Jim aren't, is a specious argument once you examine it.

Do you want a world where a virgin with a bag of gold can walk from New York to Los Angeles and never be molested? Yes, I think that is the kind of world we want. But not always has the virgin with the bag of gold been able to walk from one end of the empire to the other merely because everybody was so nice. After all you could supposedly do that in Genghis Khan's world, but that was because he left a lot of areas sparsely populated. His enforcers were very abrupt in their enforcement.

But the ideal is still there, and it is a worthy ideal. People can dedicate themselves to it; they don't need a religious excuse to do it. Religion is a potent and convenient grab bag under which you can sub-tend this golden rule. The danger is that it tends also to attract people who want to feel not only better than their neighbors who are nonbelievers, but to be in the ascendency. They want to tell others how to behave.

I don't think telling others how to behave really is the answer to this. You're not going to bring about the golden age at the point of a sword. Example is the only way to do it. I'm convinced of this. Live the best kind of life you can. If you need a religious reason for doing this, fine. If you don't, equally fine.

I've had this discussion a number of times with people in different religions. The ones who appreciate it the most and agreed with me most turned out to be Jesuits. But then Jesuits have a long history of overzealousness to overcome.

Of course I deal with religion in my books. I've studied them at great length. I've studied them both as a historical phenomenon and in their own lights. I see the thrust and necessity in some levels of consciousness for a prop to lean on. I can also make very interesting comparisons between the absolute monarchs of the early days and the forms that early religions took, and how that has carried over into present religions. The trail is there and you don't have to be an expert woodsman to follow the track of that wolf.

What I'm saying in my books boils down to this: mine religion for what is good and avoid what is deleterious. Don't condemn people who need it. Be very careful when that need becomes fanatical.

I always tell people that I'm a capitalist for a weird reason. I am a capitalist because capitalism tends to break down when it makes mistakes. Socialism requires a managerial bureaucracy that maintains itself on the basis of never making a mistake. You know damn well they make mistakes. So they bury their mistakes, they maintain their mistakes. They say that it is not a mistake, and carry it on forever because their position of power depends upon their not making mistakes.

I can simplify it in one respect. If I make a mistake in decision, it may be painful to me and to my immediate family. However, if millions of people depend upon my decision and I made a mistake in decisions, that failure is amplified by those numbers. And this is the failure of government that buries its mistakes. This is the failure of government that the people who are affected by the mistakes cannot influence. There's too much leverage.

The most successful people in bureaucracies are the people who protect the image of infallibility of those above them. Some people in the Executive Office told me a story about an interaction between Nixon and the bureaucracy. Whatever you say about Nixon, he made a few good decisions in international affairs. And one of the things he saw rather early on was that if we paid for a real land reform program in South Vietnam, we would win the support of the peasantry. And he sent through an executive order to carry out such a program. (I don't think there's any doubt it has been proved elsewhere that it works. There is no doubt that it would have been highly successful. One of the things I discovered in Vietnam was that we were losing that war very dramatically because you could see all the guerrilla war signals. No person out in that field was coming into the commanders and saying, "Hey, there are VC over there." Nobody. And only part of that was due to the fear of reprisal.)

This was contrary to many high level State Department decisions. One of the bureaucrats locked Nixon's order in a desk. He locked it up and sat on it until the transient had left. This is the thing the bureaucracy really understands: that the elective officials are transients and will be replaced. It is the bureaucracy protected by civil service which is the long-term enduring powerful factor in this government.

Now what that bureaucrat was doing was living by the rules of his employment, of his job. You can't say he was doing anything wrong. It was a conflict of interest. He knew the rules and Nixon did not. The rules are that you protect your superiors, the permanent superiors, the ones who'll be there once the transients are gone.

Also, look what happened when Proposition 13 went through in California. Instead of paring the real deadwood from the bureaucracy, they cut back primarily those services which would be felt by the population as a punishment.

The real threat in not increasing taxes was to the jobs of the bureaucracy. The bureaucracy punished the people for doing this. It's very clear that that's what was done.

I really was brought up short on the size of the bureaucracy when I used to commute across the Golden Gate Bridge. On a holiday when the state and federal workers were off, the highway was practically empty. You could drive into San Francisco at the speed limit, with no slow-downs. Everything was smooth. The minute the holiday was over, the highway was jammed.

I think there are going to be enormous shakeups in this pattern, partly because of what's happening in technology. The bureaucracy tends to offend individual dignity, and more and more people are coming to the point where they can respond violently to offenses to their dignity. And that's a hell of a world to contemplate.

That's one of the themes in my book, *The White Plague*. I found out that it's not only feasible but extremely inexpensive to create new diseases. I found out that I could do it with about six months study and research into the materials and equipment needed. Worse than that, I called every major supplier of the materials and the equipment that are needed. I introduced myself as Dr. Herbert; they never questioned it. I said, "This is Dr. Herbert and my purchasing department would like to know what procedure we go through to purchase your model AZ21." To boil it all down, basically the answer was, "When your check is cleared." Anything you wanted. Not only that, you could improvise some of the equipment.

What I am addressing is the consequences of this being so readily available. I don't intend any violence, but I can imagine a situation where someone being treated unjustly by this society would turn on it and do horrible damage. The society is going to have to reorganize itself in such a way that we don't treat anyone unjustly. And that means that the bureaucracy will have to be revitalized or made more susceptible to popular control.

It will bring the level of observation to the local level, to where it needs to be. Your neighbor will know more or less what you are doing. I'm not talking about thought police or neighborly intrusion, I'm just saying that if wrong is done your own community will know.

It's the impersonal faraway executive decision that puts human beings in the Catch-22 situation that is the danger right now. It's a terrible danger, given the levels to which technology has spread the tools of violence. I've had arguments with gun control people. If it were possible to really control guns, I'd be all in favor of it, but no way. If it were really possible to take away the instruments of violence, you'd find me right in the van doing it. But in a society such as this, when any individual could go out and stop at a hardware store, grocery store, and a drug store and come home and make a pipe bomb, which is far more dangerous than a pistol, I don't see how in the world that taking handguns away from people is really going to solve anything. When you look at New York City, which has the Sullivan law (the most stringent one in the world), you see that there are more handguns per capita in New York than any other city in the U.S.

Are we going to make iodine unavailable to people? Hydrogen peroxide? Sugar? Clorox? Diesel oil? I've just named the ingredients that, according to known formulas, can be made to make hideous bombs. What are you going to do about that? It's not the tools, because the tools are too readily available. It is the reason behind the use of them. The motivation—what do we do about that?

We cannot control. In fact the whole effort of control creates more incidents of injustice, and you need more control. And then more control to control the controllers. You're building new kinds of hierarchies. The whole controllant philosophy is at fault.

Let me make one suggestion for our society to restore the democracy. I've watched a lot of the people marching down the street yelling "Power to the people." What they're really saying is "Power to me." I think that's nonsense. I don't want to trade one set of rulers for another. But I happen to really have a lot of respect for and belief in the wisdom of masses of people. I don't think people *en masse* make too many wrong decisions without correcting them quickly. So I would like to really see a return to power to the people, and I have a thought which our computer age makes possible. It is possible right now to put into a single computer system the entire voter rolls of the United States.

I'd like to see out of those voter rolls at the federal, state, county, and city level a series of what I choose to call great juries. We would give them enormous powers, but limit their tenure and make it mandatory that they never again serve on a great jury. You choose twelve people, with six alternates. Give them the power to fire anybody in government for cause—anybody, without recourse—the executive, the bureaucracy, right down to the local state and city level.

If you gave power to a selected group produced by some sort of random walk through the rolls of people who vote, it would make voting again, like a lottery, very attractive. Right now, you read the ineffectiveness of voting by the numbers of people who don't do it. I think people know instinctively that they have little influence on what happens, so why bother.

I'm not antibureaucracy. I think some form of bureaucracy is a functional necessity of government. But what standards of excellence do you apply, and how do you enforce those standards of excellence? Right now we have none.

Once you get tenure, once you get in, you're part of the civil service system and you no longer are a transient. The behavioral pattern of the bureaucracy is such that they protect everyone up and down—it's like a feudal system. You are loyal to the duke, the duke is loyal to you.

That was one of the crudest awakenings I've had. Back when I was writing speeches for a U.S. Senator, I suddenly realized that the system didn't work the way you were taught in civics class.

I think my view of it is accurate, because with that view I'm able to predict what's going to happen far more accurately than with the civics class version of the U.S. I can tell you how people will behave in the system.

And yet there are other forces that work in our society and in our world, which lead me to believe we can change course dramatically and rather quickly. I would say in the next ten years or so, we will pay with a lot of pain. I'd rather see us not pay that way. And there's no real reason we have to, there's no moral imperative on continuing to making the mistakes we've made in the past.

But I think your earlier statement about changing levels of consciousness is one avenue which is open to us that we ought to exploit as much as possible. I see you doing this in your book. You're doing the same thing I'm doing and I agree with you. Do it. Go with it. I think that way lies survival.

New World
or No World

My name is Frank Herbert and I am a human living on the planet Earth, a condition shared by about three and a half billion of my fellows in this year 1970.

Only about one-third of us are sufficiently well fed that we can take the time to write such words as these. Food is energy is time. Pollution is lost energy.

This is insanity.

I feel constrained to say these things in just this way because of a pledge I have made. I refuse to be put in the position of telling my grandchildren: "Sorry, there's no more world for you. We used it all up."

It was for this reason that I wrote in the mid-sixties what I hoped would be an environmental awareness handbook. The book is called *Dune*, a title chosen with the deliberate intent that it echo the sound of "doom." In the pages of *Dune* there is a man named Pardot Kynes, a planetologist, which is kind of super-environmentalist. I put these words into his mouth:

> Beyond a critical point within a finite space, freedom diminishes as numbers increase. This is as true of humans in the finite space of a planetary ecosystem as it is of gas molecules is a sealed flask. The human question is not how many can possibly survive within the system, but what kind of existence is possible for those who do survive.

Population can destroy us. There exists a limit to global elbow room, a limit to how many the good Earth can support. Yet, we go our separate ways, geared to propagating separation, geared to national and racial and many other kind of distrust, actively preventing affection for each other as humans.

On the issue of birth control, Hindu deeply distrusts Moslem, and Moslem distrusts Hindu; Blacks distrust Whites and Whites distrust Blacks.

And all the time, we know we must solve our mutual problem together or be destroyed—Moslem, Hindu, Black, White . . .

Together is sane.

Fragmented is insane.

That's the message I want you to get from this assemblage of words representing the *Today Show*'s look at Earth Week: *New World or No World*.

The thing we must do intensely is be human together. People are more important than things. We must get together. The best thing humans can have going for them is each other. We have each other. We must reject everything which humiliates us. Humans are not objects of consumption.

We must develop an absolute priority of humans ahead of profit—any humans ahead of any profit. Then we will survive. . . .

Together.

On the morning of April 20, 1970, commentator Hugh Downs opened NBC's *Today Show* with the first of five days' programs focused on Earth Week. His guests for the series were to be some of the nation's leading figures in the field of environment, people such as Margaret Mead, Paul Ehrlich, Rene Dubos, Ian McHarg, Canon Don D. Shaw, Mayor John Lindsay, Astronaut Frank Borman, Senators Edmund Muskie and Gaylord Nelson, Steward Udall, and Congressman Morris Udall.

That opening show shared the spotlight with many news events—the safe return of the *Apollo 13* astronauts, disastrous tornados in the South and Middle West, the air war in Laos, President Nixon's announcement that he would report on Vietnam, a new assault on Cuba by armed exiles, new fighting in Israel, heavy snows in Northeast Minnesota and

Idaho, and freezing rain in Northwest Wisconsin...and gusty winds in Southern California.

All of this, and much more, constituted the environment of April 20, 1970.

Apollo 13 astronaut James Lovell had some words about this environment, which many probably did not associate with the air they breathed, the water they drank, with their total life-style on this spaceship Earth. He said:

"As I looked back on the Earth and saw just how wonderful we had it back there and suddenly realized maybe we would not get back, it suddenly became something much more, something we wanted to see and wanted to become part of again."

Although they may not have focused on the Earth as an oasis in space, the only place we know that supports our kind of life, many in the *Today Show*'s audience must have begun to sense vague feelings akin to those of the astronauts—that the Earth that could nurture them with its life-support systems was disappearing, and they wanted to hear what they could do to get back to that Earth.

NBC began then to conceive of its programs as a kind of Mission Control, searching out what was wrong with spaceship Earth, telling the passengers how they could participate in survival.

Awareness of the environmental crisis has been a long time coming. Many have seen our misunderstanding of our place in the biological schema.

But now the awareness breaks upon us like a thunderous pounding on our doors. We have been served with a colossal summons:

"On this date you did willfully contribute to the pollution of your world."

The penalty is upon us. We are sentenced to breathe the air we have fouled, drink the water we have polluted, to have our consciousness crushed by views imprisoned in gray walls.

Nature has no probation system to test our good intentions.

Continued offenses will only bring down total capital punishment—upon the guilty and the innocent.

In a universe that seldom gives warning of its larger death sentences, we have received clear warning. We feel the earth under our feet and we have seen the Earth from space.

It's all one world.

There are no uncharted islands here where we can run away to sunshine and sparkling white beaches. We have just this one world, and on these pages we're beginning to get a feeling for the gigantic physical project confronting us. Our awakening is touched with dismay: we must come to terms with our world or it will terminate us.

When we speak of defending the environment, we are speaking of defending our own lives.

For thousands upon thousands of years before man's first written words ever were carved into stone or punched into soft clay, language was oral. Words were for the ears. At our most primitive levels, we still know this and react accordingly. That's why there is such power in these spoken words from the *Today Show*. You see the printed words on the page, certainly, but the style is for the ears. You can sense the lips moving as these very human humans struggle with words against the apocalypse.

One thing you really feel about many of the people on this show—they have seen that words are most useful as harbingers of action. They have faced themselves and seen how the world is made. There is something essentially sane about facing up to our past mistakes, outlining the dimensions of the problem and saying:

"We must get out of our conventional stupor, away from our old and useless fears, and into a common awareness of what each of us can do."

You can hear, for example, Ian McHarg saying we need to toilet-train the nation's industrial polluters—and toilet-train ourselves while we're at it, because we're the worst polluters.

Like Pogo: "We have met the enemy and he is us."

But we allow hidden fears to constrict our minds, pull a

curtain over our awareness and limit our imagination.

None of us can afford to be mediocre under today's conditions. The sickness of our world requires our best talents and perseverance, both of these qualities together, because without talent perseverance is a much overrated trait. You can beat your head against the wall all you want, but you're more likely to get concussion than produce a hole in the wall.

Each of us can transform his own life. Together, we transform what it is to be human and to value what is human. We can learn together and achieve this new sophistication geared to human survival.

But words are not enough. The root of environmental awareness may be an understanding of consequences, but first we must achieve awareness—here and now.

We exist in a finite energy system. We can feel the dangers of permitting unbridled growth in the use of that limited energy.

Our sun, that blazing fire in the sky which has dwarfed us with its outflow of energy all through our history, shrinks to a finite thing.

Just another star.

And this planet beneath our feet?

Just another planet, but the only oasis we know for human existence, and we know for a fact it is being overwhelmed by our excesses.

We are passengers on the spaceship Earth.

We get on and we get off. And while we are here, living beneath our gaseous shell of air, we often find ourselves daunted by the vastness of the unknown universe outside. We fret about many things, including our misuse of the fuel that stokes our solar furnace. We feel nature around us more complex than we can think. We see that nature, which we had thought was tamed by our technology, rising up in the form of that technology to threaten our existence.

All this while we continue to breathe in and breathe out; we continue to get on and off our Earthly ship.

· · ·

Put this book down a moment. Do it. Go look out the nearest window or completely around you if you're outdoors. This is your world. You are here now. This is the only moment you have, this moment of now, when you can do the things that must be done to save this world. Do it.

And remember this:

Human survival is not negotiable.

Even the more sophisticated control methods leave residues of pollution. These residues increase alarmingly as the number of people in the system increases.

In the past seven thousand years, we have grown from a population on the whole Earth that would have fitted nicely into New York City to something above three and a half billion. This is the primary threat to our mutual survival, and the most disturbing single fact to the egos of many who are refusing to face up to how they are participating in the death of the planet.

Ecology is a dirty, seven-letter word to many people.

They are like heavy sleepers refusing to be aroused. "Leave me alone! It's not time to get up yet!"

They retreat into death games and other violence, hiding their awareness from the terrifying necessities of this moment.

Do we use such people as scapegoats?

But we cannot afford the time for witch hunts. We can't say: "Hey! You have nine children and I only have two. You owe me seven!"

That's more insanity.

What we can say is: "I hope your nine don't have nine each. That's something I really hope, that they wake up in time."

And we can shake the sleepers—gently and persistently, saying: "Time to get up."

Concern for the environment is no fad.

We cannot get tired of the environmental issue and turn to something else because, if we do, it will get tired of us . . . and dispense with us.

This is an issue which cannot be co-opted by any group seeking to divert us into the old bread and games. It won't go away. Band-aids won't cure it. Partial solutions will only delay the ultimate confrontation, and they will require greater and greater efforts for shorter and shorter delays.

The problem is not merely water and air and resources. It is life-style and how we develop our potential as humans. Pollution is Black Panthers murdered in Chicago. Pollution is a thousand bodies floating down the Mekong. Pollution is Russia sending planes and guns to Egypt. Pollution is Red China huddling behind its paranoid curtain. Pollution is the radical left and radical right secretly arming for a war of extinction. Pollution is the son of a dear friend being shipped home from Vietnam in a flag-draped box. Pollution is distrust. Pollution is hate.

Pollution is anything that keeps us divided.

Pollution is insanity.

We are in a worldwide crisis of sanity.

Even from the doom-sayers you hear reflection of hope. Nobody wants "it" to happen.

In his darkest moments, man is aware that, while he may be limited, humankind need not be. It's a bedazzling fact—our energy here and now may be finite; humankind need not be. Death is a limit to the individual; life is potentially unlimited. Power is limited and limiting; the human spirit is unlimited.

The questions remain there waiting for decisions.

Would you like to save the Earth?

What are you willing to do?

Ecology is a word which points to a revolution generated in the earth beneath our feet.

As any good doctor will tell you, one of the best medicines is Tender Loving Care. But we have to be certain what we're doing really is TLC. The very fact we have air pollution control agencies contributes to pollution. They tend to lull many into the false belief that everything possible is being done.

That's one of the problems about such a thing as Earth Day. We get outside together, experience the sanity of being all together on a mutual problem, and we go home feeling great.

We did something.

And that's true: we did.

But that effort is useless if we then go on about our business-as-usual, immersed in word pollution, power pollution, and sanity pollution and all the other pollutions destroying us. We are tangled in contradictions between what we say and what we do. By any clinical definition, that is insanity. Let's put the words down occasionally and pay closer attention to what we are doing.

Our goal is to become activists.

We must rely on our own actions more than on words.

And these are just words.

It's good to be reminded of that occasionally in any book which reports on mutual problems.

On Earth Day in Philadelphia, Senator Edmund Muskie said:

"Our priorities are all wrong. We cannot afford to spend more on killing humans than on saving them."

We're right with you, Senator Muskie.

Being human, that's the thing. We have to keep it in our minds all the time that people—not institutions, or laws, or theories, or science, or technology—people are more important and must always be considered first.

It may just be possible that all the governments we people have in our world have been more concerned with keeping their systems going than with doing things for people.

That's a question worth asking, anyway.

Especially if you work in government.

From the individual survival point of view, the most urgent need takes priority. If you're drowning, you go for air. On the scale of the world's population, however, humans don't appear to have the same survival mechanism.

If any human sees a clear choice between life and death, then chooses death, we call that insane. Why do we accept it when it happens on a world scale?

Birth predicts death, but we don't like being reminded we're going to die—individually. We have a big hang-up on this question of dying, one by one.

If you can say to yourself "There's nothing I can do," then you can ignore the problem. We carry a whole bag of euphemisms for saying this.

"Human nature won't change." (That's another way of saying: "I won't change.")

"It's always been this way and always will be." ("You won't catch me doing anything.")

It may be that we are unconsciously saying: "If I have to go, I don't care who I take with me."

It's a real hang-up, isn't it?

The tipoff can be seen in all these boulder-yards we scatter over otherwise useful landscape—useful to the living, that is. We call them cemeteries. Occasionally, we go there and feel sad. Most often, we're really feeling sad for ourselves, that we're going to wind up there.

Of course this sadness is proper when it puts us in touch with our own real feelings. Many people have little touch with their own feelings. It's not considered proper in Western Civilization. And the odd thing is that having repressed that touch of real feeling and its attendant sense of sanity can become a fixation. We can become fixed on death, in the hypnotic sense. Turned off and "living for death."

The sane thing for the living to do might be to plant orchards on this well-fertilized land. We could put the ancestral names on nearby cenotaphs and rid ourselves of the idea that humans should not be biodegradable.

There shouldn't be any such thing as a no-deposit–no-return human. Even the dead could help save the Earth.

Charles Luce declares the U.S. should convert to nuclear energy for generating electricity. That idea is raising more and more controversy in the world's scientific communities.

The chief thing that should be noted about it is that we have developed no suitable model of the "many nuclear plant" problem. We don't know what a lot of them will do to our environment.

This is an exquisite demonstration of the "Sorcerer's Apprentice Syndrome" in the U.S. industry and technology. We already have turned on more destruction with our technology than we know how to turn off. DDT was released after only eight months of controlled field testing and now threatens every ocean in the world.

Still, an important figure in industry can say we must turn on more nuclear power when we have not fully assessed the consequences.

We see here the extreme danger of ignoring negative information and taking at face value the authoritative pronouncements of important people, of assuming they have all the necessary basic information.

On an environmental scale, if we lack information, that is the vital information.

Of course, we do know some things about the fuel Mr. Luce proposes using to fire up our electrical systems. Much of the garbage from atomic generators has a half-life on the order of one thousand years. It is becoming increasingly difficult to store safely without enormously magnifying the disaster potential.

The waters of the Columbia River already are being thoroughly radiation-tagged by the Hanford nuclear power plant. Fisheries' scientists can determine the dispersal patterns of the Columbia in the Pacific Ocean by using Geiger counters.

We also know that genetic mutations are literally related to radiation dose, that there is no threshold effect, that all doses are cumulative and the effect is independent of dose rate or the time over which the dose is received. We know radiation-induced mutations are generally recessive and harmful.

Ecology is the understanding of consequences.

• • •

Our real foe is anything that dehumanizes and victimizes humans. It is being insensitive, unconscious, and unconcerned. That is our primary polluter. All other pollution stems from this. If we are aware of what is happening around us, we can begin to move in new ways.

If we're going to get our world back in shape for happiness and assure an open-ended future for happy descendants, we must work fast. There's a real sense of urgency to the problem because, on a world time-scale, two decades is tomorrow, not the day after.

The young especially feel this urgency because the decades ahead are their decades. The question is whether their children will have any world at all.

It is no wonder that they question many of our systems and institutions. It's quite plain to them that these institutions and systems have contributed to setting us on an extinction course.

As you encounter the questions of college students, keep in mind the fact that their world extends beyond that of many in the nation right now. If there's any place to live at all, they will live longer.

When they say: "Let the polluters pay!" they are angry, yes, but perhaps with reason.

It may be that the job of the older generations is not to resist change, but just to keep the young from throwing out the baby with the bathwater. The young have come up through an educational system which, for the most part, is one-way: from pedagogue to student. Good communication, however, requires feedback. And if education does not communicate, it fails.

What is a community of humans? How large should it be?

Lewis Mumford suggests, on the basis of much convincing evidence, that a city should be no larger than 250 thousand. But we are headed toward a "sardine can" world, with all the available spaces used and cities far larger than 250 thousand.

A community of humans requires certain attention to the individual. In a world where destructive power sources have reached such magnitude that individual decisions can extinguish all life on the planet, the needs of the individual assume primary importance.

No individual should want to destroy the rest of us.

On the basis of their actions, however, some obviously do want to wreck us.

Perhaps a community of humans requires we provide each individual with that mutual support which enables each human to withstand the disintegrating forces which assail us from without and within.

It may boil down to getting each individual to accept himself—to accept all the hungers, the sexuality, appearance, the thoughts which arise unbidden in consciousness—accept it all.

As a friend once said: "If you can accept yourself, you can accept anyone."

He was only half joking.

There's no real paradox in our problem. Individuals can destroy us. To survive, we must do it together.

What are you doing?

Bibliography

Frank Herbert is one of the most popular science fiction authors ever. His novels have appeared in hundreds of editions in this country and abroad. This bibliography does not attempt to be comprehensive: it simply lists the first edition and the currently available American editions of each of Herbert's books. It is designed to provide booksellers and readers with the titles and brief descriptions of Frank Herbert's work, including books, short stories, and newspaper or magazine articles.

The bibliography is divided into four parts. The first part lists Herbert's novels, the second his short stories, the third his nonfiction, and the fourth important works about Herbert or his books.

Novels

Herbert's novels are listed below in chronological order of publication. For each novel, there are at least two publication dates listed: the date of the first edition, and the date of the currently available edition(s). If the book was first published in serial form, the dates of serial publication are also given.

The Dragon in the Sea

> Herbert's first published novel and one of his best: a gripping story of submarine warfare in the twenty-first century. As usual, Herbert's psychological insights are a key part of the story. It is also a triumph of technological speculation: its descriptions of still-secret nuclear submarines earned Herbert accusations from some quarters that he was a communist spy; its prediction of global oil shortages required another twenty years to come true.

Serial publication: *Astounding*, November 1955–January 1956.

First book edition: New York: Doubleday, 1956, under the title *The Dragon in the Sea*. Also titled *Under Pressure*, and (unauthorized) *21st Century Sub*.

Current editions: Boston: G. K. Hall, 1980 (hardbound).
New York: Ballantine Books, 1981 (paper) (as *Under Pressure*).

Dune

The first novel of the famous *Dune* saga, in which the exiled son of a defeated nobleman recruits the outcast people of a desert planet in a religious crusade to overthrow a crumbling Galactic empire. It is hard to say what is most remarkable about this book: it blends ecology, religion, psychology, and adventure into an imaginary world so detailed that an entire "encyclopedia" has been written by fans expanding on hints left by Herbert (see *The Dune Encyclopedia* listed below). It is the standard against which all other novels of imaginary worlds are judged.

Serial publication: *Analog*, December 1963–February 1964 (Part I, as "Dune World"), and January–May 1965 (Parts II and III, as "The Prophet of Dune").

First book edition: Philadelphia: Chilton Books, 1965 (hardbound).

Current editions: Philadelphia: Chilton Books, 1965 (hardbound).
New York: G. P. Putnam's Sons, 1984 (hardbound).
New York: The Berkley Publishing Group, 1982 (trade paper).
New York: The Berkley Publishing Group, 1985 (paper).

The Green Brain

> A short novel of ecology focusing on the evolution of insect intelligence in response to human attempts to control the environment.

Serial publication: *Amazing*, March 1965, under the title "Greenslaves."

First book edition: New York: Ace Books, 1966 (paper).

Current editions: Boston: G. K. Hall, 1981 (hard-bound).
                        New York: The Berkley Publishing Group, 1985 (paper).

Destination: Void

> The story of an attempt to create an artificial intelligence in a desperate attempt to reach the stars. Herbert combines technical detail with psychological insight to produce a gripping and thought-provoking story about the consequences when people try to take too much control over the world around them.

Serial publication: *Galaxy*, August 1965, as "Do I Wake or Dream?"

First book edition: New York: The Berkley Publishing Group, 1966 (paper). (Revised edition: New York: The Berkley Publishing Group, 1978.)

Current editions: New York: The Berkley Publishing Group, 1985 (paper).

The Eyes of Heisenberg

> Another story about the consequences of science, in this case, genetic engineering. A pioneering novel that raises many of the issues that are being debated today as genetic engineering becomes a reality.

Serial publication: *Galaxy*, June–August 1966, as "Heisenberg's Eyes."

First book edition: New York: The Berkley Publishing Group, 1966 (paper).

Current editions: New York: The Berkley Publishing Group, 1986 (paper).

The Heaven Makers

Though not published until 1967, much of this novel was written in the early 1950s. It is a sometimes whimsical look at an immortal race of aliens who manipulate Earth's history for their own entertainment.

Serial publication: *Amazing*, April–June 1967.

First book edition: New York: Avon Books, 1968 (paper).

Current editions: New York: Ballantine Books, 1982 (paper).

The Santaroga Barrier

A powerful look at the power of social norms to create the framework of "reality" in which we see and perceive. An investigator is sent to uncover the secret of a small town in California that doesn't respond to advertising and other pressures from the outside world. Instead he finds himself drawn inexorably into a society based on the heightened awareness provided by a psychoactive drug. One of Herbert's most accomplished novels.

Serial publication: *Amazing*, October 1967–February 1968.

First book edition: New York: The Berkley Publishing Group, 1968 (paper).

Current editions: New York: The Berkley Publishing Group, 1985 (paper).

Dune Messiah

The sequel to *Dune*, in which many themes hidden in the first novel begin to be revealed: the dangers of hero worship and messianic leadership, and the consequences of trying to control the future. From a thematic point of view, possibly the most important of the first three *Dune* novels, and an absolutely gripping story.

Serial publication: *Galaxy*, July–November 1969.

First book edition: New York: G. P. Putnam's Sons, 1970 (hardbound).

Current editions: New York: G. P. Putnam's Sons, 1976 (hardbound).
New York: The Berkley Publishing Group, 1986 (trade paper).
New York: The Berkley Publishing Group, 1984 (paper).

Whipping Star

An ambitious novel that explores one of Herbert's recurring themes: the nature of intelligence (especially intelligence and awareness greater than our own). This is also the first novel to feature Jorj X. McKie and the Bureau of Sabotage, a government agency devoted to slowing down the passage of laws and growth of government in an all-too-efficient future. (A government without red tape, armed with the latest in information-gathering technology, can easily ride roughshod over the individual.) McKie and BuSab had previously appeared in a number of short stories.

Serial publication: *Worlds of If*, January–April 1970.

First book edition: New York: G. P. Putnam's Sons, 1970.

Current editions: Boston: G. K. Hall, 1980 (hardbound).
New York: The Berkley Publishing Group, 1983 (paper).

Soul Catcher

A gripping adventure novel that takes a penetrating look at the mind and spirit of the American Indian, and at the profound differences between their way of being and our own. Though this is not a science fiction novel, it is as powerful a story of the meeting between alien cultures as can be found anywhere in science fiction.

First book edition: New York: G. P. Putnam's Sons, 1972 (hardbound).

Current editions: New York: The Berkley Publishing Group, 1984 (paper).

The Godmakers

An expansion of Herbert's 1960 novella, "The Priests of Psi," which explores the nature of religion and the ability of worshipers to literally create the gods they worship. Picks up the *Dune* series' argument about the danger of messianic leadership from another point of view.

Serial publication: *Fantastic*, February 1960, in a much shorter form, as "The Priests of Psi."

First book edition: New York: G. P. Putnam's Sons, 1972 (hardbound).

Current editions: New York: The Berkley Publishing Group, 1986 (paper).

Hellstrom's Hive

A chilling novel that strikes right to the heart of the hero mythos in science fiction. A society of insectlike humans are trying to take over the earth. . . . They must be stopped. But the reader is left in the end to make his or her own judgment about who are the "good guys."

Serial publication: *Galaxy*, November 1972–March 1973, as "Project 40."

First book edition:	New York: Doubleday, 1973 (hardbound).
Current editions:	New York: Bantam Books, 1974 (paper).

Children of Dune

The culmination of Herbert's original *Dune* trilogy, in which all is revealed: the dark underside of the appealing dreams of *Dune*, in which the uncertain future is tamed by a larger-than-life hero and the planetary ecology of Arrakis is transformed by the wizardry of science. Here, Herbert shows the price of such dreams.

First book edition:	New York: G. P. Putnam's Sons, 1976 (hardbound).
Current editions:	New York: G. P. Putnam's Sons, 1980 (hardbound).
	New York: The Berkley Publishing Group, 1985 (trade paper).
	New York: The Berkley Publishing Group, 1985 (paper).

The Dosadi Experiment

The return of Jorj McKie in another look at the intensified consciousness that can develop when people are subjected to certain kinds of stress. This novel picks up and expands on themes from nearly every one of Herbert's other books.

First book edition:	New York: G. P. Putnam's Sons, 1977 (hardbound)
Current editions:	New York: The Berkley Publishing Group, 1984 (paper).

The Jesus Incident (with Bill Ransom)

A sequel to *Destination: Void*, in which the artificial intelligence created by the desperate engineers of that novel has become a capricious god, subjecting their descendents to endless tests designed to make them more aware (and hence worth saving) before he grows too bored and destroys the entire human race.

First book edition: New York: G. P. Putnam's Sons, 1979 (hardbound).

Current editions: New York: The Berkley Publishing Group, 1983 (paper).

Direct Descent

A short novel expanded from the 1954 story "Pack Rat Planet," which explores the conflict between a peaceful group devoted to maintaining an ancient library and barbarians who scorn what it contains. A parable about the value of information.

First book edition: New York: Ace Books, 1980 (trade paper).

Current editions: New York: The Berkley Publishing Group, 1985 (paper).

God Emperor of Dune

After completing the trilogy he had planned from the beginning, Herbert couldn't help returning to his most successful creation. This book explores the far future of Arrakis, in which Leto II decides he has held mankind in stasis long enough, and is ready to set loose a rebirth of independence and chaos.

First book edition: New York: G. P. Putnam's Sons, 1981 (hardbound).

Current editions: New York: G. P. Putnam's Sons, 1981 (hardbound).
New York: The Berkley Publishing Group, 1986 (trade paper).
New York: The Berkley Publishing Group, 1983 (paper).

The White Plague

This book focuses on two of the greatest fears of the twentieth century—terrorism and genetic engineering. A biochemist whose wife and children have been killed by terrorists seeks revenge on all mankind. Besides being an absolutely gripping novel, this book has some very profound things to say about war, terrorism, and individual violence. Possibly Herbert's best book since *Dune*.

First book edition:	New York: G. P. Putnam's Sons, 1982 (hardbound).
Current editions:	New York: G. P. Putnam's Sons, 1982 (hardbound). New York: The Berkley Publishing Group, 1983 (paper).

The Lazarus Effect (with Bill Ransom)

A sequel to *Destination: Void* and *The Jesus Incident*, which returns once again to the Planet Pandora and the demi-god Ship who was created to serve, and now rules humans.

First book edition:	New York: G. P. Putnam's Sons, 1983 (hardbound).
Current editions:	New York: G. P. Putnam's Sons, 1983 (hardbound). New York: The Berkley Publishing Group, 1985 (paper).

Heretics of Dune

A fifth *Dune* novel, taking place millennia after the fall of Leto described in *God Emperor of Dune*. Many of the same players are here: the Bene Gesserit, the Bene Tleilax, even Duncan Idaho the ghola. As usual, Herbert gives his old material a new and insightful turn.

First book edition:	New York: G. P. Putnam's Sons, 1984 (hardbound).

Current editions: New York: G. P. Putnam's Sons, 1984 (hardbound).
New York: The Berkley Publishing Group, 1985 (trade paper).
New York: The Berkley Publishing Group, 1986 (paper).

Chapterhouse: Dune

The sixth and final *Dune* novel.

First book edition: New York: G. P. Putnam's Sons, 1985 (hardbound).

Current editions: New York: G. P. Putnam's Sons, 1985 (hardbound).
New York: The Berkley Publishing Group, 1985 (trade paper).

Man of Two Worlds (with Brian Herbert)

A tongue-in-cheek sendoff of many science-fiction themes— a combination of Frank Herbert's insights with his son Brian's sense of humor.

First book edition: New York: G. P. Putnam's Sons, 1986 (hardbound).

Short Fiction

This section lists the available collections of Herbert's short fiction, followed by original publication data, including serial publication of novels. No attempt is made to list inclusion of Herbert's stories in anthologies.

Collections

The Worlds of Frank Herbert

Contains "The Tactful Saboteur," "By the Book," "Committee of the Whole," "Mating Call," "Escape Felicity,"

"The GM Effect," "The Featherbedders," "Old Rambling House," and "A-W-F Unlimited."

First book edition: New York: Ace Books, 1971 (paper).

Current editions: New York: The Berkley Publishing Group, 1983 (paper).

The Book of Frank Herbert

Contains "Seed Stock," "The Nothing," "Rat Race," "Gambling Device," "Looking for Something," "The Gone Dogs," "Passage for Piano," "Encounter in a Lonely Place," "Operation Syndrome," and "Occupation Force."

First book edition: New York: DAW Books, 1973 (paper).

Current editions: New York: The Berkley Publishing Group, 1983 (paper).

Original Publication Data

"Survival of the Cunning." *Esquire*, March 1945.

"Yellow Fire." *Alaska Life* (Alaska Territorial Magazine), June 1947.

"Operation Syndrome." *Astounding*, June 1954. Reprinted under the title "Nightmare Blues" in T. E. Dikty's *Best Science Fiction Stories and Novels*, 1955 Series.

"The Gone Dogs." *Amazing*, November 1954.

"Packrat Planet." *Astounding*, December 1954.

"Rat Race." *Astounding*, July 1955.

"Occupation Force." *Fantastic*, August 1955.

"Under Pressure" (three installments). *Astounding*, November 1955–January 1956. Published in hardcover as *The Dragon in the Sea*.

"The Nothing." *Fantastic Universe*, January 1956.

"Cease Fire." *Astounding*, January 1956.

"Old Rambling House." *Galaxy*, April 1958.

"You Take the High Road." *Astounding*, May 1958.

"A Matter of Traces." *Fantastic Universe*, November 1958. The first appearance of Jorj McKie, the hero of *Whipping Star* and *The Dosadi Experiment*.

"Missing Link." *Astounding*, February 1959. Reprinted with a brief explanatory introduction by Frank Herbert in *SF: Author's Choice*, ed. Harry Harrison. The Berkley Publishing Group: New York, 1968.

"Operation Haystack." *Astounding*, May 1959.

"The Priests of Psi." *Fantastic*, February 1960.

"Egg and Ashes." *Worlds of If*, November 1960.

"A-W-F Unlimited." *Galaxy*, June 1961.

"Try to Remember." *Amazing*, October 1961.

"Mating Call." *Galaxy*, October 1961.

"Mindfield." *Amazing*, March 1962.

"Dune World" (three installments). *Analog* (formerly *Astounding*), December 1963–February 1964. Comprises Book I of *Dune*.

"The Mary Celeste Move." *Analog*, October 1964.

"Tactful Saboteur." *Galaxy*, October 1964. Another McKie Story.

"The Prophet of Dune" (five installments). *Analog*, January–May 1965. Comprises Books II and III of *Dune*.

"Greenslaves." *Amazing*, March 1965. Expanded to form *The Green Brain*.

"Committee of the Whole." *Galaxy*, April 1965.

"The GM Effect." *Analog*, June 1965.

"Do I Wake or Dream?" *Galaxy*, August 1965. A shortened version of *Destination: Void*.

"The Primitives." *Galaxy*, April 1966.

"Escape Felicity." *Analog*, June 1966.

"Heisenberg's Eyes" (two installments). *Galaxy*, June–August 1966. Published in paperback as *The Eyes of Heisenberg*.

"By the Book." *Analog*, August 1966.

"The Featherbedders." *Analog*, August 1967.

"The Heaven Makers" (two installments). *Amazing*, April–June 1967.

"The Santaroga Barrier" (three installments). *Amazing*, October 1967–February 1968.

"Dune Messiah" (five installments). *Galaxy*, July–November 1969.

"The Mind Bomb." *Worlds of If*, October 1969.

"Whipping Star" (three installments). *Worlds of If*, January–April 1970.

"Seed Stock." *Analog*, April 1970.

"Murder Will In." *The Magazine of Fantasy and Science Fiction*, May 1970. Part of *Five Fates*, by Keith Laumer, Poul Anderson, Frank Herbert, Gordon Dickson and Harlan Ellison. Doubleday: New York, 1970. An ingenious collection where five authors complete the same story, each in their own way.

"Project 40" (three installments). *Galaxy*, November 1972–March 1973. Published in paperback as *Hellstrom's Hive*.

"Encounter in a Lonely Place," in *The Book of Frank Herbert*. New York: DAW Books, 1973. An autobiographical story.

"Gambling Device," in *The Book of Frank Herbert*. New York: DAW Books, 1973.

"Passage for Piano," in *The Book of Frank Herbert*. New York: DAW Books, 1973.

"The Death of a City," in *Future City*, ed. Roger Elwood. Trident Press: New York, 1973.

"Children of Dune" (four installments). *Analog*, January–April 1976.

"The Dosadi Experiment" (four installments). *Galaxy*, May–August 1977.

"Come to the Party" (with F. M. Busby). *Analog*, December 1978.

"Songs of a Sentient Flute." *Analog*, February 1979.

Nonfiction

Books

New World or No World (editor)

A collection of articles prepared for "Earth Day 1970," edited and introduced by Herbert.

First book edition: New York: Ace Books, 1970 (paper).

Current editions: Out of print.

Threshold: The Blue Angels Experience

Contains photos and screenplay (by Herbert) for the documentary film on the crack flying team. Herbert once again shows his fascination with the coupled subjects of pressure and human potential.

First book edition: New York: Ballantine Books, 1973 (paper).

Current editions: Out of print.

Without Me, You're Nothing (with Max Barnard)

An attempt to mix Herbert's ideas about bureaucracy and the potential dangers of government use of computers with a microcomputer primer.

First book edition: New York: Pocket Books, 1981 (trade paper).

Current editions: Out of print.

Essays and Introductions

This section lists short nonfiction written by Herbert, often in the form of introductions to other works of science fiction. These pieces give a lot of insight into the ideas behind the stories. Most are included in this book.

"Introduction to *Saving Worlds*," ed. Roger Elwood and Virginia Kidd. Doubleday: New York, 1973. (Reissued by Bantam Books under the title *The Wounded Planet*.)

"Introduction: Tomorrow's Alternatives?" in *Frontiers 1: Tomorrow's Alternatives*, ed. Roger Elwood. Macmillan: New York, 1973

"Introduction" to *Tomorrow and Tomorrow and Tomorrow*. Heitz, Herbert, Joor McGee. Holt, Rinehart and Winston: New York, 1973.

"Listening to the Left Hand." *Harper's Magazine*, December 1973, pp. 92–100.

"Science Fiction and a World in Crisis" in *Science Fiction: Today and Tomorrow*, ed. Reginald Bretnor. Harper and Row: New York, 1974.

"Men on Other Planets" in *The Craft of Science Fiction*, ed. Reginald Bretnor. Harper and Row: New York, 1976.

"Dune: The Banquet Scene." Jacket copy for *Dune: The Banquet Scene, Read by the Author*. Caedmon Records: New York, 1977.

"The Sky is Going to Fall" in *Seriatim: The Journal of Ecotopia*, No. 2, Spring 1977 (425 3rd St., McMinnville, Oregon 97128), pp. 88–89. A slightly different version of this article appeared in *The San Francisco Examiner* "Overview" column, July 4, 1976.

"The ConSentiency and How it Got That Way." *Galaxy*, May 1977.

"Sandworms of Dune." Jacket copy for *Sandworms of Dune: Read by the Author*. Caedmon Records: New York, 1978.

Newspaper Articles

"Flying Saucers: Facts or Farce?" *San Francisco Sunday Examiner & Chronicle, People* supplement, October 20, 1963.

"2068 A.D." *San Francisco Sunday Examiner & Chronicle, California Living* section, July 28, 1968.

"We're Losing the Smog War" (part 1). *San Francisco Sunday Examiner & Chronicle, California Living*, December 1, 1968.

"Lying to Ourselves About Air" (part 2). *San Francisco Sunday Examiner & Chronicle, California Living*, December 8, 1968.

"You Can Go Home Again." *San Francisco Sunday Examiner & Chronicle, California Living*, March 29, 1970. Refers to some of Herbert's childhood experiences in the Northwest.

Poetry

"Carthage: Reflections of a Martian," in *Mars, We Love You*, ed. Jane Hipolito and Willis E. McNelly. Doubleday: New York, 1971.

Works About Herbert and His Books

Frank Herbert, by Timothy O'Reilly.

> A critical study of Herbert's work, with some biographical background. Includes many interviews with Herbert and a deep look at the ideas and experiences behind his novels. Covers Herbert's work up through *The Jesus Incident*.

> First edition:　　　　New York: Frederick Ungar, 1980 (hardbound and paper).

The Dune Encyclopedia, compiled and edited by Willis E. McNelly.

> One of the most enjoyable things about Herbert's *Dune* series is the richness of the background. For years, fans have entertained themselves filling in even more background,

based on clues suggested by Herbert. This volume is an imaginative encyclopedia of the world of the series, written by fans and critics who can't get enough of *Dune*.

First edition: New York: The Berkley Publishing Group, 1984 (trade paper).

The answer to the problem posed at the end of "Listening to the Left Hand" is simple: *the numbers are listed in alphabetical order.*